AF608119

MAKING THE PUBLIC SERVICE MILLENNIAL

MAKING THE PUBLIC SERVICE MILLENNIAL

Generational Diversity in Public Service

LIZA IRENI SABAN, MAYA SHERMAN,
AND KEREN SHLOMI

Published by State University of New York Press, Albany

Printed in the United States of America

For information, contact State University of New York Press, Albany, NY
www.sunypress.edu

Library of Congress Cataloging-in-Publication Data

Names: Ireni Saban, Liza, author. | Sherman, Maya, author. | Sholmi, Keren, author.
Title: Making the public service millennial : generational diversity in public service / Liza Ireni Saban, Maya Sherman, and Keren Sholmi.
Description: Albany : State University of New York Press, [2022] | Includes bibliographical references and index.
Identifiers: LCCN 2022009666 | ISBN 9781438490779 (hardcover : alk. paper) | ISBN 9781438490793 (ebook)
Subjects: LCSH: Civil service—United States. | Generation Y—United States—Attitudes. | Diversity in the workplace—United States—Management. | Intergenerational relations—United States. | Conflict of generations in the workplace—United States.
Classification: LCC JK692 .I74 2022 | DDC 352.6/30973—dc23/eng/20220810
LC record available at https://lccn.loc.gov/2022009666

10 9 8 7 6 5 4 3 2 1

Contents

Introduction 1

Chapter 1
Diversity Management 7

Chapter 2
Generational Diversity—A Literature Overview 29

Chapter 3
Theories and Measurement of Ethical Decision-Making 85

Chapter 4
Antecedents of Ethical Judgments in the Public Service 111

Chapter 5
Generational Diversity and Public Service Ethics in Israel 125

Conclusion 151

Bibliography 155

Index 203

Introduction

> "Millennials are frequently written off as narcissistic, arrogant, and fickle. Although there is certainly some truth in such negative perceptions, the millennials also can be quite impressive in their ambitions and achievements. They are a generation of conflicting characteristics—self-absorbed but also civic minded."
>
> —Alsop, 2008, p. vii

As Generation Z (a.k.a iGen/Genzers/Genzees) gains media traction for its environmental protests and concern for the planet as a whole, the peculiarities of its predecessor—Generation Y (a.k.a Millennials/Gen Y/Generation Next)—is gradually paring down in public interest (Alsop, 2008). While such a process is expected for every generation as it reaches its apex, we assert that Generation Y has yet to entrench its generational vocation, distinctly within the workforce and precisely, within the public sector.

Researchers concur that by the end of the year 2020, Millennials are expected to be fully integrated into the labor force, just as Generation Z begins to enter it (Thompson, 2017). Interestingly, one ramification of the increase of the human lifespan is an increase in the retirement age. Therefore, the integration of Generation Z brings forth a new reality where four different generational cohorts are working side by side. Each cohort is conversant with its own habits, customs, skills, and standards, each with its own disparate needs that often contrast the others' required accommodations. From this perspective of cohort-bound forms of aging, five categories of generational cohorts are classified in literature: (a) the Traditionalists (also termed Veterans; individuals born between 1922 and 1945); (b) the Baby Boomers (individuals born between 1946 and

1964); (c) Generation Xers (individuals born between 1965 and 1980); (d) Generation Y/Millennials (individuals born between 1979 and 1990); and (e) Generation Z (born between 1991 and 2002) (Zemke et al., 2000).

Accordingly, the amalgamation of these five generational cohorts poses new challenges, never before encountered in the Westernized labor force, requiring further scrutiny and interpretation. Even though it is too early to discern the effects of iGen's integration into the workforce, much can be discussed in relation to Generation Y, particularly in terms of the distinction in ethical perceptions, values, and morals.

While the divergences in attitude and culture are taxing to all sectors, they are particularly noticeable within the public sector, presumably on account of the sector's conservative attitude and technologically incompetent nature. In opposition to previous multi-generational cohorts, however, it would appear that Generation Y's conflicting outlook with these public institutions is not only vexing to the sector but also throwing off-course the long-accustomed, quintessential modus-operandi. This is especially reflected in Generation Y's lack of loyalty to the workplace, as they've shown to frequently change career paths; and in their inability to abide by certain pre-established regulations, which they believe are no longer fitted to present realities.

> Millennials are unlike any other youth generation in living memory. They are more numerous, more affluent, better educated, and more ethnically diverse . . . They are beginning to manifest a wide array of positive social habits that older Americans no longer associate with youth, including a new focus on teamwork, achievement, modesty, and a good conduct. Only a few years from now, this can-do youth revolution will overwhelm the cynics and pessimists . . . This cohort wants to behave ethically (85%) with almost one-third willing to quit their job if they perceive their firm is behaving unethically . . . They also value working for more environmentally conscious companies (53%) and are willing to take less salary to do so . . . They are altruistic, care about volunteerism (85%), and believe it is important to give back to the community through unpaid service. (Strauss & Howe, 2000)

As a by-product, the Millennials' motivation to serve the public sector is steadily deteriorating. The 2011 survey conducted by the National

Association of Colleges and Employers (NACE), graduate students' interest in government and/or public-sector careers has dropped significantly (Bright & Graham, 2015).

The pretext behind this decline is ambivalent and is open to many interpretations. Some believe that the lack of interest in working in the public sector is a result of poor academic curriculums; weakening of the public-sector job market; the nature of governance, and subsequently, the rise of additional employment opportunities in the third sector and/or business sector—particularly the emergence of the tech industry and other opportunities made available as a result of globalization. Nonetheless, a repeated postulation is that which claims students hold the position that government organizations are not rewarding enough, as opposed to private sector organizations (Infeld & Adams, 2011).

Instinctively, one might be tempted to pair the lack of interest in government work with the preconceived notion that Millennials are "spoiled" or "sheltered"—"trophy" kids if you will. However, we would like to offer another perspective by first examining what this unique generational cohort perceives to be "rewarding" in the first place.

By the same token, we wish to challenge the commonly held belief that it is up to members of Generation Y to adjust themselves to the public sector. We maintain that the opposite is true—the system must learn to accommodate Generation Y and pay close attention to their demands. Not because they are special and must continue to be sheltered in the workplace, just as they were at home, but because a state's fate depends on it.

It is crucial to remember that unlike those cohorts before it, this cohort has plenty of other employment opportunities, often more attractive in other sectors—many of which tend to clash with the state's principal propositions and modus operandi (e.g., Facebook, Google, etc.). These other institutions offer Millennials exactly what they need to be content. As a result, they bring into their lineups the most adroit of workers, thereby depriving the public sector of the people most ideal for serving the state.

Ultimately, a lack of competent employees could, in turn, hinder—or even altogether prevent—the state's ability to address internal as well as external matters as they come, and perhaps further erode the younger generation's trust in the system. Therefore, the public sector must make an effort to cater to Generation Y, both for the sake of the younger generation's confidence in the state system and for the sake of the state's growth and development.

This book takes as its basic premise that generational diversity contributes to managing ethics and leadership in the public service that meets the public interest. In the future, the public workplace will be experiencing increased mobility and technological competencies required to satisfy social needs. Generational diversity management in public organizations may affect the public sector ethos and values and, in turn, may improve managerial efficiency, policy effectiveness, public service performance, and public trust in the public sector.

However, to benefit from the advantages of a generationally diverse workforce, public managers need to use it as a strategy through which the different experiences, workforce values, and competencies of public service employees play a part in improving performance, replacing retirees, and attracting competent staff. As such, the public service will become an attractive employer for Millennials.

Therefore, this project aims to highlight innovative practices in the pursuit and management of workforce diversity in the public sector and suggest some practical guidelines to enhance and make the most of a diverse workforce in the public service. The identification of trade-offs generated by a diverse public workforce and the measures adopted to support them are core elements of this project.

Chapter 1 discusses the development of the concept of diversity in the public service and the implementation of diversity management in recruitment, hiring, retainment, and managing a diverse workforce to enhance performance in public organizations. In this chapter, we review the literature on diversity practices in the area of human resource management (HRM). We focus on the theoretical underpinning of diversity management to evaluate HRM strategies and policies to manage diversity effectively. Our framework will also help researchers identify key areas for future research and guide practitioners to formulate and implement diversity appropriately.

Chapter 2 provides a valuable and thoughtful understanding of the theoretical foundation for generational differences based on the generational cohort approach. We first introduce definitions of generational boundaries that have been adopted in academic research and an organizational context; second, we identify generational differences in work-related attitudes and values; finally, we discuss the gaps in the literature and the implications of applying a cohort-based approach in public management and ethics. By approaching this study from a cohort-based approach, we could gain a clear and compelling picture of the similarities and differences between generational attitudes and behaviors, and their potential impact on individual and organizational decision-making and practice. In particular, it is suggested that the challenge for public-sector managers recruiting Generation Y employees, who are likely to have a distinctive set of values, beliefs, expectations, and attitudes, could affect the way this cohort approaches ethical issues and values conflicts that arise in daily practice.

Chapter 3 draws on ethical decision-making theories and models. Ethical decision-making is the process whereby individuals apply their ethical reasoning and attitudes to determine whether a given situation or issue is right or wrong. Ethical decision-making studies offer comprehensive cognitive models of ethical reasoning and examine individual and organizational variables that may facilitate or hinder ethical decision-making.

Chapter 4 aims to comprehend further why public servants engage in unethical behavior. We will briefly overview recent studies examining the antecedents and consequences of ethical judgment in public service. The scholarly discourse of public sector ethics identifies several antecedents to ethical judgment classified as organizational, environmental, and personal demographic characteristics underlying a wide array of global- and geographic-based trends.

Chapter 5 offers empirical testing of how generational diversity affects the extent to which successive generations of public service employees hold that public service ethos encourages ethical decision-making and behavior. The first objective of the research presented in the chapter is to stipulate and measure work-values differences and similarities across generations in the public service given the coming of age of a younger generation and the retirement of an older generation. It implies that understanding generational diversity in public sector values as they are inducted or socialized into normative attitudes and behaviors may facilitate the development of diversity management practices to address growing challenges spawned by age diversity. The proposed research is of special importance, given the disturbing growth of corruption and ethical misconduct in the public sector in Israel.

The second objective is to uncover the underlying mechanism of PSE (public sector ethos) by scrutinizing the effects of the three dimensions of PSE and ethical decision-making regarding ethically questionable conduct in the public service across generational cohorts. By focusing on the interaction effect between PSE and generational cohort on ethical sensitivity, rather than on the chosen variables alone, our study aims to contribute to the burgeoning exploration of the dynamic nature of the PSE construct in predicting what forms of ethical attitudes and judgments are associated with the most recent generation to enter the public service. An examination of the sort suggested here will focus on generational differences and their possible effect on public management, providing for informed management strategies to ethical training and code enforcement placed on the agenda of administrative ethics committees. Public managers need to be more proactive than reactionary in handling diversity issues involving members of different generations, including ethical issues.

For that, we define the construct of ethical sensitivity, public service ethos, and generational cohort. Second, we offer a set of propositions about how each variable influences the perceptions of ethical sensitivity in the public service and examine the effect of the interaction between PSE and generational cohorts on ethical sensitivity among public service employees in Israel. Next, we present a scenario-based instrument to measure ethical sensitivity, examining its association with public service ethos on a sample of 674 Israeli government-agency employees. We conclude by considering the implications of our findings for developing further research on the generational cohorts' understanding of PSE and public administration ethics for improving the effectiveness of diversity-management practices in organizational ethics in the future.

Finally, this book proposes to identify innovative practices in the pursuit and management of generational workforce diversity in the public sector and to provide some practical guidelines to enhance and make the most of Millennials working in the public service. Identifying trade-offs generated by a diverse public workforce and the strategies adopted to address them are core elements of demonstrating moral entrepreneurship of the public service.

Chapter 1

Diversity Management

This chapter highlights the development of diversity in the public service and the implementation of diversity management in recruitment, hiring, and retainment, to manage a diverse workforce and enhance performance in public organizations. In this chapter, we review the literature on diversity practices in human resource management (HRM). We focus on the theoretical underpinning of diversity management to evaluate HRM strategies and policies to manage diversity effectively. Our framework will also enable scholars to identify key milestones for future research and guide practitioners to formulate and implement diversity appropriately.

1.1. Conceptualization of Diversity in the Workplace

Diversity is often defined as a multifaceted concept. Robbins et al. (2012) indicate that the construct of diversity covers a broad range of attributes and conditions that distinguish individuals from one another. Therefore, diversity is hard to define. In its simplest form, diversity is associated with the distribution of concept differences among members of a given group (Babalola & Marques, 2013; Hays-Thomas, 2004; Kearney & Gebert, 2009; Konrad, 2003). A more subjective definition of diversity is offered by Loden and Rosener (1991, p. 223) as "otherness or those human qualities that are different from our own and outside groups to which we belong, yet present in other individuals and groups." A more in-depth definition of diversity, which encompasses different organizational variations and needs, and includes both business and ethical imperative reasoning is provided by Wise and Tschirhart (2000, p. 387):

> a self-conscious, programmatic approach affecting the policies, culture, and structure of an organization that incorporates a diverse workforce as a way to enhance organizational efficiency and effectiveness . . . [with a focus] on achieving positive outcomes from the interaction of individuals who vary in their degree of heterogeneity [which is] . . . the collective (all-inclusive) mixture of human differences and similarities along a given dimension.

Dimensions of diversity among workforce members include "race, culture, religion, gender, sexual preference, age, profession, organizational or team tenure, personality type, functional background, education level, political party, and other demographic, socioeconomic, and psychographic characteristics" (Wise & Tschirhart, 2000, p. 2). For example, *ethnicity and race diversity* practices were first introduced by passing the Civil Rights Act and the Equality Act in the US. Research on earlier ethnicity and race diversity in the workplace initiated during the late 1960s focused on ethnic and racial discrimination in recruitment and training and professional development, performance evaluation, and rewards (Shore et al., 2009). The impact of ethnic and racial differences between employees was measured in terms of job satisfaction, commitment, organizational motivation, and leadership (Kamenou et al., 2013; McKay & McDaniel, 2006; Williams & O'Reilly, 1998).

Nonetheless, studies on work teams yielded inconsistent findings (Jackson et al., 2003; Mannix & Neale, 2005). While it is commonly agreed that a diverse workforce contributes to an inclusive organizational environment necessary to drive innovation and foster creativity, the results of the studies on ethnically diverse work teams in comparison to homogeneous teams are not significant (e.g., Jehn & Bezrukova, 2004; McLeod et al., 1996; Watson et al., 1993; Webber & Donahue, 2001) or diverse teams produced negative effects (e.g., Jackson & Joshi, 2004; Kirkman et al., 2004). This evidence is often supported theoretically by the similarity-attraction paradigm of team composition, which maintains that members' perceptions of others, as frequently inferred based on similarity in demographic attributes, lead to attraction among team members (O'Reilly et al., 1989; Smith et al., 1994; Wiersema & Bantel, 1992). Cultural diversity engages with the effects of workforce diversity and organizational outcomes (Gelfand et al., 2007). Cultural diversity has been linked to the influence of positive organizational outcomes such as information processing, learning, and development of problem-solving competencies (Cox et al.,1991; Ely & Thomas, 2001). However, research on the implementation of cultural diversity practices in the workforce has also yielded negative stereotyping and social categorization regarding the behavior and perceptions among members of organizations (Dahlin et al., 2005). According to research, measuring the effects of cultural diversity in the workforce is challenging, especially in facilitating or restraining inter-professional collaboration in teams (; Earley & Mosakowski, 2000; Gelfand et al., 2007; Kirchmeyer & Cohen, 1992; Milliken & Martins, 1996).

The topic of gender diversity has resulted in a substantive body of literature on measuring the effects of gender differences on organizational outcomes across organizational functions, including attitudes to diversity, group efficacy and performance, organizational commitment to diversity, and a pro-diversity culture of female inclusionary policies (e.g., Bilimoria, 2006; Ely, 2004; Karakowsky et al., 2004; Lee & Farh, 2004; Mannix & Neale, 2005; Mavin et al., 2014; Rau & Hyland, 2003; Sawyerr et al., 2005). Prior research on the role of gender diversity in organizational performance has demonstrated two potentially problematic domains, namely, wage discrimination and inequality. While some efforts have been made to decrease the gender wage gap (e.g., by corrective pay measures such as merit pay awards), it remains extensive (Blau & Khan, 2006). Gender differences are assumed to play a moderating factor through the employee orientation process and subsequently to job satisfaction levels.

Disability diversity has been recently considered one of the important dimensions of diversity management in the workplace (Bell, 2012; Ren et al., 2008). Scholars have found different effects across the variety of types of disability, but as a whole, disability diversity raises negative perceptions such as prejudice, stereotyping, discrimination, and stigma in the workplace (Malo & Pagán, 2012; Schur et al., 2009). A potentially positive effect is found when the organization's management addresses disability diversity in the daily practices, with appropriate workplace adjustments or flexible work spheres and schedules, and when attracting and integrating a diverse workforce (Ball et al., 2005; Baumgärtner et al., 2014; Kulkarni & Lengnick-Hall, 2011; Wooten, 2008;). Consequently, corporate leadership and culture play a crucial role in encouraging or discouraging inclusive attitudes and practices for employees with disabilities (Schur et al., 2005).

Sexual orientation diversity management is essentially targeted at fostering positive effects of sexual orientation and mitigating its negative effects (Ozturk & Rumens, 2014; Ragins & Wiethoff, 2005). This type of diversity represents an invisible or underlying type of diversity instead of more visible traits such as race or gender. Research on sexual orientation diversity (e.g., gay, lesbian, bisexual, and transsexual (LGBT) employees) has been predominantly focused on heterosexism and discriminatory practices. The concept of heterosexism can be defined as "an ideological system that denies, denigrates, and stigmatizes any non-heterosexual form of behavior, identity, relationship, or community" (Herek, 1990, p. 316). Research has demonstrated that heterosexism in the organization can lead to a decrease in perceived productivity, job satisfaction, organizational commitment, and professional growth, as well as high turnover intentions among gay, lesbian, and bisexual employees (Berg & Lien, 2002; Blandford, 2003; Brown, 1998; Ellis & Riggle, 1995; Klawitter & Flatt, 1998; Ragins & Cornwell, 2001; Van Hoye & Lievens, 2003).

It is indicated that gay and lesbian employees may choose to work in lower-paying sectors or occupations such as the public sector, enabling them to disclose their sexual orientation in the workplace so that they feel more comfortable openly expressing their sexual orientation at work. This openness in lower-paying sectors is often more highly valued than monetary reward. The first bill on sexual orientation discrimination was introduced in the US Congress in 1974. An increase in the number of LGBT employees in the workforce was already evident to HR managers in the eighties (Day & Schoenrade, 2000). Consequently, in May of 1993, the board of the Society for Human Resource Management, the premier national association of American human resource practitioners, introduced a resolution to include sexual orientation in its statement, acclaiming the value of a diverse workforce (Day & Schoenrade, 2000). By 1994, the Employment Non-Discrimination Act (ENDA) was introduced in the United States Congress. The act would prohibit civilian nonreligious employees with at least 15 employees from discriminating against employees based on sexual orientation or gender identity. It should be noted that the bill failed several times. Until 2009, each proposal for protecting sexual diversity had failed. Currently, 21 states have laws that ban sexual orientation discrimination: California, Colorado, Connecticut, Delaware, Hawaii, Illinois, Iowa, Maine, Maryland, Massachusetts, Minnesota, Nevada, New Hampshire, New Jersey, New Mexico, New York, Oregon, Rhode Island, Vermont, Washington, and Wisconsin. Due to the limited number of states that enabled the law, LGBT people are more likely to face serious discrimination in employment, including being fired, denied a promotion, or experiencing harassment. Despite the adoption of LGBT-friendly HR practices and organizational performance (Chuang et al., 2011; Wang &

Schwarz, 2010), more research is needed to measure the effects of existing institutional mechanisms of LGBT-friendly policies by organizations on sexual orientation diversity in the workforce (Van Hoye & Lievens, 2003).

In the literature on human resource management (HRM), a distinction is being made between visible and invisible diversities when theorizing diversity (Kossek et al., 2005; SHRM, 2012). Visible diversity refers to those differences that are unchangeable and external. Visible diversity refers to certain identity groups, such as gender, race, and physical disability[1] (Foldy, 2002). In comparison, invisible diversity refers to those differences which are not instantly recognized or considered. Invisible differences can include, for example, family history, sexual orientation, political opinion, religion, culture, and education. The complexity in defining invisible diversity lies in the process of intersectionality, which addresses how intersecting social identities (e.g., gender, race, sexuality, class) interact in complex ways to construct simultaneous forms of dominance and subordination, and privilege and oppression (patriarchy, colonialism, imperialism, neoliberalism, etc.) (Brah & Phoenix 2013; Patil, 2013, p. 850; Warner and Shields 2013).

As such, intersectionality's conceptual boundaries take on various contextual meanings, interpretations, and analyses. Intersectionality, as Bose (2012) has recently argued, is becoming an emerging favorite for methodological design since it has been shown as the best tool for investigating cross-cutting themes, such as health, religion, or militarization. These themes are composed of interrelated foundations upon which broad inequalities or manifestations of oppression are built (Bose 2012; Hankivsky & Renee, 2011). The field of intersectionality grants researchers the ability to see how interlocking systems of oppression converge to create a complex interplay of multiplicity and intersecting identities within structures of power. Furthermore, burgeoning research has begun to explore the relationship between "intersectionality in action" and social movement organization. Albeit still in its fledgling stages of exploration, the interplay between intersectionality and social movements promises to demystify the various pathways to identities affected and informed by oppression within an organizational structure.

Due to socio-political context shifts, an added layer of complexity to invisible diversity encompasses generational differences. For example,

1. One should note that disability is considered both a visible and an invisible type of diversity, see the discussion in Konrad, Alison M. (Ed); Prasad, Pushkala (Ed); Pringle, Judith K. (Ed). Examining the Contours of Workplace Diversity: Concepts, Contexts, and Challenges. Thompson-Southwestern, Mason, Ohio, 2005 (chapter 16).

in the United States, older people may define themselves as "Blacks" while younger people may use "African Americans." Cultural variations influence the conceptualization of diversity, specifically in the workplace environment. For example, in the US workplace, diversity is associated with differences in gender, race, ethnicity, age (including generational age), physical disability, religion, and sexual orientation. In Europe, diversity refers to language, culture, and nationality (Mor Barak, 2005). Therefore, understanding diversity's conceptual variations across countries (and even subcultures) requires the analysis of the social meanings and relative power positions of diversity groups (Haq, 2004). This approach builds on Konrad's (2003) definition of diversity that emphasizes intergroup interaction and is inclusive of power differences, rather than concentrating on individual differences. Furthermore, one must take into account past discrimination and oppression in producing socially marginalized groups.

Gazley, Chang, and Bingham (2010) differentiate between diversity and representativeness, which are often used interchangeably. They suggest that diversity holds a different meaning from representativeness as it is "closely synonymous with a variety of heterogeneity, or having qualities or characteristics," while representativeness is viewed as a "more purposeful term, referring to the extent to which an organization reflects constituent characteristics in its governance or operations" (p. 610).

Additionally, closely related to the concept of diversity is the concept of cultural competency. Cross (1988) defined cultural competency as "a set of congruent behaviors, attitudes, and policies that come together in a system, agency, or professional and enable that system, agency, or professional to work effectively in cross cultural situations" (p. 1). Wyatt-Nichol and Antwi-Boasiako (2008) offer to define cultural competency as "the ability to effectively interact with individuals different from oneself" (p. 79). Drawing on these definitions, the concept of cultural competency is distinguished from the concept of diversity in that it provides a more inclusive framework that better meets the multi-dimensions of diversity (Norman-Major & Gooden, 2012). It is by no means suggested that cultural competency and diversity may not be integrated to foster diversity management strategies. Indeed, cultural competency is the mechanism through which diversity is managed appropriately. This goes the other way around—if diversity does not evolve, cultural competency will become a meaningless instrument (Sabharwal & Royster, 2014). Therefore, both diversity and cultural competency are needed to better account for and foster various diversity management practices across sectors.

1.2. Managing Diversity in the Workplace

Diversity management is human resource management (HRM) practice that aims to promote a diverse workforce in recruitment, hiring, and retention to improve organizational performance and efficiency as well as encourage social justice and inclusion (Cunningham, 2009; Morrison et al., 2006). It is difficult to locate the origin of diversity initiatives in the workforce. According to McCormick (2007), the first modern equal employment legislation was introduced in the United States Congress in 1943 (and subsequent legislative initiatives proposed over the next 20 years). In 1948, President Truman signed Executive Order 9981 to bring together the armed services, which is observed as introducing diversity initiative in the workplace (McCormick, 2007). The Executive Order 9981 specified equality of treatment and opportunity in the armed services but did not go further to forbid segregation. As it is stated in Executive Order 9981: "It is hereby declared to be the policy of the President that there shall be equality of treatment and opportunity for all persons in the armed services without regard to race, color, religion, or national origin" (Note the lack of reference to "sex" among the protected categories) (See Executive Order 9981, "Establishing the President's Committee on Equality of Treatment and Opportunity in the Armed Services," July 26, 1948). Both President Truman and the President's Committee on Equality of Treatment and Opportunity in the Armed Services created to administer the integration of the armed services used Executive Order 9981 to manage the integration of the armed services. This initiative has led to the integration of 95% of African American army soldiers in integrated service units (Truman Presidential Museum and Library, Desegregation of the Armed Forces Documents at www.trumanlibrary.org.). During the 1960s, social and political changes led to the passage of civil rights legislation that prohibited discrimination on the basis of race, color, religion, sex, national origin, and later, age. Indeed, in the course of the congressional debates over Title VII, amendments were proposed that would have also prohibited discrimination based on age.[2] While these amendments were defeated, Congress asked the secretary of labor to deliver insights on the effects of age discrimination (McCormick, 2007). In 1965, the secretary of labor issued *The Older American Workers—Age Discrimination in Employ-*

---

2. See 42 U.S.C. 2000e, Title VII of the Civil Rights Act of 1964, as amended, ("Title VII"); 29 U.S.C. 621, The Age Discrimination in Employment Act.

ment report, which recorded discrimination against older workers, which later became the basis for the Age Discrimination in Employment Act in 1967. Consequently, the Equal Employment Opportunity Act of 1972 signaled the beginning of raising the awareness of workplace diversity in the US by providing the regulatory framework for advancing the interest of people of color in the workplace.

During the 1990s, research on diversity focused mainly on representative bureaucracy, affirmative action, and equal employment opportunities (Grabosky & Rosenbloom, 1975; Kellough, 1990; Meier, 1975; Meier & Nigro, 1976; Nachmias & Rosenbloom, 1973; Rosenbloom, 1977). Studies aimed at evaluating the adequate representation of women and minority groups enrolled in public organizations to the extent to which government organizations mirror the composition of the larger population they are committed to serving. Scholars were interested in finding whether the government succeeded in complying with the laws and regulations governing the public service, thus prohibiting discrimination in recruitment, selection, and other human resources functions (Cornwell & Kellough, 1994; Kellough, 1990; Lewis, 1996; Lewis & Allee, 1992; Nkomo & Cox, 1999). These studies showed confusing findings as several studies documented the government's ability to manage diversity among public servants by providing equal employment opportunities to women and people of color. However, at the same time, they also showed the failure of the government to gain the advantages of this diversity to increase the effectiveness of public service delivery (Cornwell & Kellough, 1994; Foldy, 2004; Gentile, 1994; Riccucci, 2002).

In 1990, Thomas first introduced diversity management as an organizational strategy for enhancing an environment in which employees are able to reach their full potential in pursuit of organizational objectives. Thomas defined diversity as a concept that "includes everyone: it is not something that is defined by race or gender. It extends to age, personal and corporate background, education, function, and personality. It includes lifestyle, sexual preference, geographic origin, tenure with the organization . . . and management and non-management" (1990, p. 12). Such definition of diversity views individuals as different and equally valued, thus ignoring power relations between identity groups. Similarly, Ivancevich and Gilbert (2000, p. 75) defined managing diversity practice as "the systematic and planned commitment by organizations to recruit, retain, reward, and promote a heterogeneous mix of employees." Pitts (2006, p. 235) suggests that "diversity management is a multifaceted concept" and, as such, encompasses three components: "recruitment programs, cultural awareness initiatives, and pragmatic management policies." Critics of the implicit hierarchical power of the term managing diversity view it as the powerholders' "continued commitment to pursuing control . . . under the guise of liberal affirmation" (Casey, 2002, p. 143). Therefore, a hierarchy of appropriateness and differential disbursement of power within and amongst identity groups approaches regards diversity management as part of affirmative action initiatives. Following this approach, diversity management enlists with traditional affirmative action (AA) or equal employment opportunity (EEO) policies (Groeneveld & Verbeek, 2012).

Commonly, a distinction is made between managing diversity and EEO and AA (Cassell, 2001; Hays-Thomas, 2004) by arguing that affirmative action or equal employment opportunity policies (AA/EEO) engage solely in recruitment and selection processes, while diversity management embraces broader organizational policies and methods that aim to increase legitimacy, creativity, and innovation, and positive employee attitudes and behaviors, which improves organizational performance (Ashikali & Groeneveld, 2015; Ely & Thomas, 2001; Groeneveld, 2011; Groeneveld & Van de Walle, 2010; Pitts, 2009). Consequently, diversity management, AA, and EEO differ in terms of methodological operationalization, e.g., managing diversity is based on behavioral research in which the emphasis is on building employees' competencies through the rewarding system to achieve the objectives such as profit and productivity. Unlike managing diversity, affirmative action uses quantitative techniques to increase the understanding of the impact of diversity on different effects on employees and workplace outcomes (Rice, 2001; 2004).

Drawing on the differences between managing diversity and AA/EEO, it is argued that managing diversity builds on individual assessment presumably in a way that does not increase discrimination or favoritism. Managing diversity carries a legacy of management that is about control, leadership, organization, and power. Moreover, it is commonly argued that managing diversity needs to go beyond a passive (valuing diversity) to an active (managing diversity) approach. An active approach lies within the hierarchical corporate control systems where organizational authority lies with senior management. As such, diversity management should be implemented by senior managers to bring organizational change, including mentoring programs, succession planning, responsive programs, alternative work arrangements, training, and accountability (Bozeman & Feeney, 2009; Kellough & Naff, 2004; Morrison, 1992; Pitts,

2006, 2009; Pitts et al., 2010; Riccucci, 2002; Rice, 2004; Roberson, 2006; Strachan et al., 2004).

This diversity framework carries an ambiguous requirement of predicting and pre-empting the needs of multiple identity groups "lower" in the organization. Managing diversity then becomes the task of higher rank managers engaging in "double-guessing" the needs and wishes of the marginal groups (Jones et al, 2000). According to Alvesson and Willmott (1996), "emancipation is not a gift to bestow" (p. 33) and acts of assimilation and integration can "estrange the individual from the tradition, which has formed his or her very subjectivity" (p. 174).

Functionalist management scholars have demonstrated the importance of supporting managing diversity over valuing diversity for its agentic virtues. This indicates an opening for a variety of nuanced conceptualizations of affirming or valuing diversity (Kamp & Hagedorn-Rasmussen, 2004; Thomas & Ely, 1996). Diversity management is a human resource management method relying on organizational authority and control, while at the same time it "emphasizes the value of difference among people in organizations" (Kamp & Hagedorn Rasmussen, 2004, p. 535). Diversity management implies the need for managing diversity scholarship to address "mutual respect, collaborative work styles, and employee empowerment" (Betters-Reed & Moore, 1992, p. 47). In addition, diversity management highlights the need to allow more room for ethical and moral theorizing (Kirby & Harter, 2003). Diversity tolerance should be taken into account when bringing organizational change so that efforts should be made to value differences between employees of different social identity groups in a way that would not turn organizations into one of grudging tolerance. In this book, framing managing diversity may not rely solely on achieving organizational objectives but on an ethical matter, a theme we take up below.

1.3. Managing Diversity Initiatives as a "Double-Edged Sword"

Studies have set out to identify the outcomes of managing diversity practices in terms of beneficial or detrimental effects that have yielded contradictory findings. Moreover, it is also argued that one cannot demarcate a distinction between positive and negative effects of managing diversity as often the negative effects of demographic diversity appear to fade over time (e.g., Harrison et al., 2002), and positive effects of cognitive diversity are more likely to succeed when employees are faced with a broadened range of complex and non-routine tasks (Pelled et al., 1999). The underlying assumption is that diverse workgroups have a comprehensive and richer base of experience from which to approach a problem, and that allows them to enhance critical analysis in decision groups by group diversity (Cox, 1991). It is suggested that heterogeneous team membership promotes creativity, innovation, and problem-solving, hence generating more informed decisions (Horwitz, 2005). Diversity workgroups convey informational diversity, defined as differences in knowledge sources and perspectives that members bring to the group (Jehn et al., 1999). Homan et al. (2007) suggest that informational diversity and perspectives on workgroups can potentially increase performance when groups are using their informational resources and when group members are committed to valuing diversity in their organization. Therefore, diversity beliefs moderated the relationship between informational diversity and performance, such that informationally diverse groups improved their performance when they held pro-diversity beliefs rather than pro-similarity beliefs (Homan et al., 2007). The divergent effects of diversity in the workplace are also indicated by Milliken and Martins (1996) as "diversity appears to be a double-edged sword, increasing the opportunity for creativity as well as the likelihood that group members will be dissatisfied and fail to identify with the group" (p. 3).

From the decision-making/information processing approach, managing diversity may foster positive cognitive effects and mitigate negative affective effects resulting from intergroup biases (Ashikali & Groeneveld, 2015). Building on van Knippenberg et al. (2004), the elaboration of Milliken and Martins's Categorization-Elaboration-Model (CEM), which combines an "elaboration and decision-making" perspective and a "social categorization" perspective on diversity, results in positive effects of information processing in the face of negative effects of intergroup biases that may arise from social categorization processes in such groups (Ashikali & Groeneveld, 2015).

Drawing on a more general HRM and social exchange perspective, perceptions of a fair diversity climate directly affect minority group job performance (McKay et al., 2008), as well as other organizational outcomes such as organizational commitment and turnover intentions (Buttner et al., 2010).

Gould-Williams and Davies (2005) demonstrate that the mechanism of social exchange also promotes a positive relationship between HR practices, including diversity management initiatives and performance. Employees who positively value HR management practices are more likely to meet the organization's values (often referred to as employee-organization value fit) (Bowen & Ostroff, 2004; Nishii et al., 2008; Wright & Nishii, 2007). Research on top management teams has suggested that an organization's performance increases when the senior management group is more diverse (Kravitz, 2003). In addition, it is argued that gender diversity might increase performance while an absence of gender diversity might lead to increased discrimination and stigmatization (Kravitz, 2003). For example, Kravitz (2003) found that organizations with few women in senior management positions are more likely to embrace stereotypical gender roles, and women in such organizations typically have less power. Therefore, these organizations may be less attractive to women (Kravitz, 2003). This evidence is also supported by Frink et al. (2003), whose study examined whether gender diversity would have a positive impact on organizational performance. Specifically, they predicted that performance would be maximized when female employees comprised about half of an organization's workforce. In the first study, Frink et al. used a survey of personnel officers from 291 US companies, which were ranked by their gender distribution, size, and sector (services vs. goods). Performance outcomes were measured based on profitability and growth in sales. On average, these companies had 624 employees, 49% of whom were women. The research showed that there was an overall positive effect of female participation on the organization's performance. Notably, organizational performance increased with female participation up to a maximum of 50%, after which it decreased (Frink et al., 2003).

Positive effects of diversity such as productivity and employee commitment in terms of organizational performance are found in studies focusing on business strategy. These studies show that managing diversity improves "tackling market competition and enhancing corporate reputation" (Cooke & Saini, 2010, p. 480) as well as encouraging organizational change (Olson & Eoyang, 2001; Srivastava & Barmola, 2012; Stevens et al., 2008). Roberson and Park (2007) found a relationship between diversity reputation and singling investors about companies' future performance. More specifically, they demonstrated a positive relationship between top management team diversity and revenue growth such that organizations with greater ethnic minority representation in top management ranks tended to experience larger increases in annual revenues. It is suggested that capital market participants may use Fortune's list of the 50 best companies for minorities as a quality diversity reputation signal or may assess such a designation as relevant when evaluating a company's expected stock returns (Roberson & Park, 2007). Accordingly, Weigand (2007) argues that a diverse workforce becomes a strategic business asset that leads to improved decision-making, problem-solving, innovation, and creativity when developing relationships with other diverse stakeholders.

A growing interest in the diversity management literature is to evaluate managing diversity practices in organizations not only by performance outcomes but also in terms of ethical aspects (Lozano & Escrich, 2017). Ethical imperatives approaches are based upon objectives like social justice and inclusion for building "an equitable work environment, free of discrimination, stereotypes, glass ceilings, and other impediments to the full participation and inclusion of women and people of color" (Naff & Kellough, 2003, p. 1309). Johnson (2009) argued that fostering diversity should be seen as an ethical imperative to stimulate employees to act ethically and prevent them from acting unethically.

Negative effects of diversity initiatives are manifested in lower performance (Herring, 2009). For example, a diverse workforce can have an adverse effect on cooperation and collective action in terms of time consumption (Chatman & Flynn, 2001; Foldy, 2004). For example, group members who differ from the majority tend to have lower levels of organizational commitment as well as higher levels of turnover intent and absenteeism than majority members. It is also suggested that group coordination costs, such as increased communication time, seem to increase with diversity (Watson et al., 1993).

To address these challenges, an organization must hold diversity audits to determine whether its climates are supportive of diversity, better communicate organizational recruitment processes to support racial adjustments and place them in minority-rich recruitment sources, evaluate recruitment and retention effectiveness, and eliminate workplace characteristics that undermine diversity recruitment and minority retention. Skepticism of the effectiveness of managing diversity initiatives and the commitment of top management to diversity initiatives often arises when such programs are unable to effectively value the diversity among employees and encourage their participation in decisions that impact their individual and organizational objectives and values (Pless & Maak, 2004).

1.4. Managing Diversity Approaches

As seen, the organizational literature reveals a recent increase in the number of diversity management studies. This proliferation in diversity studies has been accompanied by a wide range of multidisciplinary approaches applied to organizational studies. In this section, we will discuss relevant approaches pertaining to diversity management research across public and private organizational settings.

1.4.1. Colorblindness and Multiculturalism Approaches

In organizational studies, scholars have attempted to examine diversity management practices using colorblindness and multiculturalism (Stevens et al., 2008). Using the colorblind approach, organizations are committed to treating employees equally as individuals. In addition, group differences should be disregarded when making decisions, such as hiring and promotion. This focus is on individual achievements and competencies rather than cultural characteristics (Stevens et al., 2008). Group equality is then promoted when group differences are downplayed, and the members who constitute the groups are treated as identical to each other (Rattan & Ambady, 2013). This approach is based on the assumption that individuals or institutions can only act in a racially biased manner if they are able to notice race. If they do not observe race, then they cannot act in a racially biased manner (Apfelbaum et al., 2012).

In contrast, a multicultural approach emphasizes that differences between cultural groups should be recognized and are beneficial for organizational performance (Cox, 1991; Stevens et al., 2008). The multicultural approach draws on the understanding that differences between cultural groups are seen as a source of strength to the organization. Encouraging diversity implies that different backgrounds and cultural group identities are recognized and valued (Apfelbaum et al., 2012; Plaut et al., 2011; Rattan & Ambady, 2013). Whereas majority groups show higher levels of support for colorblindness than minorities, minorities tend to support multiculturalism more than majorities (Plaut et al., 2011; Ryan et al., 2007; Verkuyten, 2005; Wolsko et al., 2004).

However, in organizational diversity practice, insights delivered from both colorblindness and multiculturalism approaches have not been frequently complemented by organizational initiatives that address management diversity but rather by national integration policies (e.g., Karafantis et al., 2010; Levin et al., 2012; Plaut et al., 2011; Ryan et al., 2007; Wolsko et al., 2004). A key weakness in colorblindness and multiculturalism is the lack of knowledge about the impact of diversity approaches on majority and minority group members in an organizational context (Jansen et al., 2015).

1.4.2. The All-Inclusive Multiculturalism (AIM) Approach

The lack of application of both colorblindness or multiculturalism as a framework for diversity management research, as well as the problems related to the ideological split between members of minority and non-minority groups in the workplace, have paved the way for the all-inclusive multiculturalism (AIM) approach. The all-inclusive multiculturalism (AIM) approach aims to provide a more applicable framework to better account for the perceptions of inclusion in the organization by minority and majority members. This approach combines colorblind and multicultural approaches by emphasizing the importance of perceptions of inclusion not only to enhance effective individual work outcomes, but also to improve the functioning of groups and organizations. In this regard, it has been suggested that as individuals perceive to be more included, they are more motivated to contribute to the group (Ellemers & Jetten, 2013).

1.4.3. Organizational Integration and Learning Approach

The organizational integration and learning approach to diversity was introduced by Thomas and Ely (1996). Thomas and Ely (1996) conceptualize diversity by valuing employees' subjective needs for belonging and differences and "removing the barriers that block (them) from using the full range of their competencies" (Thomas & Ely, 1996, p. 11). Moreover, cultural competence is strongly valued and respected, as it uses cultural differences among employees as a learning experience to help them learn from divergence rather than feeling anxious or suppressing it. Differences can become a source of improved organizational performance but only if they are acknowledged and constructively explored as they "are potentially valuable resources that the [organization] can use to rethink its primary tasks and redefine its markets, products, strategies, and business practices in ways that will advance its mission" (Ely & Thomas 2001, p. 240). Thomas and Ely call on organizations to apply the organizational integration and learning approach to diversity management for achieving competitive advantage to "incorporate employees' perspectives into the main work of the organization and to enhance work by rethinking primary tasks and redefining markets, products, strategies, missions, business practices, and even cultures" (Thomas & Ely, 1996, p. 85). The organizational learning process requires groups to employ the integration-and-learning perspective in their daily practices, whether implicitly or explicitly, thereby enabling an open discussion regarding the implications of diversity in handling tasks and finding new solutions for achieving organizational objectives (Dass & Parker, 1999). The organizational integration and learning approach differs from other organizational approaches to diversity as it accelerates the normative contribution of diversity management: "The rationale that guides people's efforts to create and respond to cultural diversity in a work group; normative beliefs about the value of cultural identity at work; expectations about the kind of impact, if any, cultural differences can and should have on the group and its work; and beliefs about what constitutes progress toward the ideal multicultural work group" (Ely & Thomas, 2001, p. 234). Organizational integration and learning approach to diversity is manifested through six universal ethical values that are closely synonymous to hyper norms (Schwartz, 2016, p. 39) based mostly on the Thomas and Ely paradigm including:

1. trustworthiness manifested by "setting a tone of honest discourse" (Thomas & Ely, 1996, p. 12) and "mak[ing] sure their organizations remain 'safe' places for employees to be themselves" (Thomas & Ely, 1996, p. 12);
2. respect manifested by "acknowledg[ing] differences among people and recogniz[ing] the value in those differences" (Thomas & Ely, 1996, p. 7);
3. responsibility manifested by "identifying important similarities and differences and managing them in the interests of long-term learning" (Dass & Parker, 1999, p. 72) and by integrating differences "to inform and enhance core work and work processes" (Ely & Thomas, 2001, p. 248);
4. fairness manifested by "equal and fair treatment of everyone" (Podsiadlowski et al., 2013, p. 160);
5. caring manifested by "actively working against forms of dominance and subordination that inhibit full contribution" (Thomas & Ely, 1996, p. 11) and by "resolving [tensions] sensitively and swiftly" (Thomas & Ely, 1996, p. 12);
6. citizenship manifested by "encourag[ing] active participation in finding better, faster, or more efficient ways of compliance beyond those legally mandated." (Dass & Parker, 1999, p. 72)

1.4.4. Contingency Approach

The contingency approach focuses on understanding the effects and relationships of certain diversity management practices and how they fit with organizational culture and needs (McGrandle, 2017). According to Kast and Rosenzweig (1973), contingency is generally defined as: "[t]he contingency view of organizations and their management suggests that an organization is a system composed of subsystems and delineated by identifiable boundaries from its environmental supra-system."

The need to match the mindset of the individual with the characteristics of the organization was introduced during the 1960s in HR management theory (Lofquist & Dawis, 1969). The adjustment to work theory focused on the role of the environment and matching its requirements to the characteristics of the individual (Dawis, 2005). It underlies the congruence of the individual and environmental factors; "interaction between individual and environment comes about because both parties have requirements that potentially can be fulfilled by the other [otherwise known as 'needs']" (Dawis, 1980, p. 268). This understanding is often described as "mutual responsiveness" (Dawis, 1980, p. 268). Following the adjustment to work theory, there are two main indicators of a successful work relationship: satisfaction (well-being of the individual) and satisfactoriness (adequate performance in the environment) (Dawis, 2005). The outcome of both satisfaction and satisfactoriness is work adjustment, or what Lofquist and Dawis (1969) have referred to as tenure, the length of time an employee stays within the organization.

Contingency theory lists eight dimensions affecting the match between the organization and the environment: socio-demographic, technological, cultural, educational, legal, political, economic, and ecological. These dimensions may lead to strong variation in terms of organizations' unique environments and members' needs (Lorsch, 1973; Pugh et al., 1973). This observable variation reflects incoherence and contested convergence lead to differentiate between intervention strategies to the extent that it is necessary to use such strategies to address organizational change problems (Harrison, 1973); and that there is no model to measure performance outcomes (Rejc, 2004).

Therefore, the contingency approach pertains to a match between individual and organizational characteristics. The ability to discern different organizational environments allows for the drawing of different lenses through which public and private organizations can encourage diversity management practices that meet their unique culture and values. For example, for the public organization, the contingency approach might be applied "to demonstrate an awareness of the roots of many public management innovations in private sector practice, and of the political context in which those innovations were applied . . ." (McCourt, 2001, p. 244).

1.4.5. Institutional Approach

An attempt is made to examine diversity management practices by using institutional theory (Yang & Konrad, 2011). The institutional approach focuses on the normative aspects within which organizations operate. A major thrust of this theory is the identification of three types of structures: regulative, normative, and cognitive structures that influence behaviors: "Regulative institutions include laws, regulations, and rules; normative institutions include social and professional norms; and cognitive institutions include cultures and ethics" (Yang & Konrad 2011, p. 12). These structures frame the antecedents of diversity management practices. For example, government regulations and legislation are crucial for enhancing employment equity programs that employ diversity in recruitment processes (Benimadhu & Wright, 1991; Holzer & Neumark, 2000), inclusion programs for employees with disabilities (Balser, 1999; Woodhams & Corby, 2007), and reducing bias and discrimination in compensation and tenure (Dobbin et al., 1993; Konrad & Linnehan, 1995). Scott demonstrates the value of the institutional approach to diversity management as "institutions operate at different levels of jurisdiction, from the world system to localized interpersonal relationships . . . by definition connote stability but are subject to change processes, both incremental and discontinuous" (Scott, 1995, p. 48).

Developing regulative rule-based belief systems is measured by legitimacy as a positive outcome of applying an institutional approach to diversity management. Legitimacy is defined as the actions of a group of social actors to gain acceptance and approval of their actions by their stakeholders (Jain et al., 2012; Harcourt, Lam, & Harcourt, 2005). The institutional theory then stipulates an analytical lens to examine how and why specific actors use their power to legitimize and institutionalize specific policies and practices (Yang & Konrad, 2011). Therefore, relations between diversity management practices and positive work perspectives underlie the idea that diversity practices may be recognized as legitimate by the organization's employees. For example, Avery and McKay (2006) showed a correlation between employment statistics to applicants' ratings of the diversity reputation of prospective employers. Notably, while Roberson and Stevens (2006) showed a correlation between employment statistics to employees' accounts of diversity-related occasions in organizations, Pugh et al., (2008) showed a correlation between employment statistics to employee ratings of the organizational diversity climate.

It is noteworthy that the institutional approach holds that institutional structural forces can be both enabling but also constraining in terms of organizational homogeneity. The homogeneity of organizations is problematic for both organizational change and considering diversity management practices as internal and external environments that influence the organization.

1.4.6. Resource-based Approach

The resource-based theory implies that the possession of strategic resources provides an organization with competitive advantages over its competitors. The primary focus of the resource-based approach is on organizational performance heterogeneity. While institutional theory emphasizes social and normative aspects of an organization's functioning, it stresses firm strategy and performance (Yang & Konrad, 2011, p. 28). The resource-based approach entails a performance-management system being flexible in order to recognize and respond to the changes of operating inputs and resources over time and dynamically adapt the system accordingly.

Among the variety of organizational resources that affect organizational performance heterogeneity are physical, financial, and human capital and corporate capital resources (Yang & Konrad, 2011, p. 19). In this regard, diversity is valued in terms of its efficiency or effectiveness in attaining financial gain. For instance, Ely (2004) shows that employee participation in diversity education programs was related to increased sales productivity. Jehn and Bezrukova (2004) demonstrate that supervisors' evaluations of employees' cultural competencies were positively associated with pay supplement; however, no significant relationship was found with group or individual performance assessments. Pitts's study (2009) found that employee perceptions of their managers' commitment to diversity practices positively impacted employees' perceptions of organizational performance and quality of work. Few studies have shown a positive relationship between rewarding diversity actions within an organization and financial performance (Roberson & Park, 2007; Weigand, 2007; Wright et al., 1995). Kochan et al. (2003) suggested using diversity management practices as a moderator of the relationship between the diversity of human capital and performance outcomes. His suggestion was based on the assumption that diversity management practices enable organizations to gain value in terms of financial gain from a diverse employee system. As stated in HRM terms, the resources can be managed to create effectiveness and do so in a highly efficient manner that can handle uncertainty in the environment through employee-oriented organizational culture, and a customer-oriented business strategy enhances the positive effects of gender diversity on constructive group processes. As such, diversity management practices may extend our understanding of how increased employee diversity can contribute to a competitive advantage over time.

Nonetheless, this perspective presents a major drawback, especially for private organizations, as it overlooks other dimensions of diversity management, such as equal opportunities and long-term sustainable development (Bleijenbergh et al., 2010, p. 414). Methodologically, the main effects of diversity management practices on performance from a resource-based theoretical lens hinge on relationships among diverse stakeholders, yet there is no consensus on measuring these relationships, thus making it difficult to evaluate the effectiveness of diversity management practices (Yang & Konrad, 2011). In addition, the resource-based approach often ignores the pressures of internal and external environments on the application of diversity management practices (Priem & Butler, 2001; Yang & Konrad, 2011).

Although there is no scholarly consensus on an acceptable theoretical framework for diversity management, the issues highlighted above in the applications of various theoretical and methodological frameworks indicate that diversity management has promise as an area of study, especially its normative effects to better account for and improve its application across sectors. In this book, we will focus on age diversity. The next chapter focuses on age, and generational age differences, and their implications for the field of public administration.

1.5 Window on Management

This chapter provides an in-depth review of literature dealing with the conceptualization of diversity in the public service, its evolutionary steps, and the implementation of diversity management in recruitment, hiring, and retainment, to manage a diverse workforce. Through the varied theories analyzed, we review the prevalent diversity practices in the field of human resource management (HRM): colorblindness and multiculturalism approaches, all-inclusive multiculturalism (AIM) approach, organizational integration and learning approach, contingency approach, institutional approach, and resource-based approach. For about a decade, global organizations have been managing to enhance diversity. CEMEX,[3] for example, a global building materials company that provides products and services throughout the Americas, Europe, Africa, the Middle East, and Asia, developed a job opportunity policy to ensure employees can apply for open positions to support their professional growth. Hiring decisions are not made based on an employee's race, color, age, religion, mental or physical disability, sex, or nationality. In addition, CEMEX compensation packages are based on the responsibility level of the position and not related to race, gender, religion, age, or any other protected traits.

Orange,[4] one of the foremost telecommunications operators in the world, has recruitment procedures that structure positive discrimination in the case of the most socially disadvantaged people, which establish that to cover any vacancy, the pool must contain at least one disabled candidate and one woman. At Ericsson,[5] which is also a world leader in supplying and developing 2G, 3G, and 4G mobile technologies and telecommunications services, has a program for the integration of new employees into the company through which they are guided by their direct supervisor and their "buddy" (a person with experience in the company who acts as a guide for the new employee).

---

3. See, https://www.cemex.com/documents/20143/160187/cemex-position-diversity-inclusion-2020.pdf/1c33a0ab-adb5-7882-cc77-9cd23c7759d2

4. See, https://www.orange-consulting.de/files/doc/downloads/_de/oc_portfolio/Orange-Consulting-Diversity.pdf

5. Diversity and Inclusion drives innovation—Ericsson, see https://www.ericsson.com/en/about-us/diversity-and-inclusion

Chapter 2

Generational Diversity

A Literature Overview

The year 2020 marks the start of a new decade and the dawn of unprecedented changes in the omnipresent workforce. In virtue of scientific developments, the average human lifespan continues to increase, and as a result, the average age of retirement increases accordingly. Researchers have determined that the year 2020 will be the first year to integrate four distinct generations under one roof, unifying within it the following cohorts: the Boom Generation, Generation X, Generation Y, and Generation Z (Thompson, 2017). In practice, this unprecedented reality presents a likely occurrence that two employees within one place of work may have an age difference of nearly half a century.

Though a seemingly innocuous affair, prior research has manifested that integrating multiple generational cohorts presents a wide range of challenges. If these challenges were to be left unattended, they could potentially disrupt the functionality of a workplace.

While this is germane to all sectors and industries, these changes are expected to be especially consequential within the public sector, which has gained a reputation for being archaic and incapable of adapting to the new globalized world (Mulgan, 2014).

As each generational cohort is unique in its strategies and techniques, managing multiple generations under one workforce also requires a disparate management style, and distinct terms and conditions perfectly designed for each cohort. Having said that, however, research by Sullivan et al. (2009) found that the difference between Boomers and Generation

X is non-existent in terms of their needs and challenges in the workforce. Therefore, it should also be taken into account that, in theory, if a workplace were to be comprised solely of these two generations, it may not require autonomous terms and conditions. However, this does not mean that such a workplace would be exempt from making an effort. It remains consequential to better understand the characteristics and needs of these two generations on the whole, because even the mere fact that the two may require similar management requires understanding in and of itself. Paying tribute to generational experiences is still necessary to obtain a healthy work environment. The sooner these matters are attended to, the better of a workplace will be.

The forthcoming amendments in the workforce are presumed to evolve into subsidiary challenges for employees and managers alike. Failure to properly adhere to these impediments may negatively impact the functionality of the labor force. Therefore, it is important to take proactive action and ensure that pertinent adjustments are made, ones that ultimately enable the four cohorts to collectively and effectively operate together.

2.1. Generations and Age

Before we begin our core analysis of generational gaps and their implications on the public sector at large, we must first take a gander at the notion of generations and differentiate between generation and age. Even though most individuals may manage to innately gather some discrepancies on their own, the notion of generation and age is not quite as straightforward as it would initially appear. In fact, oftentimes, elements that should be taken into account are unfortunately disregarded. An understanding of these precise nuances allows for a more in-depth comprehension of generational concepts, particularly the concepts related to generational gaps. In a broader sense, paying observation to even the subtlest of disparity allows us to comprehend better the manners in which our society has changed, how it has evolved over time, and finally, how it has managed to ameliorate our future.

In this next section, we will explore the concept of *age* to differentiate between *age* and *generation*. According to Cleveland and Lim (2007), Kooij et al. (2010), and Sterns and Doverspike (1989), chronological age refers to the year in which a person was born, or alternatively, how long a person has been alive. These measures are directly related to components of human development such as physical, emotional, cognitive, and social developments that are, more often than not consistent with one's numerical age (Parry, 2014). Additional means used to define age are through functional capabilities or through a comparison of humans alongside other organisms. Nonetheless, age is ultimately a representation of a certain set timeframe and though a person's age changes as they grow older, a person will forever remain part of the same generation. That is, once you are a member of a generation, you are part of it for the rest of your life. But what exactly is a *generation*? The term *generation* possesses multiple definitions yielded by numerous scholars throughout the years. While most are similar in essence, each of the provided definitions has its own point of emphasis, occasionally related to the scholar's hypothesis and argument and sometimes given in a broader sense.

For example, Kupperschmidt (2000) defined a generation in the following manner: "An identifiable group that shares birth years, age, location, and significant life events at critical developmental stages" (Kupperschmidt, 2000, p. 66). Important to mention, this definition was given within an article arguing that a manager's understanding of their employees' generational characteristics as well as the influential points in times of their upbringing, which could have impacted their perspective, would potentially avoid various points of conflict within the workplace.

One may infer that this definition puts an emphasis on times and highlights potential influences that may have had an impact on each generation. These include age, location, and life events. Likewise, Johnson and Johnson (2010), whose book provided a comprehensive perspective on obstacles facing the different generations, including those within the workforce, defined a generation as: "A group of individuals born and living contemporaneously who have common knowledge and experiences that affect their thoughts, attitudes, values, beliefs, and behaviors" (Johnson & Johnson, 2010, p. 6). This definition accentuated the idea that the obstacles and difficulties each generation experiences are potentially a reflection of their ethical values and, inevitably, the same ethical values that they bring with them to the workplace.

Similarly, Steele and Acuff (2012), whose book intended to apply the theory of generations in the realms of international relations and politics, defined a generation as: "A cohort of individuals in a particular setting (local, corporate, national, or transnational) that is shaped by a set of interrelated processes, including specific formative experiences and a set of cultural tropes constituting a collective set of ideas, causally relevant assumptions, and expectations about the world within a particular historical period" (Steele & Acuff, 2012, p. 5). Though universal in nature, this definition places noticeable cynosure on national components and historical elements that influence individuals' expectations of the world they live in.

Finally, Strauss and Howe (1991), who established the "generational theory," a leading theory in this subject of study, defined a generation as a group of individuals who are born to a particular political and social movement and build a set of defined values, belief systems, and peer personalities (Strauss & Howe, 1991). This definition discusses the influence of individuals' experience and also directly correlates to their generational theory, which will be further elaborated on in the upcoming pages.

While many other definitions of *generation* have been established, our work will utilize the definition provided by Strauss and Howe—who are considered to be leading experts in the study of generational cohorts, and more relevantly, dominant scholars in the subfields of Generation Y (also known as Millennials) and Generation Z (sometimes referred to as iGen).

Though the study of generations had indeed been justified in scholarly research, it has also received its fair share of criticism. For example, some had given prominence to the issue of age ranges that make up a generational cohort. As seen in scholarly work, the years that ultimately make up a particular generational cohort vary significantly and are assigned in a somewhat unsystematic order (Parry, 2014). For example, in some works, Millennials may be regarded as those born in the early 80s, and in others, as those born in the late 80s or even to the early 90s. This, in turn, entangles the study of generations and could potentially furnish variances when applied in empirical research. That is if hypothetically, one wishes to understand how two separate generations feel about a particular topic (e.g., loyalty in the workplace), surveying a subject born in 1981 (Generation X) and 1982 (Generation Y/Millennials) could potentially yield a similar result, even though the two subjects are considered to be members of two distinct generations.

The term *Cuspers* was established to address these concerns. According to Thompson (2017), Cuspers are individuals born between generations, ultimately making them part of two distinct cohorts (Thompson, 2017). Presumably, this means that certain individuals may not suit the precise attributes and characteristics of the generation they are connected to and instead better complement the characteristics of the generation before or after their own. This term provides some acknowledgment of the issues of variance between cohorts, as it recognizes that certain members of two distinct generations may be closer in their mindset and attitudes.

Additional critiques of the intergenerational gaps are based on disregarding discrepancies within generational cohorts. This refers to the placement of a set of individuals in one group, tying them down into one bracket of characteristics, attitudes, behaviors, etc., while failing to recognize their differences and potentially overgeneralizing the group as a whole (Parry, 2014).

Indeed, it is difficult to grasp how a particular time frame can accurately depict how such great quantities of individuals can be bracketed and categorized into a multitude of characteristics shared by them, just as some may find it difficult to understand concepts such as astrology for example and how it groups individuals based on the day in the year they were born.

So why, then, is classifying individuals into a particular bracket effective, and why is it necessary to distinguish between generations at all?

2.2. The Foundation of Generations

At large, the notion of generation has been extensively used in the everyday world to differentiate between age groups in a particular society and a set of scattered individuals who are extant during a distinct historical timeframe (not necessarily within proximity) (Pilcher, 1994).

As many readers would attest, the term generation is frequently used in our daily conversations and everyday lives. For example: "In my generation, kids weren't so spoiled"; "Our generation can understand technology better than anyone"; "This generation is so stubborn in their ways"; and so on. It has become part of our culture and our universal language and has furnished individual connections founded solely on generational idiosyncrasies. That's not to say our individualism and self-direction have been entirely set aside, but instead, these distinctions have offered us prospects to many questions we often contemplate with ourselves; why we act a certain way, and ultimately, why we are who we are.

Nowadays, one's tendency to differentiate between generational cohorts has increased, and in fact, sometimes provided one with entertainment. As it would appear, society has frequently enjoyed pointing out unique characteristics in each generation. For example, "Millennials are spoiled and entitled," or "Boomers are too set in their ways." Moreover, Generations Z and Y have even started social media trends such as the #OKBoomer hashtags, which ultimately plays on the idea that the older generations do not understand the reality of the world they are living in.

Without realizing it, we have somewhat innately been able to recognize the existence of a particular generational gap, giving it full justification. Our understanding of generational differences has been deeply entrenched in our cultural norms and within our society, so it is somewhat of a surprise that institutions fail to recognize, or even acknowledge that there are certain gaps that require adjustment on their part.

As it would show, when it comes down to recognizing these generational gaps in practice (particularly within formal institutions or professional organizations), not enough effort is being made to gain a profound understanding of the distinctions between members of generations, and as a result, not much is being done to tackle quandaries and complications these eventually engender (Pilcher, 1994). Interestingly, we can recognize these incongruities for entertainment purposes and have given them validity, yet, we still have not been able to recognize the importance of learning how to work around them. We have essentially accepted generational gaps as they are, without bothering to even consider the idea that attending to the issues such gaps precipitate may furnish positive results that would not only benefit us as individuals but also become beneficial to our close surroundings, communities, and society as a whole.

To address the matter, our book will first provide an outline of famous generational theories and later present an overview of generational cohorts, which will lay out a summary of each generation's typology, including the mention of notable, formative experiences believed to have shaped each generation's unique traits and quotidian perceptions.

This review is believed to entrench a solid understanding that a generational gap exists, and secondly, that paying tribute to disparities across the different generations will allow us to see how these differences come about within the workforce, and more specifically, the public sector. Better yet, this section will act as a foundation to bring forth concrete elucidation to the issues the workforce is faced with today.

Over the years, sociological scholars have developed several theories to prove that occurrences encountered by one generational cohort significantly impact their comprehensive viewpoints and general day-to-day conduct. The first of such theories was the theory of generations (also known as sociology of generations), postulated by Karl Mannheim in 1928.

In his essay, "Das Problem der Generationen" (translated to English in 1952 as "The Problem of Generations"), Mannheim asserted that human beings are influenced by their socio-historical surroundings, particularly during their youth, while contending that a series of events shared by one group eventually influences and determines the future proceedings of the generations to come (Edmunds & Turner, 2005).

The basis for Mannheim's work was the belief that the problems of generations are to be taken seriously, as they enable us to further comprehend the structure of social movements. Mannheim further stated that in practice, the significance of intergenerational issues becomes all the more noteworthy, particularly if one aspires to understand "the accelerated pace of social change characteristics of our time" (Mannheim, 1952, p. 286). In his essay, he distinguished between *generational location*, *generation as actuality*, and *generation units*, terms that will be briefly touched upon in the pages to come (Purhonen, 2016).

To gather a coherent understanding of the generational phenomenon, Mannheim attempted to elucidate the distinct interrelations of individuals that make up a generational unit. In doing so, he established that: "The unity of a generation does not consist primarily in a social bond of the kind that leads to the formation of a concrete group, although it may sometimes happen that a feeling for the unity of a generation is consciously developed into a basis for the formation, as in the case of the modern German Youth Movement" (Mannheim, 1952, p. 288).

In this section, Mannheim clarifies that the case of the German Youth Movement is unique in that these groups are:

> Most often mere cliques, with the one distinguishing characteristic that group formation is based upon the consciousness of belonging to one generation, rather than upon definite objectives. Apart from such a particular case, however, it is possible in general to draw a distinction between generations as mere collective facts on the one hand, and concrete social groups on the other. (Mannheim, 1952, p. 290)

Interestingly, Mannheim chose to discuss the German Youth Movement during a time when these were first being initiated and presumably, during a time this particular generational cohort was still forming and unknowingly establishing their unique traits and characteristics. Having said that, however, Mannheim had argued that generations are not a solid group in a communal sense. That is, unlike communal groups, a generational group can and certainly does continue to exist even when its members do now know each other or when they are not located within proximity of each other. The German Youth Movement, then, is not a generation but merely a small part of one.

Over and above, Mannheim stated that a generation does not form for a specific purpose and is not knitted together by "a deliberate act of foundation, written statutes, and a machinery for dissolving the organizations" (Mannheim, 1952, p. 292). Instead, his perspective of generation was justified on the basis of historical process and consciousness, advocating that members within a certain generation are tied together on the grounds of historical events encountered during the same or similar points in time (Edmunds & Turner, 2005). Mutual experiences shared by individuals during a specific phase of their lives (childhood, coming of age, etc.) determine whether they are members of the same generation or not.

As far as Mannheim's conceptual definition goes, the closest one established by him is as follows: "A concrete group, a union of a number of individuals through naturally developed or consciously willed ties" (Mannheim, 1952, p. 307).

Overall, Mannheim's essay remains the foundation of generational study. The theory of generations has been regarded as the "most systematic and fully developed treatment of generation from a sociological perspective" (Bengtson et al., 1983, p. 56), and was used to explain several historical events and phenomena in America, as well as across the world throughout the years. For example, the effects of the Great Depression (Elder, 2018), the second wave of the feminist movement (Schnittker et al., 2003), civic engagement patterns (Rotolo & Wilson, 2004), and many more. However, despite the many accolades Mannheim's theory has received, scholars examining the notion of generations and the influence of external factors on a particular set of individuals have pointed out both its surpluses and deficiencies over time.

According to Pilcher (1994), Mannheim's "The Problem of Generations" "firmly locates generation within socio-historical contexts, and moreover, plays a significant part of a wider sociological theory of knowledge" (Pilcher, 1994, p. 482). In this work, additional attention was called to Mannheim's concern of social location in terms of generational factors, pinpointing it as being an indispensable element in his theory: "Generational location points to 'certain definite mode of behavior, feeling of thought' and the formative experiences during the time of youth are highlighted as the key period in which social generations are formed" (Pilcher, 1994, p. 490).

With that, Pilcher (1994) brings forth another key element in Mannheim's theory, stating that:

> Contemporaneous individuals are internally stratified by: their geographical and cultural location; their actual as opposed to potential participation in the social and intellectual currents of their time and place; and by their differing responses to a particular situation so that there may develop opposing generational "units." (Pilcher, 1994, p. 483)

In opposition to Pilcher (1994) who lauded Mannheim's contribution to the study of generations, referring to it as an "undervalued legacy," some of the criticism placed on Mannheim's work regarded the notion that the theory appeared to apply primarily to the Western world, lacking an all-embracive cultural understanding beyond it (Vandegrift, 2016). Additional criticism claimed that the theory requires further development to coincide with the globalized essence of modern society, as it does not presently reach a global scope (Edmunds & Turner, 2005).

Nonetheless, perhaps one of the most significant criticisms of Mannheim's work came from McCourt (2012), who had asserted that Mannheim failed to define generations with "any great precision" further adding that he "conflates the impact of generations with age- and cohort-effects, leaving underspecified, the links between generations and other social factors, including class" (McCourt, 2012, p. 47).

McCourt (2012) then mentioned that political scientists have shown that political views are not inherently predicted by generational cohorts, which, on his account, puts additional doubt on "the appropriateness of a generational account of political change." Having said that, McCourt does recognize that generational analysis should indeed be based on the foundation of Mannheim's theory, yet believes that the theory is "overly deterministic," lacking both a social mediator between social position (or as he refers to it, generational membership), and lacking shared knowledge and behavioral dispositions (Cutler & Bengston, 1974).

As McCourt's (2012) article views the theory from a political science perspective, it is worth mentioning here in our book as well. This is so that further on, we may be able to make use of such theories as we dive into the impact of generational gaps on the public sector.

In McCourt's view, much of Mannheim's theory was founded on the grounds of his intellectual and personal background, ultimately hinting that Mannheim's theory was biased.

The first matter addressed by McCourt was that Mannheim was a philosophy student and did not major in sociology. In his view, this then gave the impression that Mannheim's prospects were shaped and developed through alternative disciplines entirely. Secondly, McCourt mentions that Mannheim lived in Hungary in the 1910s, a time when calls for cultural restorations were supported by either romantic principles (those who believed in reason and reality through experience) or idealistic principles (those who took a spiritual stance and accepted whatever had come). Nonetheless, Mannheim chose an amalgamation of the two. That is, instead of siding with one school of thought, Mannheim chose a combination of both, and more relevantly, exhibited that his preference resided with a synthesis between two concepts (McCourt, 2012).

With that, through the amalgamation of both philosophy and sociology, Mannheim was ultimately able to justify his theory. Nevertheless, in doing so, he merely provided an ambivalent, somewhat equivocal point of reference, which lacked several key elements potentially crucial to the study of generational cohorts and, in particular, elements more relevant to the realm of political science—a domain Mannheim was said to be somewhat ignorant of (McCourt, 2012).

Ultimately, and as previously mentioned, McCourt maintained that: "Mannheim's essay, which stresses the importance of formative experiences and shared social perspectives, was very much a reflective conceptualization of his own intellectual origins and position in the scholarly field of his time" (McCourt, 2012, p. 47). This would imply that the theory, which acts as a foundation to the study of generations, is projective and not necessarily reflective of the broader cultural norms.

Additionally, McCourt stated that Mannheim "had a more sophisticated appreciation of the necessary underpinnings of a sociology of knowledge than the charge that he was a naïve relativist betrays" (McCourt, 2012, pp. 54–55), meaning that while he attempted to confront the historical authenticity of systems, and their correlation to particular social formations, he still did not discredit scientific evidence of cultural modifications, leaving the final salient point, up for interpretation (McCourt, 2012). More specifically concerning generations, McCourt claims that:

> [Mannheim], despite drawing out the main elements of a sociological approach to the problem of generations, includ-

> ing a delineation of generations into "generations as actuality, generation-units" and "generational location," Mannheim did not manage to specify with sufficient accuracy the relationship between generations as social locations and the forms of thought they underpin. (McCourt, 2012, p. 55)

This, in turn, brought McCourt to suggest that generational analysis, particularly when scrutinizing generations through the subfield of international relations, should certainly be based on Mannheim's insights but must also draw on the works of Bourdieu and remain strictly "within the context of the sociology of international political knowledge" (McCourt, 2012, p. 58). With that, we will briefly discuss the works of Bourdieu in terms of generations.

Unlike Mannheim, Bourdieu was a sociologist whose work focused on the dynamics of power within a society and the manners in which social order is maintained within and across generations. However, and as mentioned by Purhonen (2016), the theme of generations in Bourdieu's work was marginal at best.

Instead, Bourdieu discussed the generational phenomenon at irregular intervals and failed to refer to or even cite Mannheim's essay in his work despite being aware of its existence (Purhonen, 2016).

Even though our research does not relate directly to the works of Bourdieu or the subfield of international relations, it is of value to see how much of a role these changes in definition and other nuances play in this particular field of study. More importantly, however, is recognizing the additional generational theories established since Mannheim's time.

2.3. Additional Generational Cohort Theories

To this point in our overview, much emphasis was placed on Mannheim's essay primarily because it acts as a premise for all generational theories. Nevertheless, and since 1928, additional theories have been developed, and the study of generational cohorts has further expanded.

The most notable of the modern theories are found in the works of Strauss and Howe—the generational theory (also known as the fourth turning), which was first released in their 1991 book *Generations—The History of America's Future 1584–2069*. In this generational handbook, the two presented the generational theory and established that historical events have a connection to certain generational personas (approximately 20–22 years):

> Like medieval French villagers, modern Americans carry deeply felt associations with what has happened at various points in their lives. We memorize public events (Pearl Harbor, the Kennedy and King assassinations, the Challenger explosion, 9/11) by remembering exactly what we were doing at the time. As we grow older, we realize that the sum total of such events has in many ways shaped who we are. Exactly how these major events shaped us has much to do with how old we were when they happened. This is how generations are formed: Historical events shape peer groups differently depending on the phase of life they occupy. In other words, generations are shaped by the intersecting tides of life and time.[1]

To their account, each generational persona furnishes a new era (or as they refer to it, *turning*) and brings with it a regenerated social, political, and economic climate, making them a part of what Strauss and Howe (1991) refer to as a "cyclical speculum," which means a long human life spanning between 80–90 years: "Because members of a generation are shaped in lasting ways by the eras they encounter as children and young adults, they also tend to share some common beliefs and behaviors, including basic attitudes about risk taking, culture and values, civic engagement, and family life."

The theory proclaims that (roughly) every 80 to 90 years, history repeats a crisis that is then followed by a recovery phase. Throughout the recovery phase, political theories such as institutionalism (trust in institutions) and philosophies such as communitarianism (the connection between individuals and their communities) are vividly manifested (Strauss & Howe, 1991). That is, if one generation commends its institutions in one phase, the next generation often resents institutions in the next phase and has also been known to try and weaken them. This primarily happens when a certain generation processes the tendency to value individualism over a collective group. Clashes such as these often lead to disorderly conduct within the political domain and engender ambiance for the next crisis, all the more reason why generational gaps must be taken into account when endeavoring to manage an organization of some sort.

An interesting observation has to do with the fact that according to past research, members of different generations often feel as though they

1. LifeCourse website (established by Strauss and Howe): https://www.lifecourse.com/about/method/phases.html.

have a different outlook on certain matters than the generations before and/or after them: "Aware of the experiences and traits they share with their peers, members of a generation tend to have a sense of common perceived membership in that generation. Numerous surveys have shown that most members of various generations identify themselves as a unique group with a different outlook from those outside their generation" (Strauss & Howe, 1991).

What this shows is that as a society, we have managed to justify the existence of generational gaps. However, generational gaps do not just end with groups. Generational gaps go well beyond groups and touch upon ethical conduct and even a list of attributes these generations share.

In their work, Strauss and Howe (1991) not only looked at generations but also generational values and how, over a certain period, each generation's characteristics and experiences repeat themselves: "Members of a generation share an age location in history. They encounter key historical events and social trends while occupying the same phase of life. For example, the G.I. Generation, who came of age during a crisis era of depression and world war, were shaped very differently from their Boomer children, who came of age during an awakening era of values experimentation and youth rebellion." (p. 58–68).

As can be inferred, members of different generations are significantly influenced by the historical events and social norms that have been present during their early phases of life. To explain this matter, Strauss and Howe (1991) established a four-stage cyclical model that focuses on generational events (also known as turnings), which emphasize the mood of a particular era. These turnings in consecutive order are the High, the Awakening, the Unraveling, and the Crisis (Strauss & Howe, 1991).

The High (first turning) is the stage that occurs after a certain crisis, for example, post-World War II. During this stage, institutions are said to overpower individualism and societies have been known to act as a collective. However, there are some exceptions, as some individuals within the society and generation may feel suffocated by the unified atmosphere (Strauss & Howe, 1997).

The second turning, the Awakening, is quite literally an awakening. It is when the tables turn on the institutions, and they are censured in pursuance of individualism and autonomy. As society reaches its unified apex, people become more spiritual, and project the need for authenticity and individualism to be recognized. Looking back, many that lived through this turning view it as a time of "cultural and spiritual poverty" (Strauss & Howe, 1997).

The third stage of the cycle (third turning) is the Unraveling and it is a time when individualism thrives, as institutions experience a significant lack of trust from society. During this time, people look to simply lay back and enjoy their life without disturbance, for example, the Culture War in the 1980s (Strauss & Howe, 1997).

The fourth and final phase of the cyclical model is the Crisis (fourth turning), and it is referred to as an era of wreck and havoc, where there is typically an occurrence of a war of some sort or a revolution. After a crisis such as this, establishments regain their authority, society once again begins to act as a collective, and individuals begin to see themselves as a unified group. To give a timelier example, and according to the scholars, this is where we stand today and what is to be expected: "In the Fourth Turning, we can expect to encounter personal and public choices akin to the harshest ever faced by ancestral generations" (Strauss & Howe, 1997).

In their 1997 book, *The Fourth Turning*, Strauss and Howe put a greater emphasis on a four-fold cycle of generational personas and recurrence of mood eras. They explained that just as each generation is part of a turning, each turning also encompasses generational "character values." Strauss and Howe classified these values into four different archetypes, each of which represents unique traits and characteristics that follow these generational patterns. The archetypes are today known as Hero, Artist, Prophet, and Nomad (Strauss & Howe, 1997) and these archetypes will be further elaborated on in greater depth.

In addition to the four archetypes, the scholars also saw fit to differentiate between a "dominant" and a "recessive" generation. Meaning, the scholars put each generation under one of the two classifications based on the generation's formative experiences as young adults. Dominant generations are regarded as independent within a defining era, whereas a recessive generation takes on a dependent role in a particular defining era. These classifications formed a pattern: once a generation comes of age and forms a collective persona, a contrasting generation reaches its midlife pinnacle of power (Strauss & Howe, 1997).

Referring to the archetypes in their relation to the classifications above, recessive generations are the nomad archetype and the artist archetype. Nomads experienced an unraveling during their young adult lives, a time when institutions were weak, and individualism and autonomy thrived; and artists lived through their adult lives during a "high" period where institutions are the driving force of society and individualism is undervalued and substandard.

As for dominant generations, the two remaining archetypes are prophets, who were young adults during an "awakening" period and had lived during a time when autonomy and individualism were valued (causing them to attack their institutions); and heroes, who experienced a crisis during their young-adult lives, a time when institutional power is rebuilt following a crisis that had threatened a nation's survival (Strauss & Howe, 1997).

The mention of the ladder is important to make a note of, particularly as we dive into Generation Y (Millennials) and attempt to understand what influence and/or impact this generation has on the public sector. That is, understanding the archetype and their formative experiences ultimately provides coherent insights into this generation's vocation. More specifically, we can now presume that Generation Y will be responsible for rebuilding the present institutions in response to a theoretical, potential threat to the nation's survival.

However, before we analyze the impact of Generation Y on the public sector, it is beneficial to understand better the four archetypes described by Strauss and Howe, to gain further insight into each generation's characteristics and experiences. This next section will outline the four archetypes—hero, artist, prophet, nomad—and provide greater context to their distinctions.

2.4. Hero Archetype

The hero archetypes enter their childhood after the awakening stage of the cycle model established by Strauss and Howe. The individuals who suit this archetype are described in the literature as individuals who grew up being good, overprotected children, and eventually become underproductive parents themselves. As heroes reach their coming of age, society enters a crisis, and as a result, they live up to their name (hero) and shape up to be empowering individuals who focus primarily on the well-being of the outer world (Strauss & Howe, 1997). Once again, this is particularly relevant when discussing Generation Y, as they too fall under the hero archetype and presumably feel as though it is up to them to empower and take good care of society so that it does not collapse.

Additional traits that accompany the hero persona are optimism, determinism, and overcoming hardships. Heroes are selfless, rational, and competent but can also be unreflective, mechanistic, and overbold.

They are often described as proud, self-confident, and individuals who possess a collegial and expansive leadership style and tend to be viewed as powerful throughout their adulthood. As a whole, hero archetypes value community, affluence, and technology, and are considered to be selfless, rational, and competent. Once these individuals reach their elder years, they are financially rewarded (Strauss & Howe, 1997).

Out of the generations we shall be analyzing in this work, the two generations who fall under the hero archetype are the G.I. Generation and Generation Y (Millennials). Other generations include Arthurian (1433–1460), Elizabethan (1541–1565), Glorious (1648–1673), and Republican (1742–1766).

2.5. Artist Archetype

The artist archetypes begin their childhood following the unraveling phase and grow up during a time of crisis. As children, they are overprotected, yet are said to still grow up placid. Due to their unfulfilling coming of age and the fact that society enters a high phase just as they reach the ladder phase of their lives, artist archetypes become interdependent. Additional personality traits of artists are as follows: they are caring, open-minded and expert, but are also sentimental, complicated, and indecisive.

When artists reach adulthood, they experience a change in mindset. From being conformist young adults, they shift to being experimental fully-grown adults. Leadership-wise (due to the lack of leadership), artists are pluralistic and hesitant. As elders, society views them as sensitive individuals, but they are also well-liked by others.

Out of the generations we will be discussing in this book, the Silent Generation (1925–1942) coincides with the artist archetype. Other generations in this archetype are Humanist (1460–1482), Parliamentary (1566–1587), Enlightenment (1674–1700), Compromise (1767–1791), Progressive (1843–1859), and Generation Z (2005–?).

2.6. Nomad Archetype

The third archetype of the four archetypes established by Strauss and Howe is the nomad archetype. Nomad children are brought up during an awakening period and are said to be bad children who were under-protected by their parents. This, in turn, leads them to eventually become over-protective parents themselves.

During nomads' coming of age, they are alienated, and their main focus tends to be on self-sufficiency. Moreover, as young adults, they are competing, and once they transition into their midlife, they are said to be frenetic and exhausted. Nomad leadership styles are pragmatic and solitary, two traits that align well with their reputation as tough elders. Nonetheless, it was also said that nomads are abandoned once they reach the golden age.

Nomads are savvy, practical, and perceptive but can also be unfeeling, uncultured, and amoral. What depicts them overall is liberty, survival, and honor. The generations that fall into this category are Reprisal (1512–1540), Cavalier (1618–1647), Liberty (1724–1741), Gilded (1822–1842), Lost (1883–1900), and Thirteenth (1961–1981).

2.7. Prophet Archetype

The final archetype of the four archetypes discussed by Strauss and Howe is the prophet archetype. Prophets begin their childhood following a high phase of the generational theory. They are regarded as spirited children who grew up in nurtured and relaxing environments, and their coming of age was sanctifying. When growing up, this generation places focus on the inner world and become reflective young adults. Later in life, as prophet archetypes transition into adulthood, their mindset becomes detached from judgment, and as a result, members of this archetype tend to receive the reputation of being righteous and austere leaders, who are founded based on religion, vision, and value. Once prophets reach their elder years, members of this generational archetype are viewed as wise elders, gaining much respect and appreciation from society.

Personality-wise, prophets are said to be a driven, idealistic, and determined bunch who aim to rebuild society. Moreover, additional personality traits for this archetype include principled, resolute, and creativity as their more positive attributes; and narcissistic, presumptuous, and ruthless for more negative characteristics. Other generations in this archetype include Reformation (103 years), Puritan (part of the New World, 1640), and Transcendental (part of Civil War, 1831).

In terms of the generations we are focusing on in this book, the Baby Boom Generation is the generation that directly correlates to the prophet archetype. Judging solely by the description and characteristics mentioned above, one may get a sense that the Baby Boom Generation has set forth the norms and values presently occupying the workforce as we know it, particularly the public sector. This is especially conspicuous when considering the fact that the executives in the public sector (in America especially) tend to be members of this generational cohort. In this case, it should come as no surprise that Generation Y is potentially the first generational cohort to struggle with coming to terms with the Baby-Boom mindset and, specifically, their workforce etiquette. It is also worth mentioning that both of these generations are regarded by Strauss and Howe as dominant generations, and both cohorts place value on individualism. Instinctively, one might say that the fact that these two generations hold similar values should actually be fruitful and beneficial to the workforce. However, it appears that this may be another case of having too many chefs in the kitchen. Both generations are set in a particular mindset, hoping to lead the world into a better tomorrow, but cannot quite come to terms with what is the best manner of doing so.

This is presumably because the Baby Boom Generation consists of driven, idealistic individuals who are determined to rebuild society the way they see fit. In addition, Generation Y represents a generational cohort that has taken it upon themselves to instill values and shape society in a way that suits their perspective.

Nonetheless, in opposition to the Baby Boom Generation, Generation Y (hero archetype) focuses on the well-being of the outer world, while the Baby Boom Generation has been regarded as a generation that is more self-centered. It would appear that this is where the conflict comes about, especially since the other two generations, X and Z, are referred to as recessive generations and tend to take on a dependent role within a defining era. That is, they potentially do not care enough to bring about changes, which also may be why the complications in the workforce have become more noticeable with the entrance of Generation Y.

Overall, and according to Strauss and Howe, the four archetypes provide a good balance for America (and potentially additional countries worldwide) and aid us in understanding why each generation has come to be as it has. Nevertheless, it should be mentioned that the two scholars have determined that understanding the impact of these generations together is actually more substantial than understanding what occurs to each generation on a separate basis:

> Of more importance to history is what happens to generations together. They age in place in a manner that François Mentré described as "tiles on a roof"—overlapping in time, corrective in purpose, complementary in effect. As generations age, they together form new archetypal constellations that alter every aspect of society, from government and the economy to culture and family life. (Strauss & Howe, 1997, p. 99)

Meaning, as we aim to understand how these generational gaps are impacting the workforce, and in particular, the public sector, understanding the impact of these generations together is just as important, if not more so, than learning about these generations separately:

> Most researchers focus on age brackets, as though the people in these brackets were constant and unchanging. We believe this approach is deeply misleading. People never "belong" to an age bracket. Rather, they belong to a generation that happens to be passing through an age bracket—a generation with its own memories, language, habits, beliefs, and life lessons. (Chitiga et al., 2011, p. 19)

Following the discussion mentioned above, we can infer from the generational theory that Strauss and Howe examined both the notion of generation and how each generation's characteristics and experiences impacted the individual approaches over time.

This, in turn, further emphasizes that generational gaps play a huge role in the way people act, react, and function throughout their day-to-day lives. As we apply the proclaimed theory to our current research, it's important to pay close attention to the hero archetype, as this is the archetype that describes Generation Y/Millennials, who act as our main research subject. Nevertheless, just as established by the generational theory, when examining all generations in the context of the omnipresent workforce, it is important also to examine other generations, both as a collective and on their own (Strauss & Howe, 1997).

Interestingly, 2020 is the first year to encompass all four archetypes alive, requiring individuals to adapt to and comply with, one single set of demands—unless these gaps are recognized and acknowledged accordingly. In that regard, workplaces across the world will be required to deal with four different archetypes who hold different values and beliefs, and therefore, it is expected that having all generations under one roof will engender its own set of challenges—challenges this book endeavors to solve.

Though many workplaces today tend to ignore generational gaps and not pay them any consideration whatsoever, in this book we will emphasize why non-recognition of the matter will negatively impact the workplace and ultimately prevent it from reaching its full potential. More importantly, the following chapters will pay close attention to how these gaps impact the public sector, and as a result, the nation-state at large.

All in all, generational gaps deserve greater scholarly scrutiny along the challenges they bring so that at the very least, the workforce does not deny itself an opportunity to scale and grow. This next section will therefore discuss the generational gaps currently present in the workforce and how those impact employees, managers, and organizations as a whole.

2.8. Generational Gaps in the Workplace

According to Smith (2000), generational conflict is a prevalent component in human society and continues to challenge organizations within the workforce (Smith, 2000). Though the integration of multiple generations within the workforce furnishes positive aspects such as innovation and diversity, it also engenders conflict among employees (Smith, 2000). This becomes particularly evident when employees of two distinct cohorts are required to either perform tasks of similar nature or cooperate on the same task through different strategies and/or work techniques.

For example, the younger generations may prefer to utilize technologies to complete a certain conceptual task, while the older may prefer to approach the same task through more traditional means. Therefore, and considering these means of conduct wholly contrast one another, friction is bound to be present and bring with it an additional range of opinions. More in that regard, Yang (2019) provides additional examples that relate to each generation's stance on prevalent matters. The fact that generations view social and/or political matters differently may also bring forth disputation among employees. Some examples include climate change, abortion rights, and immigration. Inevitably, and considering each person within a generational cohort has gone through different life experiences before joining the workforce, each member/cohort then possesses diverse work ethics, motivations, and leadership needs. When ignored, however, struggles are expected to be amplified.

Thompson (2017) found that the workplace is often challenged by intergenerational conflicts and attributed these conflicts to the "manifestation of generational descriptors in a particular workplace." In this school of thought, Thompson is not alone. Likewise, Dwyer (2009) discussed the potential challenges and conflicts of an intergenerational workforce and attributed them to the unique characteristics each cohort brings to the table (Dwyer, 2009). If we refer back to Strauss and Howe's theory, these characteristics are fairly well defined using the four archetypes: hero, artist, prophet, and nomad, which act as another indication of the differences between generations, and therefore, also exhibit yet another indication that generational gaps remain present.

In addition, and over the past few years, scholarly studies have determined that divergences in generational cohorts remain extant and that they must be scrutinized, particularly within the workforce. They have determined that meeting the needs of each cohort will benefit individual employees and increase the functionality of a workplace overall. Not only that, but these will also aid in understanding the regarded differences in a way that will also be beneficial to managers and to the organizations they manage.

The fact that generational gaps have not been properly acknowledged in the workplace until this point brings significant consequences that are becoming more and more noticeable by the day. In particular, these come to view when examining the present motivation to work for old-fashioned organizations, and more relevantly to our topic, the public sector.

According to the 2011 survey conducted by the National Association of Colleges and Employers (NACE), graduate students' interest in government and/or the public-sector careers has significantly declined. The survey shows that out of over 37,000 students surveyed, only 6% of students stated that they plan to work at any level of government. This finding is especially staggering when one considers previous research that suggested that students who studied public administration in academia were more interested in pursuing public service careers when they first started their programs than they were as they got closer to their completion (Dwyer, 2009).

The pretext behind this choice is unclear and is open to many interpretations. Some believe that the decline in government work is a result of poor academic curriculums, weakening of the public-sector job market, the nature of governance, and, subsequently, the rise of additional employment opportunities in the third sector and/or business sector. This particularly holds true when taking into account the emergence of the tech industry and opportunities made available as a result of globalization (Raffel, 2009). Nonetheless, a repeated postulation claims that government organizations are not rewarding enough (Infeld & Adams, 2011).

Instinctively, one might be tempted to pair the lack of interest in government work to the preconceived notion that the younger generations, and amongst them the Millennials, are "spoiled" or "sheltered"—"trophy" kids if you will. However, another perspective is worth looking at by first examining what this unique generational cohort perceives to be "rewarding" in the first place. By the same token, it may also be worth challenging the commonly held belief that it is up to members of Generation Y to adjust themselves to the public sector. We maintain that the opposite is true—the system must learn to accommodate Generation Y and pay close attention to their needs and demands. Not because they are special and must continue to be sheltered in the workplace (as believed they had been at home), but simply because a state's fate depends on it.

It is crucial to remember that this cohort, unlike generational cohorts before it, possesses plenty of other employment opportunities in other sectors. These opportunities are often more appealing, and many of them actually tend to clash with the state's principal propositions and modus operandi (e.g., Facebook, Google, etc.). In fact, other employment opportunities offer millennials exactly what they need to feel content, and as a result, bring into their lineups the most adroit of workers. This, in turn, deprives the public sector of employees most ideal for serving the state. It is important to realize that the relationship between the cohorts must be understood to tackle these matters in the most efficient manner possible.

According to Park and Gursoy (2012), placing focus on the dynamic relationships between the cohorts and yielding a comparison between them may allow managers to better understand and maintain their employees (Park & Gursoy, 2012). As this is an especially prevalent matter in the public sector—particularly on account of the fact that the younger generations' motivation to work for the sector has decreased over the past few years (Bright & Graham, 2015)—studies examining the dynamic relation of cohorts are especially essential.

However, it should be noted, and as stated by multiple scholars, that while a decent amount of research had been conducted to understand the influence of generational gaps within the workplace, not much had been directly geared towards the public sector, and in fact, the studies conducted have been specific toward the private sector (Yang, 2019). While we are able to gather some significant knowledge from these studies and may be able to apply them here as well, the dissimilarities between the sectors are so vast that a distinct study would allow a true understanding of the present dilemmas and difficulties that are encompassing the public sector today.

That is, given the peculiarities between the two sectors (public and private), we require a separate and more specific understanding as the public sector, which is unable to conduct changes in its modus operandi as efficiently as the private sector may be able to due to its bureaucratic nature.

Another important issue that should be addressed is the challenges that come with the present retirement wave of the Baby Boom Generation. As previously regarded, the Baby Boom Generation represents the leaders of the workforce. With their retirement, the workforce finds itself having to recruit new leaders, retain employees, and bring in new employees altogether (Green, 2008).

Ultimately, different historical events have made an impact on each generation, and these are responsible for shaping different generations. According to Stefaniak and Vetter (2007), these historical events have to do with technological inventions. Some of the examples provided include the Hoover dam for the Veterans, the microwave for the Boomers, the cell phone for Generation X, and the Internet for Millennials (Stefaniak & Vetter, 2007).

Moreover, and as asserted by Lancaster and Stillman (2003), understanding generational characteristics is a good starting point when looking to diminish present generational gaps (Lancaster & Stillman, 2003). Therefore, the following will present an outline of each living generational cohort and expand on their unique traits.

2.9. The G.I. Generation (1901–1924)

The G.I. Generation is the second-to-last generational cohort of the Great Power Saeculum, lasting 81 years and including the Third Great Awakening, Great Depression, and World War II. They are the successors of the Lost Generation (born before 1901), entering childhood in a time when schools had become more popular. Though this generation is formally known as the G.I. Generation, a more prevalent term is the Greatest Generation, a term that was first coined by American journalist Tom

Brokaw in 1998, and one that has become popularized amongst scholars in the field (Strauss & Howe, 1991).

The most discernible trait of this aging generational cohort is the value they place on collective identity. Today, as this concept begins to dissipate, the last remaining generation members tend to view their successors as nugatory replicas of themselves. They are frustrated by the lack of community spirit manifested worldwide as they are very patriotic in nature and process a strong sense of morality (Eisner, 2005).

Moreover, they believe that all people are the same and find it difficult to grasp the idea that this perception is no longer viewed to be accurate in present times. While such an attitude may seem unrelenting, the events of their upbringing better justify it. One must remember that these individuals lived and survived through the Great Depression, World War II, and the Cold War. As a result, their outlook on life has forever been rational and collective, and for this reason, their stance on these matters has remained pertinent in just about everything they do (Strauss & Howe, 1991).

Though this generation is long retired, it is worth mentioning their attitude in the workplace to be able to compare them with another hero archetype, otherwise known as Generation Y.

Lancaster and Stillman (2003) asserted that the G.I. generation is very faithful to their place of work, and the values they hold dear are dedication, loyalty, and respect. This, of course, does not come as a surprise, considering the G.I. Generation is known for their conservative attitudes, practical approach, and embrace of unity (Jenkins, 2019).

As Tolbize (2008) describes, this generation is disciplined, formal, and believes in a top-to-bottom hierarchal structure in the workplace. They oppose risk-taking and tend to base their decisions on past experiences (Tolbize, 2008). These individuals have a preference for formality, social order, and strongly detest change.

Referring back to the generational theory presented by Strauss and Howe and the archetypes, this generation falls under the hero generation and quite possibly the one we should most pay attention to when examining Generation Y, who also fall under the hero archetype.

2.10. The Silent Generation (1925–1942)

The Silent Generation grew up during a time of war and depression and is a generation who, unlike their previous cohorts, possess a more open mindset. They are more easily persuaded, described as being balanced and adaptive in their general outlook and approach, and finally, are a bit more receptive to diversity and change (Yang, 2019).

Having said that, this generation has struggled to develop conclusive viewpoints and has had a tendency to respond ambivalently in whatever they address (Strauss & Howe, 1991). Therefore, and as suggested by Strauss and Howe (1991), the idea that millions of people can fit into one bracket of personality seems absurd to them. They prefer to take a compromising stance, sticking to the notion that everyone needs to remain open-minded. For the silent generation, their word is their bond; they respect authority and always prefer social order.

Lancaster and Stillman (2003) described this generation as loyal to the institutions they work for and mentioned that one would typically choose to stay at a job out of loyalty to their clients or customers. This generation cherishes long-term careers and requires a sense of security and stability (Lancaster & Stillman, 2003).

According to Zemke et al. (2000), members of this generation are practical, dedicated, and respectful. They support national pride and embrace unity. In addition, Watson (2010) mentions that they are detail-oriented, thorough, and are some of the most hardworking and reliable workers in the workforce.

Tolbize (2008) mentions that they are frustrated when time is wasted, are past-oriented, and as Hayes (2013) suggests, they exhibit a command-and-control leadership style. This generation values formal communication and will always use respectful tones in memos and letters. Even though they seek digital advancements, technology today makes it difficult for them to act in the way they'd like to, and more specifically, communicate in the same manner they have been accustomed to all these years. Communication today is no longer as simple as it used to be for them, and as a result, they tend to struggle to communicate (Tolbize, 2008).

Finally, much like the previous cohorts, this generation embraces uniformity and patriotism and cares the most about doing their job right (Williams et al., 2010).

When Zemke et al. (2000) also add that the Silent Generation has a love-hate relationship with establishments and institutions and that quite frankly, the two prominent reasons that they would remain working at a particular place are their loyalty or to get a chance to work somewhere they would be able to make a difference in these institutions (Lancaster & Stillman, 2003).

2.11. The Baby Boom Generation (1943–1960)

The Baby Boom Generation is the generation born between 1943 and 1960. They grew up influenced by the Vietnam War and the Civil Rights movement. They are the wealthiest out of all the other generations mentioned (Stefaniak & Vetter, 2007) and tend to be the most distinct and rather popular generation of our time. Lancaster and Stillman (2003) describe this bunch as being workaholics and add that they are the utmost "idealistic, optimistic, competitive, and suspicious of authority" generation (Lancaster & Stillman, 2003).

Interestingly, however, due to the upbringing they received from their traditionalist parents (the Greatest Generation), they are very hardworking and loyal, no matter the workplace they work at, and they wholeheartedly believe that they must work hard and make sacrifices if they ever wish to be successful.

According to Lancaster and Stillman (2003), the Boom Generation wants to be well paid to reshape the state establishments and bring about the changes they wish to see. Watson (2010) claims that they want things done the way they want them and tend to be judgmental of anyone who thinks differently. Hayes (2013) claims that in terms of communication, they are a tad less formal than their parents were and usually communicate via phone call or face-to-face.

2.12. Generation X (1961–1981)

Generation X is the generation born between 1961 and 1981. Lancaster and Stillman (2003) refer to this generation as innovative, eclectic, independent, and pleasant at work. However, much like their previous cohorts, they also do not trust institutions and are skeptical about the connections they make at their place of work. They are especially suspicious of Boomers since their values do not align with their own. Nevertheless, this generation often strives to become the Boomers' boss. They are independent, self-reliant, and interestingly, unlike the previous generations discussed, they are comfortable with changes, and they "work to live, not live for work" (Stefaniak & Vetter, 2007). Moreover, as mentioned by Tolbize (2008), unlike the generations before them, they are not motivated by money and therefore not particularly loyal to their institutions.

Generation X leads a rather balanced lifestyle and works hard so that they are able to spend time pursuing personal interests and/or spend time with their friends and family. Communication-wise, Hayes (2013) proclaims that they are more technologically advanced and will usually communicate through phone and email. Moreover, and with regard to the prominent characteristics of this generation, Watson (2010) mentions that Generation X is adaptable, pragmatic, and not intimidated by authority. In addition, and once again, unlike the previous generations, they do not work particularly well in a team but do multitask very well. Unfortunately, however, they also tend to be stereotyped as being "slackers, aggressive, and annoying" (Lancaster & Stillman, 2003).

2.13. Generation Z (2006–Present)

Though it would have made more sense to discuss Generation Y following the outline of Generation X, we will now briefly touch upon Generation Z before we dive into the discussion on Millennials.

Generation Z is the most recent generational cohort to be joining the workforce, and therefore, there is not enough data to allow us to understand this generation's impact on their place of work, or more specifically, the public sector. Having said that, and since we are unable to fully determine the kind of implications this generation will have on the workforce, we will only briefly touch upon some of their characteristics and other elements that have been established in the literature so far.

Generation Z is a generation born around 2006 to the present. They are a product of Generation X (a generation that had grown up during the post-Watergate and post-Vietnam War) and, therefore, were given a childhood that centers around protection. That is, because Generation X grew up during a time of chaos, they chose to provide their children with a safe and secure environment, unlike the one given to them.

Generation Z was constantly being provided with organized activities by the parents, and more so, activities that make sure both boys and girls are included, encompassing the values of diversity (Chi et al., 2013). In addition, this generation is also the first generation to be raised with smartphones, and most of them cannot recall a time before social media existed (Williams, 2015; Seemiller & Grace, 2018).

Notably, the available literature has described members of this generational cohort as conscientious, hardworking, anxious, and mindful of the future. Some have even referred to them as "grandparents" considering such characteristics tend to also suit the Golden Age.

Members of Generation Z grasp information quickly but also tend to lose interest just as quickly. This is virtually why everything that is being marketed today does so within a very short, designated timeframe. For example, TikTok videos tend only to be between 15–60 seconds long (Williams, 2015).

Curiously enough, Generation Z is growing up during a time where multiculturalism and acceptance are on the rise. To give a more specific example, this generation was basically born into a world where same-sex marriage is no longer some political or controversial matter, but rather a constitutional right in the United States (or protected by law in other countries across the world). As Malloy (2012) mentioned, Generation Z may not have any recollection of a time when diversity was not a cultural norm.

Nonetheless, this generation's upbringing is not as perfect as it may seem. Generation Z also grew up during a time of global conflict and economic hardships, which have undoubtedly shaped their outlook on life. As previously mentioned, these hardships and times of uncertainty are what led this generation to play it safe, or rather, be extra conscious about the decisions they make in life. More so, and in virtue of social media, Generation Z no longer seeks to find a regular summer job, but instead, they opt for starting their own business during their summer break.

While this generation is relatively close to Generation Y in terms of age, they have shown some differences in multiple arenas. What we found to be interesting is that they value their privacy tremendously, unlike the previous cohorts. Generation Z tends to be more mature than Millennials and constantly abide by the rules. If we wanted to compare one of the generations we previously mentioned and see which one best correlates to Generation Z, the most suitable one would be the Silent Generation. When interviewed for the New York Times, Williams (2015) recognized the similarities and differences as well and provided further examples as to what may be expected for Generation Z[2]:

---

2. Williams, A. (2015) Move Over, Millennials, Here Comes Generation Z, The New York Times, Sept. 18 see at https://www.nytimes.com/2015/09/20/fashion/move-over-millennials-here-comes-generation-z.html.

> The parallels with the Silent Generation are obvious . . . There has been a recession, jobs are hard to get, you can't take risks. You've got to be careful what you put on Facebook. You don't want to taint your record . . . Those children of the New Deal, epitomized by the low-key Warren Buffett, didn't want to change the system, they wanted to work within the system. They were the men in the gray flannel suits. They got married early, had kids early. Their first question in job interviews was about pension plans.

Luckily for members of this generation, Williams also said that members of the Silent Generation cohort are the most career-focused generation and the richest of the generations discussed. It seems as though Generation Z has something to look forward to, but before we forget, it is just as beneficial first to take a gander at where the previous cohorts of Generation Z are these days and understand their struggles so that we can both learn from what (if anything) has changed since the entrance of Generation Y into the workforce, and what is to be expected as Generation Z becomes fully incorporated in the workforce in the next few years.

2.14. Generation Y (1982–2005)

The final generation we will be analyzing is Generation Y, also known as Millennials or Y Gen. This generational cohort was born in the early 1980s to late 1990s or early 2000s.[3] According to Sauser and Sims (2013), and much like other generations, Millennials have been exposed to a motley of experiences that have significantly impacted their attitudes, outlook, and values (Sauser & Sims, 2013). These include historical, cultural, economic, and technological changes, all of which have shaped their approaches to social interaction, beliefs in workplace etiquette, personal concerns, desires, and more.

Millennials grew up in the midst of technological expansion, new media, and during a time when immigration policies were brought to the political agenda. Therefore, it should come as no surprise that they are

3. Specific years tend to vary between different sources. The same is of course also true for other generational cohorts.

"globally concerned, cyber-literate, and technologically savvy" (Zemke et al., 2000, p. 20).

As mentioned by Sullivan et al. (2009), this generation values diversity, and moreover, as regarded by Zemke et al. (2000), Generation Y holds unique character traits such as being hopeful, determined, and inclusive. Stefaniak and Vetter (2007) add that Millennials are a generation that accepts challenges, but at the same time, welcomes the advice of others and approves of supervision. Nevertheless, and though they remain ambitious and busy, this generation does have a problem staying focused.

Watson (2010) points out that Millennials are a generation who loves to learn as much as they can but as Lancaster and Stillman (2003) have suggested, Millennials are typically stereotyped as being completely oblivious to their lack of skill.

Specifically, concerning the workplace, Generation Y values "recognition, status, and autonomy," (Ng et al., 2012), meaning they care about getting recognition for their hard work; are impressed by titles, as well as career advancements; and they prefer to be independent and enjoy flexible hours and unique working environments. Though Millennials tend to expect a lot from their place of work, their loyalty is rather questionable. In the words of Alsop (2008), this is what needs to be done in or to keep this generation engaged properly: "To improve their retention rates, companies must work harder to keep Millennials engaged in their jobs, showing them value and impact of their work, creating a collegial and team-oriented culture, and offer them a rich variety of opportunities to advance" (Alsop, 2008, p. 48).

As can be seen above, Generation Y is not particularly faithful to any given work and has shown the tendency to switch between jobs rather frequently. For them, the number one reason to eventually leave a place of work is if they feel that they are no longer making a difference or adequately serving the greater good/making the kind of difference they thought they would when starting the position (Yang, 2019). Similarly, Williams et al. (2011) have pointed out: "Millennials are on track to become the best educated and best behaved adults in history. But since many of them have never worked outside the home, they frequently lack business etiquette and social skills" (Williams et al., 2011, p. 44–45).

Nonetheless, this cohort has plenty of positive attributions and can be quite an asset for any sector. In fact, Williams et al. (2011) argued that Millennials actually have a great amount of respect for teachers and institutions—attributes that suit the public sector particularly well. As for additional traits and characteristics, Alsop (2008) states: "Millennials are frequently written off as narcissistic, arrogant, and fickle. Although there is certainly some truth in such negative perceptions, the Millennials also can be quite impressive in their ambitions and achievements. They are a generation of conflicting characteristics—self absorbed but also civic minded" (Alsop, 2008, p. vii).

Moreover, Howe and Strauss (2000) have stated that:

> Millennials are unlike any other youth generation in living memory. They are more numerous, more affluent, better educated, and more ethnically diverse . . . They are beginning to manifest a wide array of positive social habits that older Americans no longer associate with youth, including a new focus on teamwork, achievement, modesty, and good conduct. Only a few years from now, this can-do youth revolution will overwhelm the cynics and pessimists. (Howe & Strauss, 2000, p. 4)

Finally, in the words of Burgess (2011):

> This generation shows promise. They are technologically savvy, hyper connected through mobile devices, instant messaging, and texting. The Internet is second nature. Furthermore, as social libertarians in their outlook, they are comfortable with diversity in race, culture, and sexual orientation. Millennials are joiners: Early signs suggest they may endanger a renaissance in civic participation and the rebuilding of social capital. (pp. 9)

Referring to the public sector for a moment, it has suddenly become abundantly clear that the motivators, perceptions, and outlook that Generation Y processes will be extremely beneficial to the public sector on the whole. However, for this to work and eventually yield some fruition, the public sector must learn to cope and adjust itself to the needs of Generation Y accordingly, and moreover recognize that by doing so, they'll in fact bring in a group of quality employees who would be there for all the right reasons. Nevertheless, and despite any positive attributes these may yield, adjusting the present norms of the public sector to suit the needs of millennials is not so much an easy task.

That is, the nature of these organizations is so different from the kind of environment Generation Y/Millennials require to thrive in (based on their characteristics). Moreover, since Generation Y is not the only generation that will be working at a particular place of work, even greater adjustments must be made. Judging solely by the archaic and slow-paced nature of the public sector, these changes would not come about quickly, making matters more difficult for both the public sector and the members of this generational cohort.

Not only so, and quite inevitably, the fact that every generation has gone through its own formative experiences and developed its own outlook on how things should play out tends to lead to clashes between Millennials and the older generations (who are usually well established at their workplace and hold senior positions). This is partly because Generation Y does not hesitate to challenge their authoritative figures when receiving constructive criticism (Williams et al., 2011), further increasing already expected tensions. Nonetheless, we believe that common ground can be found, even within the public sector and that learning more about generational gaps within the public sector will aid us in finding pragmatic solutions to the matters discussed above. With the emergence of new technologies, the generational gaps have been exacerbated, and therefore following the generational analysis, we will review the notion of digital generational gaps and scrutinize the inter-generational discrepancies from a technological prism. In addition, we will examine the impact of digital inter-generational diversity in the public sector.

2.15. Intergenerational Overview of Digital Gaps

Analyzing the intergenerational gaps in the public sector requires an in-depth overview of the modern technological evolution, including the digital tools and innovative measures taken by the younger generations alongside the adaptation of the older counterparts.

Within this review, the generations are referred to by the following names: Baby Boomers, Generation X (Gen Xers), Generation Y (Millennials), and Generation Z (Gen Zers). Important to mention, we firmly posit that any analysis of generations older than the Baby Boomers shall be less relevant for the new multigenerational workforce since they are less likely to show a digital affinity or proficiency. Therefore, the generational focus is restricted to the generations mentioned above.

Broadly, technology serves a crucial function in modern society, often used as a tool for intellectual and social purposes, such as communication, information, and entertainment (Luppicini, 2005). The technological differences are more likely to relate to the users' usage level and frequency. In this regard, intergenerational analysis is essential to predict the preference for different technologies within society.

In addition, analyzing the digital intergenerational gaps may enable us to understand the new leading workforce in the public sector, which is required to connect the traditional physical world with the innovative digital sphere. Unlike the business and entrepreneurial sectors, known for their digital innovation and operational flexibility, the public sector is based upon traditional and fixed perceptions and procedures and usually consists of relatively older servants.

Nonetheless, the globalization and digitalization processes have yielded society with significant opportunities in all human fields, and therefore the public sector is required to adapt its old doctrines and prisms to the new era. This chapter aims to offer a critical analysis of digital gaps between the varied generational cohorts, elaborate upon their digital usage patterns, and indicate the potential role of the Millennials as tech mediators in the public sector. To better discuss the Millennials' role, we will employ a comparative analysis between the older and younger generations since technological exposure and knowledge is a core relative discussion impacted by varied sociocultural factors. In this regard, the literature elaborates upon this sociocultural context of each generation and enables us to create different digital profiles of younger and older generations.

2.16. Intergenerational Gaps Triggered by Technological Development

Broadly, the advent of new technologies has led to significant business and public sectors changes. Consequently, this digital amplification creates greater gaps between the younger generations who grew up with technology and the older counterparts, who need to adapt to these innovative tools (Harber, 2011; Lancaster & Stillman, 2003). As articulated by Vaterlaus et al. (2015):

> During the last five decades technology has undergone dramatic shifts, including the transition from being limited to non-interactive technologies (e.g., television, movies) to providing access to a broad array of interactive technologies

> (e.g., Internet, cell phones). Technology users are no longer limited to viewing media, they can also communicate socially with others across the globe [. . .] the interactive nature of these technologies may provide more relevant implications for parent-child relationships. (p. 2)

Therefore, despite the widespread progress brought by the varied technologies, the digital expansion has led to an inherent obstacle for older generations due to the technical skills and exposure, which differ between the varied generations (Linnes & Metcalf, 2017). Dimock (2019) reinforces this notion and claims that: "Technology, in particular the rapid evolution of how people communicate and interact, is another generation-shaping consideration."

Additionally, Gafni and Geri (2013) highlight the digital gaps as a matter of generational, cultural distinction: "While it may be claimed that younger people are more adaptable to new technologies, the proclivity to use mobile Internet services may be influenced by generational cultural differences, so it may be more appropriate to cluster age groups according to generations" (p. 20).

In this regard, several studies mention the relevance of the age factor and show the relatively lessened affinity of older adults to technologies compared to young individuals. The examined indicators comparing the generations tend to be the level of interest in technology, variety of technological mediums used, and attitude concerning technologies (Czaja et al., 2006; Purcell et al., 2012; Van der Kaay & Young, 2012). Consequently, younger users are more likely to be experienced with various technological tools and functions compared to their older counterparts (Olson et al., 2011). An additional insight raises the gaps in the ability to adapt to new technologies, as younger adults can adapt to technologies more quickly than older adults (Zickuhr & Madden, 2012).

Important to mention, while young individuals seek to engage with new technologies (Brown et al., 2006), older people may become interested in technologies if they watch the younger generations using them (Paz, 2004). In addition, one can mention the possible knowledge sharing of children and their parents in terms of acquiring technological skills. In this regard, several researchers reinforced this educational process and argued that the younger generations seek to learn new technologies and attempt to teach their parents how to use them as they are the representatives of the older generation (Kolodinsky, et al., 2002; Oksman & Turtianinen, 2004; Livingstone, 2003).

Notably, there is a substantial body of research dealing with the importance of intergenerational analysis in organizations and companies to enable hiring managers and executive directors to suit different candidates with the proper position. However, there raises a significant controversy due to the generalizing perspective of the age factor as an inherent predictor of intergenerational gaps. This notion is based upon a dichotomic division between the generations, such as Baby Boomers, Gen Xers, Millennials, and Gen Zers. Meaning, the age-based division of generations might lead to a superficial and inaccurate understanding of modern digitation processes among different populations, which do not focus as much on the inner gaps within each age cohort (Gilleard & Higgs, 2005; Parry & Urwin, 2011; Reither et al., 2009). This leads to a broader question regarding the cultural and sociological factors impacting our ability to learn new technologies and use them within society.

One of the most prevalent studies in the field of intergenerational gaps was offered by the scholar Marc Prensky (2001). He offered two core terms, "digital natives" and "digital immigrants," which enable us to distinguish between varied levels of technological users. The digital natives are defined as "native speakers of the digital language of computers, video games, and the Internet" (Prensky, 2001, p. 1). They were born after 1980, including the Millennials and the Gen Zers, and grew up alongside the amplified processes of digitization. They are known for their ability to adapt to new technologies quickly, compared to their parents and older colleagues (Zickuhr, 2010). Notably, Prensky suggested the technological sphere has altered the brain structure, and therefore young individuals process data and think differently compared to older cohorts (Prensky, 2001). As further articulated by Prensky: "Digital natives are used to receiving information really fast. They like to parallel process and multi-task. They prefer their graphics before their text rather than the opposite. They prefer random access (like hypertext). They function best when networked. They thrive on instant gratification and frequent rewards" (Prensky, 2001).

In this regard, Vaterlaus et al. (2015) explored the differences in knowledge about interactive technologies between young adults and their parents. Their study, which examined several technologies such as cell phones, social networking, email, and video chat, showed that young adults are perceived as more knowledgeable than their parents in all the technological mediums. The most significant gaps were found with the newer interactive technologies, with emphasis on the field of social networking. Additionally, their study raised: "Perceived differences between parents and their young adult children were smaller among the technologies that have been in use longer (such as such as email), and larger among the newer modes of interactive technology (e.g., video chat)" (p. 1).

Different from the digital natives, digital immigrants are usually identified with the older generations, which were exposed to technologies at an older phase of their lives and had a certain learning curve when being exposed to new technology (Prensky, 2001a). One may assume that different factors impact one's learning curve, but several studies highlight the technological obstacles older generations need to face. For instance, Walker et al. (2011) suggested that parents are more likely to become uncomfortable when acquiring advanced digital skills, such as creating new online accounts on social media platforms.

In addition, Roman and Colle (2002) posited that generational distinctions might exhibit an obstacle for community development and mentioned the example of the telecenter project, in which separate locations were provided for young individuals and adults to participate (Bailey & Ngwenyama, 2010). Nonetheless, some scholars emphasize certain benefits resulting from the technological gaps, including knowledge sharing, as depicted above, and a better understanding of intergenerational interactions (Caskey, 2003; Kolodinsky et al., 2002). These benefits can possibly strengthen multigenerational relationships, in terms of both personal and professional communication.

In this regard, a study by Pew Research Center examined the generational gaps between one's perception of technologies. For instance, compared to Baby Boomers, more Millennials and Gen Xers respondents believe that technology facilitates traditional human practices. Another notion regarding the importance of technology in connecting people differed between the Millennials and Gen Xers that support the technological contribution of getting people closer, compared to the Baby Boomers, who were more divided in their opinion (Zickuhr, 2010).

Following the discussion above, intergenerational differences are examined within the adoption of new technologies. Based on Forrester Research (2006), the younger generations are more likely than their older counterparts to use technologies in most of their life domains. Nonetheless, each generation has its own technological features, which suit its inherent needs. Broadly, the digital generational gaps are depicted as:

> [w]hen the e-mail and messenger started with the development of the Internet, more gaps developed between youth and their grandparents that could not cope with this type of commu-

> nication technology. When the Baby Boomers interacted with the technology of the Atari games and video recorders, this created a big gap with their family and their parent. Today, Y, Z and Alpha generations teach their parents how to maneuver with different technology gadgets starting from mobile phones and social media. (Buheji, 2019, p. 13–14)

The literature shows that each generation is influenced by different social and cultural criteria, such as technological exposure and usage (Bartley et al., 2007). While the Baby Boomers grew up next to the television expansion, the Gen Xers faced the beginning of the computer age. The Millennials experienced the hi-tech evolution and Internet development. The Gen Zers were born into a fully digitized era.

Despite the common digital distinction between the younger and older generations, there has been a continuous rise in tech adoption among Gen Xers and Baby Boomers since 2012. Notably, the Baby Boomers are more likely to use certain technological tools, such as cell phones and tablets (Lapoint & Liprie-Spence, 2017). According to a recent analysis of Pew Research Center, more than 93% of Millennials, 90% of Gen Xers, and 68% of Baby Boomers possess smartphones. However, another study by the Pew Center highlighted the varied obstacles faced by the older generations when adopting new technologies, which are expressed in an alleged lack of confidence and physical challenges (Anderson & Perrin, 2017).

In this regard, an interesting study reviewed the Internet skills variation between different groups based on gender, age, and education (Litt, 2013). For instance, the study found that the older generations tend to use non-interactive media online more than their younger counterparts, who participate in a higher number of interactive Internet activities (Zickuhr & Madden, 2012; Zickuhr, 2010). For instance, as the early adopters of instant messaging and social networking, the mobile use of Millennials is also higher in varied functions such as listening to music and emailing (Lenhart et al., 2010).

2.17. Comparative Analysis of the Millennial Worker and his Technological Use Patterns

An interesting study was raised by Haeger and Lingham (2014), which depicted the different technologies each generation uses and the way these technologies characterize their generational profile. Exploring the intergenerational perceptions, one can suggest that the older generations have become more comfortable working in the digital space but still separate it from their personal lives. In contrast, the Millennials do not separate between the digital and physical spheres, as the virtual sphere has become an inherent component of their work and life management. As articulated by the authors, the Millennials have adopted a new trend of work-life fusion, which highlights the implementation of new technologies within one's personal and professional domains.

Broadly, the Millennials represent the first generation to experience the digital sphere from a relatively young age. This technological affinity leads them to use the digital sphere in most aspects of their lives, from work to entertainment. It, therefore, diminishes any constraints of using new and known technologies. According to Glass (2007), they represent the "first adapters," who are not afraid to try experimenting with technologies for the first time, and the literature highlights this digital orientation as one of the greatest intergenerational gaps (Espinoza et al., 2010; Martin, 2005; Patterson, 2007; Smola & Sutton, 2002; Wisniewski, 2010; Zemke et al., 2000).

For instance, by the age of five, most Millennials use a computer and therefore tend to prioritize videos and interactive content over printed materials (National Research Group, 2020). Kane (2010) adds that they prefer to communicate via email or by messaging text and clearly prioritize online technologies and webinars over traditional mediums and presentations. Generally, they find technologies a reliable tool for communication and prefer using mobile instruments (Dalton, 2012).

Based on a survey from 2015, including a sample of 2,228 respondents, additional findings were raised regarding mobile usage among Millennials. For instance, the Millennials may use the Internet on their mobile phone or their computer, but most of the respondents claimed that their mobile usage is the most frequent for regular online activities, compared to other devices like the computer. Additionally, most Millennials are more likely to exchange images or stream music while using their mobiles. Moreover, they also use their mobile to organize their life routines and be informed with global news, such as getting online access to their banking account and financial information, plan meetings, or stream videos (DOMO, 2015).

Some suggest that the omnipresent usage of technologies significantly impacts the Millennials' expectation of instant gratification. In this regard, technology is an inherent part of their work and their personality and psyche (Sujansky & Ferri-Reed, 2009). As Dalton (2012, p. 168) argues: "Millennials grew up relying not on their parents' old collection of encyclopedias to answer any questions they might have, but instead depending on the Internet as a preeminent informational nexus, 'because in their world, the Internet knows everything.'"

Following the above, the technological impact upon Millennials has been highly studied among journalists, scholars, and policymakers. A more recent report scrutinized the way the digital sphere shapes the Millennials' personal habits and thoughts and differentiated the findings between racial and ethnic groups. Despite the ethnic-racial gaps in varied online services and products, there is a consistency in the policy preferences of all Millennials regarding the positive support of net neutrality, online copyrights to content creators, and increased digital education of programming and coding (Cohen et al., 2018).

Important to mention, some argue that the Millennials represent the first digital generation who grew up with the varied digital tools and applications but who takes these technologies for granted (Ahmad & Ibrahim, 2015; Amayah & Gedro, 2014; Hendricks & Cope, 2012; Robbins, 2013; Sherman, 2014). Furthermore, they are known for their ability to multitask, need for feedback, prioritization of electronic communication, optimism, and high confidence (Church & Rotolo, 2013; Coulter & Faulkner, 2014; Ferri-Reed, 2013; Gursoy et al., 2008; Kuhl, 2014; Mencl & Lester, 2014). In comparison, the older cohorts are more likely to fit the label of Prensky's digital immigrants, as they are less comfortable with the usage of new technologies compared to the Millennials and Gen Zers (Gursoy et al., 2013).

Nonetheless, as depicted above, there is a constant increase in the technological use of older generations. Internet usage is relatively high among all generations—nearly 100% of Millennials, 91% of Gen Xers, and 85% of Baby Boomers use the Internet. However, there is a distinction regarding mobile online activities, as only 17% of Gen Xers and 11% of Boomers use the Internet on their smartphones (Vogels, 2019).

In this regard, several studies found that Baby Boomers will use the Internet to examine health, shopping, and religious data differently than the younger generation and will probably not use it for entertainment purposes, such as playing games or watching online videos. All of the above may indicate a relative skepticism of the older generations toward technologies (Chung et al., 2010).

Additionally, as the Millennials were raised in an entrepreneurial culture, they care for workplace flexibility and using the latest technological tools, and are more likely to expect to complete tasks at home to be more creative, efficient, and innovative (Waldrop & Grawich, 2011; Sujansky, & Ferri-Reed, 2009). Therefore, the Millennial worker is expected to maximize his or her usage of the Internet and other technological mediums in the workplace and bring an innovative angle to the traditional cohorts (Zemke et al., 2013; Lancaster & Stillman, 2003).

2.18. Between Millennials, Gen Xers and Baby Boomers: Social Media Usage and Intergenerational Gaps

Within the intergenerational analysis of technological adoption, the use patterns of social media platforms have gained substantial scholarly attention. There are significant gaps between the older and younger generations in their social media usage from an intergenerational prism. For instance, the Millennials tend to use social media much more frequently in their day-to-day routine, compared to the Baby Boomers, whose digital exposure occurred at an older stage, and therefore may be more prudent when using these digital platforms, with emphasis on creating social media accounts (Leung, 2013). Furthermore, while the Millennials aspire to get updated about political information through shared social media posts, the Baby Boomers will prefer to rely on the traditional platforms, such as newspapers and television (Towner & Lego Munoz, 2016).

Moreover, the Millennials are known for creating and publishing varied digital contents and mediums, and not just passively sharing existing contents, as the older cohorts: "Most Generation Y users use social media to interact with others and prefer social media to more traditional methods of communication. Users create content as well as consume it, unlike older generations who prefer to browse" (Bolton et al., 2013).

It is important to mention that this widespread social media usage has led to certain criticism against the Millennials, for being perceived as narcissistic and egoistic individuals and for over-relying on social media to maintain their social and personal interactions. Additionally, one may suggest that the Millennials have enabled the older generations to access social media and digital culture, but consequently the Millennials have become more vulnerable to social media addictions and increased narcissism: "Their addiction means spending increasing amount of time online to produce the same pleasurable effect, and it means social media is the main activity they engage in above all others" (Rao, 2017).

Compared to Baby Boomers, the Gen Xers are considered active on social media and use it for keeping personal communication with their friends and relatives and for consuming online news and videos. As articulated by Madden (2010): "Social networking use among Internet users ages 50 and older has nearly doubled from 22% to 42% over the past year."

According to Anderson and Perrin (2017), approximately 76% of Gen Xers use their smartphones most of their free time, with emphasis on online shopping or social media usage. Other findings showed that 80% of them use Twitter and Facebook, but only half of the latter maintain active accounts (Bose, 2017). In this regard, Facebook is known as the most popular social media platform among the Gen Xers, but Instagram is an additional common platform they use (Gordon, 2014).

Interesting to mention, a recent study found that older generations are responsible for sharing most online fake news on social media, compared to the younger cohorts: "11 percent of users older than 65 shared a hoax, while just 3 percent of users 18 to 29 did. Facebook users ages 65 and older shared more than twice as many fake news articles than the next oldest age group of 45 to 65, and nearly seven times as many fake news articles as the youngest age group (18 to 29)" (Newton, 2019).

2.19. Millennials Versus Generation Z

As the Millennials and Gen Zers have become a more prevalent part of the contemporary workforce, their professional aspirations and aptitude for technological adoption requires greater scrutiny (Pricewaterhouse Coopers, 2016). Nevertheless, due to the novelty of the Gen Zers in the business and public sectors, with emphasis on managing roles, most of the intergenerational literature deals with the comparison between the Millennials and its previous cohorts. To research the next generation of managers, there is an urgent need to explore the Gen Zers from a younger stage, to further comprehend their future managing patterns and preferences.

Broadly, the hyper-digitalized character of the Gen Zers exhibits enormous opportunities and obstacles in the digital sphere compared to its preceding generations. Compared to the older cohorts, the Gen Zers are known as smarter, individual, fast learners, and experienced multitaskers (Adecco, 2015; Igel & Urquhart et al., 2012; Wiedmer, 2015). In addition, compared to the Millennials, often characterized as lazy, the Gen Zers claim that only by hard work can they get into significant achievements (PPT Solutions, 2018).

Following the Millennials, the Zers are born into a fully technological reality, facilitated by social media platforms, AI, wearable devices, and cryptocurrencies (IPSOS MORI, 2018; Lanier, 2017; Madden, 2017). As suggested by Meehan (2016), the technologies enable the Gen Zers to explore the world without any physical boundaries, and they are more likely to be the workers who bring the "tech fluency to the workplace" (Lanier, 2017, p. 289). Compared to the older generations, technology fills an inherent part of the Gen Zers' life cycle and routines. For instance, they tend to interact primarily through their mobile phones and therefore expect full mobile functionality. Additionally, in similarity to the Millennials, the Gen Zers are more likely to be content creators on social media than be passive users and data consumers (Madden, 2017).

However, the technological gaps lead to increasing criticism by the older generations toward excessive smartphone usage among the Gen Zers (Dimock, 2019; Jamie, 2018; Maier, 2011). As further articulated by the Pew Research Center about the uniqueness of the Gen Zers:

> In this progression, what is unique for Generation Z is that all of the above have been part of their lives from the start. The iPhone launched in 2007 when the oldest Gen Zers were 10. By the time they were in their teens, the primary means by which young Americans connected with the web was through mobile devices, WiFi and high-bandwidth cellular service. Social media, constant connectivity and on-demand entertainment and communication are innovations Millennials adapted to as they came of age. (Dimock, 2019)

Therefore, their excessive use of online platforms has become an inherent feature of the Gen Zers in the literature: "Gen Z spend nearly nine hours a day listening to media, looking at a screen or on a device. Including time spent multitasking; they are exposed to over 13 hours of media a day on average" (IPSOS MORI, 2018, p.78).

In this regard, Madden (2017) mentions the negative implications for the younger generation, such as a constant need for entertainment and a higher rate of distraction. Moreover, there are additional threats of excessive technological usage, such as bullying, anxiety, peer pressure, and lower self-esteem.

Additionally, the Gen Zers are more likely to lack interpersonal, and communication skills and are therefore considered a "silent" generation compared to their older counterparts. They have known the world in its modern digital version and always seek technological tools to solve their problems (Cushing, 2019; Mondres, 2019). According to Bejtkovský (2016): "They take the Internet for granted and consider web sites such as Orkut, Google, and Facebook as their community. Within this community of cyberspace, a person can have many acquaintances without personally meeting anyone" (p. 109).

However, despite the negative implications, the Gen Zers have a digital and creative mindset and can adapt to different situations quickly (E&Y, 2015; Lyons et al., 2017; Madden, 2017).

Interestingly, several argue that the Millennials possess higher communicational skills in the physical sphere than the Gen Zers who completely rely on the digital sphere. Consequently, the Millennials are better known as those who can balance online and physical communicational vectors. This notion is monumental in understanding the new leaders of the public sector and the needed multigenerational approach in leading the digitalization and mentoring processes of this sector.

2.20. Ambiguity in Prensky's Definition of Intergenerational Gaps

Nonetheless, it is important to emphasize that the intergenerational gaps do not necessarily show any gaps in technological knowledge, as one's digital habits and preferences are not an exclusive indicator of technical capacity (Koutropolulos, 2011). In this regard, an interesting study analyzed the ambiguity of Prensky's terms "digital natives" and "digital immigrants," based on Mannheim's (1952) theory, which highlights the inner gaps within generations, creating separate generational subgroups (Litt, 2013).

As articulated by Gumpert and Cathcart (1985) and Bolin and Westlund (2009), there is a distinct term called "media generations," which suggests a separation by media experience and not by the age factor. The inner variations between subgroups of the younger generations prove this notion (Litt, 2013). As a result, one should not address a generation, with emphasis on the younger ones, as one coherent group, but understand its inner variations (DiMaggio & Hargittai, 2001; Facer & Furlong, 2001; Hargittai & Hinnart, 2008; Livingstone & Helsper, 2007). One may suggest that the digitization and globalization processes lead to significant changes within certain generations, and therefore the variation increases for the Millennials and the Gen Zers and creates additional subgroups.

In this regard, several scholars have criticized the common definition of Prensky (2001), arguing that digital orientation and proficiency is a complex term that is not determined solely by chronological age, as one's chronological proximity does not inflict upon identical values and attitudes (Bennett et al., 2008; Bullen et al., 2011; Hargittai, 2010; Hargittai et al., 2010; Helsper & Eynon, 2010; Koutropolulos, 2011; Litt, 2013; Parry & Urwin, 2011; Reither et al., 2009).

For instance, the Millennials are considered the most racially diverse generation and more technologically oriented and educated compared to all generations (Cekada, 2012). Additionally, there is a notable variance in social media usage among Gen Zers. The young Gen Zers prioritize Snapchat and Instagram, while their older counterparts continue to use Facebook. As articulated in another study: "Reflecting many other characteristics of Gen Z [. . .] there has been a decline in Facebook's dominance among this cohort of young, but it remains a vital part of their social media mix" (IPSOS MORI, 2018, p. 74).

Furthermore, examining the digital intergenerational gaps may require an understanding of the existing gender differences. Meaning, males and females of the same cohort may have different technological skills. Several scholars posit that there are gender differences in using new technologies, and women tend to use more text messaging, video calls, and social media than men. Nonetheless, women have been traditionally perceived as less technological compared to men (Kimbrough et al., 2013). As a result, the intergenerational analysis does not lead to clear results within the cohorts and increases the inner-generational variance, and therefore requires additional factors when examining the digital generational gaps.

As a result, one may deduce the existence of different generational units (Mannheim, 1952) or media generations (Bolin & Westlund, 2009; Gumpert & Cathcart, 1985) among the young cohorts. Further research should be attributed to exploring the technological proficiency of each subgroup, based on additional socio-cultural factors. Therefore, in modern times, the age factor alone is not a sufficient indicator of practical knowledge, as each individual reacts differently to digital exposure and comes from a different socio-economic or cultural background. This notion leads to the need to create more in-depth and detailed generational prototypes, enabling them to maximize their potential and moderate their rooted obstacles (Vaterlaus et al., 2015).

2.21. Critical Overview of the Multigenerational Workforce

The generations above exhibit a varied scale of personal and professional traits in their workplace. Modern employers must understand the motivational sources of each generation and establish proper communicational and operational processes to enhance productivity and mitigate intergenerational conflicts. In this regard, Seitel (2005) suggested the term "generational competence," which depicts the needed organizational adaptations of employers to match the varied multigenerational needs in the modern marketplace.

A notable theory in this regard is the transformational leadership theory, which was raised by the political sociologist James MacGregor Burns (Bass & Riggio, 2014; Northouse, 2016). The theory is defined as follows: "[t]he process whereby a person engages with others and creates a connection that raises the level of motivation and morality in both the leader and the follower" (Northouse, 2016, p. 162).

Moreover, Bass and Riggio (2006) argue that transformational leadership impacts both the manager and the worker in the organization, as the leader should recognize the organizational needs and establish the vision to instruct the workers (Burns, 1979; Northouse, 2016).

As offered by the Boston College Center (Fraone et al., 2008), any data about the number of employees per generation and their occupational and personal priorities may enable organizations to develop long-term strategies for recruitment and engagement. However, there are notable differences between multigenerational workforce issues globally. The Boston College Center added that: "Historical events, culture, and economics have played an important role in the development of these generational characteristics" (2008, p. 4).

For instance, the hierarchy concept in India is considered more impactful for older generations than younger counterparts. In addition, the manufacturing transformation in Brazil has enabled better education and employment for younger employees. Therefore, one may suggest the relevance of socio-cultural factors on the evolvement of intergenerational gaps and the needed state-driven analysis.

Additionally, several scholars argue that the intergenerational gaps focus on varied values and beliefs, job commitment, motivation sources, communicational vectors, and need for feedback (Hill, 2002; Wade-Benzoni, 2002; Yang & Guy, 2006). Notwithstanding, these gaps may lead to intergenerational conflicts based on the literature, which fill the workforce with collisions, disagreements, and clashes between the employees (Lancaster & Stillman, 2003; Martin & Tulgan, 2006)

Notably, these intergenerational conflicts rely upon rooted stereotypes and biases in the workforce, which may inhibit the workers from acknowledging the essential contribution of multigenerational diversity to team productivity. For instance, the employers' aspiration of the absolute adaptation of the workers to the organization's needs and character may undermine the employers' understanding of the younger and older workers' perspectives in terms of values, motivation sources, and working styles. As raised above, the varied generations may define organizational success differently (Fraone et al., 2008). Therefore, the productivity of the multigenerational workforce relies upon the managers' attempt to shape the organizational culture and promote communication diversity and cross-generational values.

In this regard, intergenerational communication represents a salient obstacle to the establishment of an efficient multigenerational workforce. The digital gaps between older and younger generations, in terms of exposure and proficiency, aggravate this obstacle (Fraone et al., 2008, p. 4):

> As the first generation to grow up with computers as a constant in their lives, Millennials prefers to use email, texting, and Instant Messaging over face to face meetings, memos, and other more formal communication techniques. Baby Boomers may misinterpret this as disrespectful or avoidant behavior, while the younger generation may simply see it as a way to expedite work and maximize productivity.

2.22. Multigenerational Mediators of New Technologies

In addition to the above overview of the multigenerational workforce, one may suggest that the different characteristics of each generation create a distinct worker profile in a certain organization. For instance, Harber (2011) highlighted the professional gaps between the younger and older generations:

"Members of the older generations show characteristics that accommodate customer service and loyalty to an organization. Members of the younger generations have the technical knowledge and the ability to train others in order to use this technology to the benefit of the organization" (p. 2).

Therefore, each generation's advantages and disadvantages in the workforce and combining intergenerational features may enable better profits and professional efficacy. As a result, the ability to mediate between generations is a crucial component in the intergenerational ecosystem, as each generation is likely to communicate with both the preceding age group and the following one and therefore possibly bridge any digital and cultural gaps. This socio-cultural understanding exceeds the traditional discourse of technological adoption among different age groups since it provides a multigenerational approach to solving the intergroup gaps stemming from any modern changes in human reality.

In this regard, the digital use patterns of the Gen Xers highlight their possible role as mediators between the Baby Boomers and the Millennials (Lyons & Schweitzer, 2017; Urick, 2017):

> The gap between Baby Boomers and Millennials is staggering, but Generation Xers find themselves in the middle of the two, sometimes overlapping in both directions, serving as a "mediating generation." Members of Generation X find ease in relating to members of the Baby Boomer generation because many of them also had to learn to use technology and social media sites as they arose, but can also relate to the Millennial generation, as those are their children and their children's lives are saturated in the ever-changing world of technology. (Downs, 2019, p. 4)

Consequently, overviewing each generation as one exclusive cohort prevents the prevalent opportunities of strengthening the intergenerational relationships in the personal and professional sectors. Relying solely on the personal and family-based connections between the younger and older generations may inhibit a full multigenerational workforce and better educational processes. Therefore, we would like to suggest the institutionalization of multigenerational education in the public sector as an efficient vector to bridge the existing digital gaps between the older generations with their traditional perceptions and the younger ones with the hyper-digitized views.

2.23. Generational Gaps and the Public Sector

First and foremost, it is important to state that according to Yang (2019), many types of research on the generation gap have been conducted, but only a few of them have been carried out in the public sector.

That being said, and as established earlier in this chapter, generational gaps tend to bring forth many conflicts between members of varying generations, particularly when they are required to work side by side. Cho and Lewis (2012) stated that age and work experience play a large role in employee turnover, particularly within the public sector. Cho and Lewis also found that employees are less likely to leave a job in their 30s, 40s, 50s, or in cases where they have worked for the government for a total of eight years or more. In fact, their study actually determined that age and experience play a role in whether an employee will leave a job or not (Cho & Lewis, 2012). According to Mayer (2014), aside from education and occupation, age is one of the characteristics that is very different from the private sector. Compared to workers in the private sector, public-sector employees tend to be older (Mayer, 2014).

Statistically speaking, it was said that employees in the public sector are older than private-sector employees: 51.7% of public-sector employees were between the ages of 45 and 64, while 42.4% of full-time private-sector workers were part of that age group in 2013 (Mayer, 2014).

Up until this point in the book, we have managed to lay out the explore how these generational gaps are ultimately impacting the public sector (despite not having very much data to work with at this time):

Critically, we shall observe the outline and distinct characteristics of the public service organizations, as determined by Pratt et al. (2007). First, public service organizations operate not just as one hierarchy but as multiple hierarchies. Second, the nature of public service organizations is that they provide services, not products. Third, the purpose of public service organizations is that they serve the common good.

Judging solely on the characteristics listed above, and by what we already know about Generation Y, it would seem that these traits and characteristics coincide well with both the public sector as well as Generation Y. This is because Generation Y's values are, in a way, very similar to the characteristics of the public sector, as listed.

That is, the fact that there are multiple hierarchies instead of one potentially allows for flexibility and open-mindedness at the place of work; secondly, providing services also means conducting meaningful tasks that genuinely make an impact on the world; and finally, the fact that the purpose of the public sector is to serve the common good is something that resonates very deeply with Millennials, particularly because they strive for this in nearly all that they do.

This, in turn, raises the question of why Millennials are not jumping at the opportunity to work for the government these days and why they have persistently opted for the private sector. Could it be a lack of trust in the government, perhaps?

As it would turn out, and according to the findings presented by Molyneux and Teixeira (2010), there is a significant disparity between Millennials and non-Millennials when it comes to trust in government: "62% of Millennials, compared to 46% of non-Millennials, believed a strong government was needed to handle today's complex economic problems; 44% of Millennials expressed their confidence in the federal government's ability to resolve problems; and only 30% of non-Millennials believed so" (Molyneux & Teixeira, 2010, p. 36).

In this case, it is interesting to learn that Millennials are more pro-government than any other generation: "Since Millennials are a pro-government generation, an assumption can be made that Millennials are more willing to work for the government than the previous generation" (Yang, 2019, p. 11).

Nonetheless, this does not seem to be the case. Why is it that Millennials are more supportive of the government, but simultaneously, the desire to work for the public sector continues to decrease? Yu and Miller (2003) stumbled upon the interesting observation and stated that cultural diversity also has an impact on people's work ethics and values. Ultimately, Yang (2019) concluded the following:

> The challenges associated with the generational gap may be context-specific and contingent upon demographic structure and values in an organization. Therefore, a more specific government organization or agency needs to be studied in order to assess the impact of the generation gap in the public sector. (Yang, 2019, p. 3)

What then are additional elements that may cause Generation Y to refrain from working for the government? This partitions into two parts.

The first: as noted by Sauser and Sims (2013), this generational cohort places a great emphasis on ethics, and while they may still trust the government, it could still be that the ethical conduct is not quite up to their standard. Second explanation is leadership styles, and management found within the public sector. Since up until recently, the public sector was dominated by the Baby Boom generation, now that they have reached retirement age, a lot of adjustments must be made, just as stated by Pate et al. (2007) that there is a persistent lack of trust in senior management in the public sector.

Whatever their reasoning may be, our world cannot afford to give up on a generation and wait for the next one because a lot can happen during this time. At the rate processes and changes occur, we cannot allow the most educated generation to not take part in and/or contribute to the well-being and survival of the state, and it is crucial we find a way to strengthen their engagement in the public sector as soon as possible.

In sum, in this chapter, we first discussed the discrepancies between generation and age and soon after dived into the conventional generational theories, both old and new. Once we found the most suitable definition for our work, we further elaborated on the generational theory as established by Strauss and Howe.

In addition, we discussed Strauss and Howe's four-stage cycle model, also known as the fourth turning, and provided a circumstantial definition for each phase. Upon completing this phase, we then took a gander at the four archetypes established by Strauss and Howe (hero, nomad, artist, and prophet). Soon after, we discussed the initial issues that generational gaps bring forth. Finally, we provided a comprehensive explanation of each generation and ended with the discussion on the characteristics of the public sector and how Generation Y perceives it. Ultimately, and in the words of Wood (2005): "The older the generation, the longer the list of positive stereotypes; the younger the generation, the longer the list of negative stereotypes" (Wood, 2005, p. 87).

Not one single generation will ever be able to fully understand the other; however, the mere act of recognizing these differences, and later on, making some minor adaptations to try and accommodate the needs of others, will ultimately only benefit the public sector, the workforce, and perhaps even society as a whole.

2.24. Multigenerational Reform in the Public Sector

To create an efficient multigenerational workforce in the public sector, widespread reforms can be enacted. Notable studies dealing with a multigenerational workforce in the business sector may provide initial insights and guidelines for the implementation of the educational and professional processes to mitigate the intergenerational gaps between public servants.

From the business prism, modern organizations have developed advanced methods and training programs to address the obstacles stemming from the creation of a multigenerational workforce and a tolerant culture. However, there is a scholastic need to change the traditional analysis of the Gen Xers and Millennial leaders (Burke, 2015; Cahill & Sedrak, 2012; Jenkins, 2008; Pili, 2018; Stanley, 2010; Smola & Sutton, 2002; Tolbize, 2008), into a combination of Millennial and post-Millennial managers, when addressing the new multigenerational workforce.

In this regard, Heskett (2007) posits that the Millennial-driven cohort of professional leaders is capable of managing dynamic and global environments. Their focus is likely to rely upon enhanced teamwork, technological tools, and keeping the work-life balance. Nonetheless, greater scholarly scrutiny should be attributed to the post-Millennial leader and its ability to cooperate with its precedent generations. Important to mention, notable issues of the Millennial leaders are relevant for the new generation of managers, which were depicted by the Boston College Center (Fraone et al., 2008).

First, the issue of knowledge transfer is of paramount importance in the public sector due to its consolidating multigenerational character, combining the older generations and the younger counterparts. As the Baby Boomers and Gen Xers get closer to the retirement age, it is essential to form organized procedures of knowledge transfer from the experienced workers to those who will fill the new leading positions. Therefore, there is a need for better documentation, communication, and relationships to facilitate the knowledge transfer within the public sector personnel.

In this regard, managers should promote organizational tolerance and respect for all workers. To do so, the public organizations must hone their culture to promote multi-generational values. For instance, the Boston College Center posits: "Millennials, who value social responsibility and activism, are attracted to values-based organizations. Volunteer opportunities can be one way of showing the organization's commitment to others, while also allowing all four generations to work together toward a goal outside of their work responsibilities" (Fraone et al., 2008, p. 6).

Consequently, there raises a need for additional training and development programs, which will qualify the managers to develop the needed interpersonal skills to supervise the multigenerational workforce (Fraone et al., 2008): "Managers need to be in tune with the preferred working styles of the different generations and how they receive and react to feedback, especially with Millennials who react more positively to coaching than traditional constructive criticism" (p. 5).

Additionally, the workers need extra training, focusing on the importance of diversity, as expressed in the workshops of Ernst & Young LLP, aimed at fostering efficient teamwork and emotional intelligence. Following the training programs, the public sector could use mentoring and pair the younger workers with their professional counterparts to develop new ideas together. This may assist in the knowledge transfer and facilitate multigenerational relationships (Fraone et al., 2008).

Following the above discussion, there is a notable study consulting the federal government regarding the formation of an American multigenerational workforce (Hannam & Yordi, 2011). Based on this study, one of the significant milestones of this multigenerational workforce is the advent of new technologies and innovation, which bridge the traditional obstacles of the physical world. While generational variance is not a unique feature of the modern workplace, it is important to mention the technological affinity of the new worker and the abundant opportunities he or she may bring. As Meister and Willyerd (2010, p. 5) posited: "Never has a generation entered the workplace using technologies so far ahead of those adopted by their employer."

To deal with the generational variance, Meister and Willyerd suggest that managers pay additional attention to the new communicational technologies to avoid misperceptions and a less productive work ambiance: "A diverse and inclusive workplace requires open communication with an awareness of these growing generational differences. It is a matter of strong leadership, embracing new approaches, and communicating in a way that engages all employees" (Hannam & Yordi, 2011, p. 9).

Additionally, the multigenerational workforce raises the need for increased innovation to promote organizational success. However, despite the 2010 OPM Federal Employee Viewpoint study, which highlights innovation as the major field the federal government should focus on, only 60% of federal employee responded that they felt encouraged to promote innovative initiatives, in comparison to 73% in the private sector (Fernandez et al., 2015). This finding exhibits a notable gap between the government and private sectors, which should be minimized to increase the profits of the multigenerational workforce in the public sector. In this regard, Hannam and Yordi (2011) argue:

> With the increased emphasis on innovation, managers will need a collaborative leadership style that supports innovation. Traditionalists and Boomers bring a vast amount of knowledge and wisdom, while Xers and Millennials bring technological savvy. In addition, the Millennials have grown up working in teams, and have the collaboration skills that are essential to innovation. By forming teams that combine members from multiple generations and ethnicities, organizations can benefit from the strengths that each brings to the table. (p. 15)

As the public sector becomes younger and filled with Millennials, policymakers and regulators have greater opportunities to maximize the full potential of emerging technologies in the public sphere. Nonetheless, the Millennials possess a special role in this regard, as they need to mediate between the traditional perceptions of the Baby Boomers and the Gen Xers to the Gen Zers. Meaning, the digital contribution of the Millennials is twofold since they are familiar with the digital world but have still experienced part of the non-technological reality of the Gen Xers and Baby Boomers.

Therefore, to digitally adapt the public sector to innovative and advanced working methodologies, there is a need for a multigenerational approach that uses the Millennials as tech mediators of the new era. Since the Gen Zers are hyper-digitalized in their personal and professional habits, we assume the Millennials will establish the digitization processes in the public sector as the new leaders, and the Gen Zers will pursue their work.

Notably, this multigenerational knowledge and skills transfer cycle is neither novel nor unique. Notwithstanding, the amplification of globalization and digitization processes magnifies the intergenerational gaps and therefore requires ameliorating personal and professional multigenerational relationships. This raises the importance of developing strategic mentorships and materials transferring between the varied cohorts and establishing the inner relationships between the public servants in the long run.

In this regard, it is essential to understand the dynamic character of the tech mediator since the Millennials' digital knowledge and exposure will probably become increasingly irrelevant compared to the post-Millennial cohorts. As society is likely to experience additional technological progress and change, the generational shift will become more prevalent until the Gen Zers replace the Millennial mediator.

As much as the public sector is often blamed for its traditional perceptions and high levels of bureaucracy, the multigenerational shift and aligned digital adaptation might be able to reshape the traditional perception of the public sector as a whole. Meaning, once tech-savvy public leaders and/or servants can guide the older counterparts and transfer crucial technological processes and data, the public sector may alter its inherent image of inefficiency and fixation.

Important to mention, this multigenerational mediating is highly dynamic and ambivalent, as each generational cohort possesses different characteristics, and therefore, the learning processes from one generation to another are different. Additionally, one cannot compel intergenerational relationships in all circumstances, especially in the hyper-politicized public sector.

Nonetheless, creating this mediating function provides several opportunities for the public sector and the modern workforce. First, it requires the public sector leaders to be more aware of their employers' preferences and needs. Additionally, it enables employers to thrive in a tolerant environment in which their personal traits matter. Furthermore, having the tech mediator bridges the old and new spheres and connects the previous leaders' knowledge with the innovative thinking and digital orientation of the new cohorts.

Despite the relative inaccuracies in Prensky's classification of digital natives and digital immigrants and the aligned critics raised above, his scholarship serves crucial support to the needed training of tech mediators between the different generational cohorts. Therefore, those who speak the digital language should be able to make technologies accessible for those who come from a less digital environment.

Following the intergenerational review above, we recommend using the digital affinity of the Millennials as a bridge between the pre- and post-Millennial cohorts in the public sector. Broadly, the digital era in which we live provides the younger individuals with unique traits and capacities, which the older counterparts do not necessarily possess or struggle to adapt to. Meaning, the traditional age-based seniority is not as relevant to the public sphere as traditionally perceived. Consequently, analyzing the digital differences between the generational cohorts is a crucial step in the establishment of tech mediators and the facilitation of digitization processes in traditional and fixed spheres as the public sector.

Window on Management

This chapter introduces an initial glimpse into the leading notions and theories dealing with generational diversity. To offer a contemporary prism, we elaborate upon the digital generational gaps in the workforce and in the public sector. Specifically, we offer to manage generational diversity in the public sector by enabling Millennials to take the role of tech mediators of the new digital era. Since the Gen Zers are hyper-digitalized in their personal and professional habits, Millennials will apply the digitization processes in the public sector as the new leaders, and the Gen Zers will pursue their work. In terms of management practices, this raises the importance of developing strategic mentorships and materials transferring across the varied cohorts and establishing the inner relationships between public organization employees in the long run. Our core argument is that a multigenerational reform is needed in the public sector in a bid to fully maximize the potential of the digital generations while balancing its deficiencies compared to the traditional cohorts managing the public sector.

Chapter 3

Theories and Measurement of Ethical Decision-Making

Several incidents of ethical misconduct in the business sector have driven researchers to examine the origins of unethical behavioral patterns. These studies enable us to comprehend the triggers of unethical conduct of businessmen and businesswomen (Christie et al., 2003). One can mention the relative frequency of unethical behavioral practices within big corporations, such as Enron and WorldCom, which were accused of fraud and misuse of funds. As a result, the scholastic fields of business ethics and ethical decision-making (EDM) have gained increased interest among scholars and businessmen. Whereas a plethora of studies have dealt with the implications of unethical business acts, some claim that the predictors of unethical conduct identified with decision-making have not received the proper scholastic observation (Nguyen et al., 2008). Nonetheless, the study of EDM has been enriched and reviewed for a few decades, and various scholars have analyzed the vast theoretical and empirical literature on the subject. Important to mention, contemporary ethics research adheres to one's ethical development, as influenced by the work of several researchers, with emphasis on the psychologists Lawrence Kohlberg and James Rest.

3.1. Kohlberg's Theory

A substantial body of research dealing with EDM relies upon the psychological foundation of Kohlberg's theory of cognitive moral development (Kohlberg, 1969). This cognitive model is considered one of the most prominent paradigms of moral judgment in the scholarly discourse of this field, which also served as a basis for Rest's four-component model (Bailey et al., 2010; Lovell, 1997; Ponemon & Gabhart, 1994; Rest, 1983; 1986).

According to Trevino (1986), Kohlberg's model suggests a theoretical framework analyzing how managers recognize and perceive ethical issues. It highlights the cognitive aspect of EDM, as it shows "how the cognitive processes of moral decision-making become more complex and sophisticated with development" (Trevino, 1986, p. 604). Therefore, the model emphasizes the cognitive process rather than the outcome of a certain action.

Following the discussion above, the Kohlbergian theory argues that one's moral reasoning is established through various cognitive stages. In terms of the model's structure, the theory divides ethical development into three main stages: the pre-conventional level, conventional level, and the post-conventional level, where each stage indicates a higher level of ethical development. Therefore, the first stage is considered the lowest level of cognitive moral development as external authorities and self-interest influence it. The second conventional stage focuses on society's norms and laws. Ultimately, the post-conventional level is the highest ethical stage, as it is shaped by universal values of fairness and justice (Kohlberg, 1969).

Nonetheless, it is essential to consider the limitations of Kohlberg's model (Trevino, 1986). For example, moral judgment is not an exclusive predictor of moral behavior, and the correlation between thoughts and actual behavior is still relatively moderate in empirical studies (Blasi, 1980; Kohlberg & Candee, 1984). Therefore, one may undermine the relationship between moral judgment and actions, which is an inherent part of Kohlberg's model.

In order to properly address the theoretical and empirical foundation of EDM, this chapter will elaborate upon the prevalent theoretical models suggested by Rest (1986), Hunt and Vitell (1986), and Jones (1991), alongside additional notable EDM theories and the relevant empirical literature supporting or refuting these models.

3.2. Ethical Decision-Making Theories

3.2.1. Rest's Four-Component Model

Rest's (1983; 1986) four-component model enables one to scrutinize the moral thought processes and behavior from a cognitive-developmental perspective. It is divided into four components: moral awareness, moral judgment, moral motivation, and moral character. Rest defines the model's stages as follows:

> [t]he production of moral behavior in a particular situation involves (1) interpreting the situation in terms of how people's welfare is affected by possible actions of the subject, (2) figuring out what the ideally moral course of action would be, (3) selecting among valued outcomes to intend to the moral course of action, and (4) executing and implementing what one intends to do. (Rest, 1983, p. 559)

Therefore, the individual follows a cognitive process, in which one must perceive the ethical aspect within a situation, create a responsive, ideal consequence, be driven to execute the idyllic action and finally decide how to perform it. This model suggests that the stage of ethical judgment is often led by moral awareness and reflects only a part of the psychology of morality. Therefore, the awareness stage is prior to one's judgment attempting to prioritize the most ethical action in a well-structured process (Rest, 1994).

Important to mention, Rest's four components are labeled differently among scholars and even within the different writings of Rest. As a result, there are varied measurement instruments aimed at evaluating different aspects of each component (Chambers, 2011). This semantic and methodological variance is an inherent and repetitive loophole within the scholarly discourse of EDM and will be further analyzed.

For example, one can mention the researcher Bebeau (2002), who has written extensively about Rest's model and the DIT measure in the field of dental practice and education. She has interpreted Rest's four stages as ethical sensitivity, ethical judgment, ethical intention, and ethical behavior, whereas Rest and other scholars do not use the same labels for the two final stages. Hence, Bebeau posits the first phase as addressing one's ability to interpret a questionable ethical action. It is then followed by another stage in which one decides which action is morally right or wrong, in order to prioritize certain moral values. The model ends with a practical outcome of the motivation turning into a behavioral pattern.

Similar to Bebeau (2002), Barnett and Valentine (2004) provided an overview of the steps of the EDM process based on the previous models, turning from one's ethical recognition into actual behavior. It begins with the initial recognition of an ethical dilemma and is followed by an individual judgment and the formation of behavioral intentions. The model considers these intentions a predictor of actual conduct, thus turning the initial recognition into a practical phase. This intention-behavior correlation is highly explored in the EDM literature.

3.2.2. Trevino's Person-Situation Interactionist Model

Based on Kohlberg's theory (1969), Trevino (1986) proposes the person-situation interactionist model. This interactionist model suggests that one's cognitive model development shapes his or her reaction to an ethical issue. Moreover, it adds the interaction of individual and situational variables in order to examine and predict the EDM processes in organizations. As articulated by Trevino (1986, p. 602):

> [c]ognitions of right and wrong are not enough to explain or predict ethical decision-making behavior. Additional individual and situational variables interact with the cognitive component to determine how an individual is likely to behave in response to an ethical dilemma.

Both the individual and situational factors are depicted as influencing the individual's moral development. Whereas the individual factors include the variables of ego strength, field dependence, and locus of control, the situational factors relate to work and organizational contexts, as explained in the article:

> Situational variables arising from the immediate job context and the broader organizational culture [. . .] These include the organization's normative structure, referent others, obedience to authority, responsibility for consequences, reinforcement contingencies, and other pressures [. . .] characteristics of the job itself, and the moral content of the organizational culture. (Trevino, 1986, p. 602)

Trevino did not mention Rest's model directly but mainly addressed the DIT as an example of a measurement instrument. However, one may argue that she has suggested an alternative model in her research, which builds on Rest's findings. Her model begins with an existing ethical dilemma and pursues the cognitions stage. This stage leads to moral judgments, which are affected by individual and situational factors. As a result, the model suggests that moral judgments affect ethical or unethical behavioral patterns.

3.2.3. Ferrell and Gresham's Model

From the marketing perspective, Ferrell and Gresham (1985) suggested an integrated model, which is mainly applicable in ethical dilemmas related to marketing. As articulated in their article, the model: "clarifies and synthesizes the multiple variables that explain how marketers make ethical/unethical decisions" (Ferrell & Gresham, 1985, p. 87). It further analyses the direct and indirect effect of individual and organizational factors on the process of EDM, with emphasis on ethical or unethical marketing behavior. Whereas the individual factors include values, attitudes, knowledge, and intentions of the decision-maker, the organizational factors include people who are significant, such as a direct manager, and opportunities for action.

The researchers employed a teleology-deontology dichotomy through this model as their core foundation. Although the authors claim that this model is not one-dimensional and may be applicable in other organizational fields, they confessed that the odds of deviating from ethical behavior are mainly salient in marketing-based fields. This may have an impact on its alleged relevance in non-marketing fields (Ferrell & Gresham, 1985).

3.2.4. Hunt and Vitell's General Theory of Marketing Ethics

The theory of Hunt and Vitell (1986, 1993, 2005, 2006) offered a general theory of marketing ethics, which includes notable core stages. Their model addresses a scenario in which one needs to deal with an ethical issue and examine the possible alternatives to solve this issue. After he or she perceives the alleged alternatives, one can choose between theological and deontological evaluations. As a result, the model highlights the importance of philosophical evaluations as a basis of ethical judgments.

Within the deontological evaluation, the individual examines the appropriateness or wrongness of the behaviors led by each alternative. He or she must compare each alternative's behavioral practices based on fixed deontological norms. Pan and Sparks (2012, p. 413) explain that deontological evaluations: "occur as decision makers employ laws, rules, codes, or behavioral norms to each perceived alternative." Important to mention, these norms or laws do not have to be highly general nor specific, and the individual examines the degree to which the perceived decision alternative disrupts these socially applicable codes. The theological evaluation suggests that the individual scrutinizes the perceived outcomes from several criteria. He or she examines each alternative for numerous stakeholder groups, its assessed probability, the level of its desirability, and each stakeholder group's importance (Hunt & Vitell, 1993, 2006). Therefore, the theory argues that deontological and teleological evaluations influence one's formation of ethical judgments. As a result, the variance between individuals relies upon their inner choice between deontological and teleological reasoning as part of their ethical judgments.

3.2.5. Dubinsky and Loken's Model

Dubinsky and Loken (1989) suggest a framework for analyzing EDM in marketing, which elaborated on the theory of Fishbein and Ajzen (1975) and the reasoned action. In order to examine their theory, sales personnel filled out questionnaires on sales-driven conducts, intentions, beliefs, and attitudes.

According to their model, one's intention to perform an ethical or unethical action immediately affects the engagement in this action. Moreover, one's attitude toward the behavior influences the intention and possibly his or her subjective norms. Therefore, the intentions enable one to predict one's behavior, but are first affected by one's attitudes and/or subjective norms. However, the relative importance given to attitudes or subjective norms in predicting intentions and their followed behavior diverges between various ethical behaviors or different subgroups.

3.2.6. Jones's Issue Contingent Model

Continuing Rest's writing (1986), Jones's (1991) issue contingent model highlights the multidimensional principle of moral intensity, which is divided into six issue contingencies. These six components include the dimension of the magnitude of the consequences, social consensus, probability of effect, temporal immediacy, proximity, and concentration of effect.

Jones (1991, p. 372) defined moral intensity as the "extent of issue-related moral imperative in a situation." He argued that moral intensity substantially affects Rest's model, and various studies have measured the different dimensions of this principle (Barnett et al., 1999; Singhapakdi et al., 1996). Moreover, notable studies examined its correlation to judgment and showed that moral intensity is a predictor of ethical judgment (Leitsch, 2004, 2006). Other studies found that moral intensity and judgment predict moral intentions (Karacaer et al., 2009).

Jones's theoretical notion has been empirically validated in various studies discussing business- and marketing-related dilemmas (Barnett, 2001; Singhapakdi et al., 1996, 1999). For example, based on Jones's theory (1991), Barnett and Valentine (2004) highlight the issue-contingent model and argue that the features of the issue itself impact ethical actions. As a result, their article analyses the effect of issue contingencies on the EDM process of marketing professionals.

Following the above, Barnett and Valentine (2004) claim that issue contingencies may predict one's recognition of ethical issues. Their explanation relies upon Hunt and Vitell's and Jones's models, which indicate that one must recognize an ethical issue before any judicial or active phase. Due to the variance of issue contingencies, an individual may expose a different extent of sensitivity to some ethical issues compared to others.

Most of these EDM models include, to some extent, an ethical judgment stage. Rest (1986) and Trevino (1986) posit cognitive moral development as a crucial component in the judgment phase. This is in comparison to Hunt and Vitell (1986) and Dubinsky and Loken (1989), who highlight the importance of moral evaluation based on teleological or deontological reasoning.

Moreover, Trevino (1986) and Ferrell and Gresham (1985) created a direct transition from the moral judgment phase to a substantial behavior. Compared to Rest (1986), Hunt and Vitell (1986), and Dubinsky and Loken (1989) included a prior stage of moral intent before any practical output.

3.2.7. Schwartz's Ethical Decision-Making Model

Based on the previous models, Schwartz (2016) suggested a holistic approach, as he argued that most theoretical models contradict each other. His model attempted to synthesize the previous theories and aimed at bridging the scholastic gaps in the literature. Moreover, it combined the factors of rationality and non-rationality and claimed that ethical behavior depends on ethical biases and environmental factors.

This integrated model is built upon Rest's model but includes the rational and non-rational factors as intermediaries and individual and situational factors as moderating variables. Compared to the other EDM models, this model has not been broadly examined in studies. However, one can note a recent study (Latan et al., 2019) that used this model. The goal of the study was to evaluate the influence of the variables above on the ethical judgments of auditors in reaching the decision to blow the whistle.

3.2.8. Additional Ethical Decision-Making Models

One can mention additional EDM models based upon the models above. For example, Cooper's (2006) model includes six stages prior to the resolution phase: ethical perception, situation description, ethical issues definition, alternatives identification, consequences estimation, and alternative election.

Moreover, Wittmer (2005) proposed a general behavioral model of EDM. It consists of seven components: ethical situation, ethical sensitivity, ethical judgment, ethical choice, ethical behavior, individual influences, and environmental influences. Important to mention, this study considers ethical sensitivity as an independent element that shapes ethical behavior.

Both Wittmer and Cooper highlight the stage of ethical reasoning and cognition in their models, thus arguing that in order to act ethically, one must begin with the perception of an ethical issue. Nonetheless, numerous scholars neglect this phase of perception and adhere to discussing the stage of moral reasoning or ethical conduct. Moreover, some suggest that the study of ethical perception is relatively lacking due to its methodological obstacles for research (Choi & Perry, 2010). Consequently, this raises a question about the needed enhancement of the existing methodological framework of ethical perception and other complex variables within EDM literature.

3.3. Reviews of Ethical Decision-Making Literature

Notable reviews of the empirical studies in the field of EDM are offered by Craft (2013), Ford and Richardson (1994), Loe et al. (2000), and O'Fallon and Butterfield (2005). Important to mention, the reviews indicate the dynamics and scholastic evolution of this theoretical field, as each review focuses on a different time frame and coverage, thus having an impact upon theoretical and empirical progress.

The first literature review on the subject was provided by Ford and Richardson (1994), which was based mostly upon non-empirical research between 1978 and 1992. Their findings indicated the scholarly focus on individual factors of decision-makers, such as gender, age, nationality, and religion.

Adding to Ford and Richardson, Loe et al. (2000) focused on the empirical research between 1992 and 1996 and added Jones's (1991) model of EDM and moral intensity. Additional factors to age, personality, and religions were explored, such as education, employment, and the personal locus of control. An additional change within this time frame relates to the examination of cognitive moral development, ethical judgment, moral philosophy, and value orientation.

Following the two reviews, one can mention the extensive review of O'Fallon and Butterfield (2005), which examined a greater number of studies between 1993 and 2003. It is considered one of the most widespread reviews in EDM and is highly mentioned in EDM studies. Their review integrated Rest's model and Jones's moral intensity factor and showed the scholarly focus on similar factors raised above. However, the review's uniqueness arises from the classification of the findings according to Rest's dependent variables, including awareness, judgment, intent, and behavior.

Important to mention, O'Fallon and Butterfield (2005) recommended expanding the theoretical foundation of EDM in order to elaborate on the existing theories, such as Rest's (1986) four-component model, Jones's (1991) moral intensity construct, Kohlberg's (1969) theory of cognitive moral development, and Ajzen's (1985, 1989) theory of planned behavior. Ajzen's theory argues that one's beliefs and evaluations of the outcomes of behavior determine his or her attitude towards the behavior. Therefore, one is more expected to assess the likelihood of an action's outcomes and its circumstances. In this regard, the issue contingencies may also affect the formation of attitudes towards a certain behavior (Jones, 1991).

Moreover, O'Fallon and Butterfield (2005) mentioned the relatively high frequency of measures in different empirical studies, including but not limited to Reidenbach and Robin's (1988, 1990) multidimensional ethics scale, Rest's (1986) defining issues test, the Rokeach value survey (1973), and Forsyth's (1980) ethical position questionnaire. They claim that the repetitive usage of these measures inhibits the practice of innovative research methods and theory development. Nonetheless, as raised above, some of the EDM variables are empirically challenging, such as ethical perception. This could potentially lead the researchers to focus on existing measurement instruments.

Furthermore, the updated review by Craft (2013) focused on 84 studies between 2004 and 2011. It suggested that the variable of moral awareness in Rest's model received more scholastic coverage in the literature than in previous reviews. Moreover, Craft's review raised the need for more longitudinal studies in this subject (Awasthi, 2008; Herington & Weaven, 2008; Marta et al., 2008), in addition to a request for increased research focus on moral intensity (Hayibor & Wasieleski, 2009; Vitell et al., 2009). It is also mentioned that demographic variables generate higher amounts of findings due its relative methodological ease (Craft, 2013).

Within the framework of EDM, one can note the attention given to the stage of ethical judgment, which is a notable predictor of one's behavior. Therefore, the chapter will elaborate upon ethical judgment, its measures, constraints, and usefulness in various empirical studies.

3.4. Definition of Ethical Judgment

Generally, ethical judgments refer to one's perception of the rightness of a certain ethical action (Reidenbach & Robin, 1990). Nguyen et al. (2008, p. 421) reinforce this explanation and define ethical judgment as a "respondent's perceived ethicality of an action." Nonetheless, the literature highlights the definitions offered by the prevalent theories of EDM, including Hunt and Vitell's model and Rest's four-component model. A comparison between both definitions, which was given by Pan and Sparks (2012), enables a proper understanding of ethical judgment as a core issue in ethics research, as from different scholastic prisms.

Hunt and Vitell (1986, p. 763) define ethical judgments as "the belief that a particular alternative is the most ethical alternative." As Pan and Sparks (2012) interpret this definition, one must identify the most ethical option among chosen alternatives, and they emphasize the needed comparison between all options. Similar to Hunt and Vitell, Rest (1986) claims that ethical judgment leads the individual to choose among various options but emphasizes the psychological aspect of the process. Nonetheless, Rest (1986) does not see the comparison act as compulsory and suggest a singular-based perspective: "Moral judgment is a psychological construct that characterizes a process by which an individual determines that one course of action in a particular situation is morally right and another course of action is morally wrong" (Rest et al., 1997, p. 5).

Similar views to Rest's observation arise within the definitions of Schwepker (1999) and Valentine and Rittenburg (2004). Meaning, while Hunt and Vitell define ethical judgment as a comparison between behavioral alternatives, the others accept an ethical evaluation in isolation and without an explicit comparison (Pan & Sparks, 2012).

Moreover, different than Hunt and Vitell, whose definition suggests a range of ethical evaluations ("the most ethical"), the other scholars emphasize the deterministic nature of ethical judgments, as people judge certain actions in a binary way of "right or wrong" or "ethical or unethical." Therefore, the researchers do not present a coherent stance regarding one's judicial expressions of an ethical issue.

To solve this ambiguity, Pan and Sparks (2012, p. 409) suggested their own definition, which argues that: "an individual's personal evaluation of the degree to which some behavior or course of action is ethical or unethical." This definition manages to combine Hunt and Vitell's judicial spectrum and the singular observation provided by Rest and the other scholars.

3.5. Empirical Studies of Ethical Judgments

Within the framework of EDM, a substantial body of ethics research has dealt with the formation of ethical judgments. This led to numerous theoretical and empirical studies, which demonstrate its inclusive importance to the analysis of ethical and unethical behavioral patterns (Barnett & Valentine, 2004; Rest, 1986). For example, Flory et al. (1993, p. 418) claimed that the study of ethical judgments enables one to properly assess an unethical behavior, as stated in their article: "the explanation, prediction, and control of unethical behavior."

As raised above, the prevalent models of EDM present ethical judgments as a crucial explanatory variable (Hunt & Vitell, 1986, 1993; Jones, 1991; Rest, 1986). For instance, Rest's (1986) four-component model found that ethical judgment is a crucial component in the EDM process as it mediates between one's recognition of an ethical issue and the formation of behavioral intentions.

Similarly, the Hunt and Vitell theory suggests a process in which one's deontological and teleological evaluations lead to the formation of ethical judgments. This judicial phase predicts the creation of behavioral intentions, which ultimately result in actual behavior. Moreover, Jones (1991) discussed a similar EDM process as raised by Rest, and he posed the ethical judgment as a direct antecedent of ethical behavioral intentions.

Following the above, Pan and Sparks (2012) raised notable issues of the existing ethical judgments literature by an extensive review and meta-analysis of previous theoretical models and empirical studies. According to their review, ethical judgment studies are considered relatively ambiguous in certain criteria. Thus, inconsistent findings are raised by their empirical research and seem to be in contradiction to the prevalent EDM theories.

Moreover, there is a wide array of measurement tools used by the researchers. There are single- and multi-item instruments, and each consists of different scaling responses. In addition, one may mention the variances in sample composition, which prevent to some extent the findings' comparability. Pan and Sparks suggest that these scholastic issues may inhibit "research generalizability and hinder the testing of ethical decision-making theories" (2012, p. 84).

3.6. Overview of Notable Antecedents to Ethical Judgments

The literature raises various antecedents to EDM, with emphasis on the stage of ethical judgment. Most empirical studies discuss its correlation with numerous factors, including but not limited to age, education, gender, and religion. For example, some studies have proven that one's ethical ideology impacts one's ethical judgment (Barnett et al., 1994, 1996; Callanan et al., 2010; Kleiser et al., 2003; Kim, 2003). Moreover, several studies explored the outcomes of ethical judgments and their impact on behavioral intentions (Barnett & Vaicys, 2000; Hunt & Vasquez-Parraga, 1993).

One may classify the antecedents into categories of variables such as personal demographic, philosophical, psychological, and environmental factors. Pan and Sparks (2012) offered another classification of these variables in two categories of individual or organizational factors. The individual factors include both demographic factors, such as age, education, gender, work, and psychological factors such as cognitive moral development, Machiavellianism, and locus of control. In comparison, the organizational factors include organizational ethical climate, industry type, and the existence of codes of ethics.

Among the demographic factors, one can mention age and gender as the most researched variables in the study of business ethics (Robin & Babin, 1997). The empirical results of the age variable differ and tend to be inconsistent. Several studies predict a positive correlation between age and strictness of ethical judgments (Chiu, 2003; Peterson et al., 2001; Vitell & Paolillo, 2003). This finding may indicate that older people tend to become more ethically strict.

Moreover, Valentine and Rittenburg (2007) raised a positive correlation between ethical judgment and older age and experience. Nonetheless, studies contradict this correlation and indicate that younger people exhibit stricter ethical judgments than older ones (Ede et al., 2000; Vitell et al., 2009), and others that do not show any significant relationship (Barnett & Valentine, 2004; Marques & Azevedo-Pereira, 2009; Schepers, 2003).

In addition to age, the gender variable has shown inconsistent findings in the study of ethical judgments. Most studies showed minimal differences in ethical judgment or no gender differences at all (Hartikainen & Torstila, 2004; Landry et al., 2004; Loo, 2001; Radtke, 2000; Serwinek, 1992; Shafer et al., 2001; Sikula & Costa, 1994; Stanga & Turpen, 1991). Nonetheless, Marques and Azevedo-Pereira (2009) showed that men are stricter than women when making ethical decisions.

However, several studies reported contradicting results showing a higher level of ethical strictness among women. Nguyen et al. (2008) found that the female students' rankings of ethical judgment are higher than those of male students across most moral issues overviewed. Similar findings were raised in additional studies, which reported that women are more sensitive to unethical conduct than men (Cohen et al., 2001; Eweje & Brunton, 2010;). Moreover, Boyle (2000) found significant gender differences in a study of ethical judgment of salespeople, and women were reported to be more ethically sensitive compared to men.

Due to the inconsistent findings, one may claim that there are no major differences between men and women in the study of ethical judgment. However, a gender-based insight is extracted by the authors: "when differences do occur women seem inclined to judge questionable activities as less appropriate than men" (Mudrack & Mason, 2013b, p. 13).

Following the above, the education variable has mainly shown a negative correlation with ethical judgment in empirical studies (Chiu, 2003; Fullerton et al.,1996), while other studies did not manage to find any significant correlation (Deshpande, 1997; Laczniak & Inderrieden, 1987; Merritt, 1991; Serwinek, 1992; Shafer et al., 2001). Nonetheless, Swaidan et al. (2003) reported a positive correlation between the level of education and being ethical. Following these findings, one may argue that higher levels of education lead to more strict ethical judgments.

Similar to the antecedents above, the income and work variables do not show a clear correlation to ethical judgment. While Chiu (2003) showed that work experience diminishes the strictness of ethical judgments, Kidwell et al. (1987) and Weeks et al. (1999) reported the opposite findings. Notably, other studies did not find any correlation (Barnett & Valentine, 2004; Schepers, 2003). Moreover, the impact of religiosity on ethical judgment remains ambiguous in the literature. Vitell and Paolillo

(2003) and Sarwono and Armstrong (2001) found a positive correlation between the two. However Barnett et al. (1996), Chiu (2003), and Zopiatis and Krambia-Kapardis (2008) did not find any significant relationship.

Furthermore, Forte's (2004) study on the moral reasoning ability of managers examined the correlation between ethical judgment and numerous antecedents mentioned above. One can mention the loci of control, age, work tenure, and education among the independent variables. However, the findings did not raise any significant correlation. Nonetheless, another study examined the ethical perception of managers and found significant correlations between the antecedents of religiosity and loci of control and ethical perception (Ho, 2010).

Among the philosophical characteristics, idealism and relativism have also been examined relating to ethical judgments. Studies have shown that idealists tend to be strict in their ethical judgment, compared to relativists who reject universal moral principles (Bass et al., 1999; Kleiser et al., 2003; Vitell & Paolillo, 2003).

Moreover, Pan and Sparks (2012) examined the possible outcome of ethical judgment resulting in behavioral intentions. To measure one's behavioral intention, he or she is asked about the likelihood of any engagement in the activities depicted in the vignettes. Numerous studies show a negative correlation between the strictness of ethical judgments and the possibility of engaging in certain activities (Valentine & Rittenburg, 2004). As a result, Pan and Sparks argued that: "As the strictness of ethical judgments increase, the expressed behavioral intentions decrease" (2012, p. 86). Consequently, one can predict a negative correlation between one's ethical judgment and behavioral intentions.

3.7. Nomenclature Issues in the Study of Ethical Judgments

Mudrack and Mason (2013b) overviewed several nomenclature issues in the study of ethical judgments, with emphasis on the measurement methods. Among the issues they identified was the lack of a consistent nomenclature in various studies, as some claim to measure "ethical judgments," while others addressed it as "ethical evaluations." Moreover, several studies have not explicitly claimed to measure judgment, but mentioned different terms such as "moral philosophy," "ethical awareness," and "ethical sensitivity" (Clark & Dawson, 1996; Cohen et al., 1998; Davis et al., 2001).

For example, Mudrack and Mason (2013b) mentioned the study of Bucar et al. (2003, p. 276), which evaluated ethical "sensitivity" and "responsiveness." In addition, the study of Beekun et al. (2003, p. 276) is highlighted as an additional reference, as it evaluates "the ethical content of a decision." Furthermore, the study of Cohen et al. (1998, p. 254) examined the "ethical orientation on a number of moral constructs" but claimed that the multidimensional ethics scale (MES) is an instrument that measures ethical judgments. In addition, Herndon et al. (2001, p. 76) measured "individual moral values" while using MES survey items. As a result, there remains a semantic and methodological ambiguity regarding the proper labels of ethical judgments in the literature and its relevant measures.

This claim was reinforced by Pan and Sparks (2012) as the definition of ethical judgments is not unified in the literature. Several studies mention similar variables to ethical judgments, such as "ethical beliefs" (Erffmeyer et al., 1999; Muncy & Vitell, 1992; Vitell et al., 2005), "ethical perceptions" (Ergeneli & Arikan, 2002; Honeycutt et al., 2001; Stevenson & Bodkin, 1998), "ethical attitudes" (Christie et al., 2003; Emerson & Conroy, 2004; Gelso & Peterson, 2005; Levin et al., 2004), and "ethical evaluations" (Jones & Middleton, 2007; Spicer et al., 2004). They suggested putting these variables under the realm of ethical judgments and enabling a more unified conceptual domain for EDM researchers.

The implications of the above were analyzed by Mudrack & Mason (2013b, p. 9), stating: "Any words or phrases suggesting that a construct other than ethical judgments has been assessed with an ethical judgments measure potentially hinder the development of knowledge in this important area." Moreover, they emphasize that the labels used instead of judgment do not necessarily reflect clear synonyms. This could possibly lead to possible methodological deficiencies when using a measurement tool aimed at assessing ethical judgment. As a result, one may raise the need to develop additional measurement instruments or refine the differences between the labels used in the study of EDM.

3.8. Notable Measurement Instruments

The EDM literature raises an abundant number of measurement instruments aimed at evaluating different ethical stages. The methodological basis of ethical judgment mainly relies upon Kohlberg's (1964, 1969) measures and Rest's defining issues test (DIT). Kohlberg created a method of evaluating one's cognitive moral development, known as the standard issue scoring (SIS). A previous version was proposed by him with the moral judgment test (MJT), consisting of two ethical scenarios, which aimed at evaluating one's moral judgment competence, including his ability to make decisions and form ethical judgments (Kohlberg, 1964). Important to mention, a central feature of the MJT is the counterarguments to the respondents.

In order to properly overview the methodological framework of ethical judgments, this chapter will elaborate upon several advancing and modern instruments, which are widely used in the literature.

3.8.1. Usage of Ethical Vignettes

Vignettes are considered highly common in business ethics research: "the use of multiple scenarios is preferable in ethics research" (Morris & McDonald, 1995, p. 719). These ethical scenarios enable scholars to exhibit substantial decision-making situations that simulate real-life processes (Alexander & Becker, 1978). One can note an abundant number of ethics studies from multiple disciplines, which have employed ethical vignettes in their empirical research (Fritzsche & Becker, 1983; 1984; Reidenbach & Robin, 1988, 1990). For instance, the measures of ethical awareness and behavioral intentions tend to employ vignettes to examine the respondents' reactions (Pan & Sparks, 2012).

Broadly, the study of business ethics tends to provide the participants with detailed vignettes, in order to measure one's ethical evaluations and judgments. In the vignettes, an agent commits an ethically controversial act, which the respondents are asked to examine according to certain criteria. Mudrack and Mason (2013a, p. 640) scrutinized the vignette themes used in the study of ethical judgments. The traditional methodology usually presents the respondents: "one or more vignettes that depict an ethically questionable activity, and then evaluate the appropriateness of the action described with one or more survey items."

In addition, they claimed that this method is different from typical survey research, as the researchers must provide an object to judge. Therefore, there is an emphasis on the specifics of each ethical activity, agents, and operational vectors to enable the respondent to provide an ethical evaluation.

As a result, the studies of ethical judgment require greater accuracy and attention to detail. Mudrack and Mason (2013b) elaborated upon the deficiencies of vignettes in ethics research. For example, researchers rarely provide clear explanations for choosing specific vignettes, and others do not address vignette contents and tend to focus on the technical aspect of choosing the survey items and less on the content of what is being judged (Chiu, 2003; Chiu & Erdener, 2003; Cohen & Bennie, 2006; Shafer, 2008). This may present a superficial usage of vignettes by some of the scholars as an addition to the existing complexity of vignette selection in ethics studies.

Moreover, one can note two popular ethics vignettes, which are widely used in ethical judgments studies (Emerson et al., 2007; Ismail & Ghazali, 2011). These vignettes were developed by Clark (1966), Harris (1991), and Longenecker et al. (1989) and depict questionable ethical actions. While the first vignette discusses the alleged underreporting of a business' income to lessen taxation, the other depicts accounting deceits that are legally applicable (Ismail & Ghazali, 2011). The difference between both vignettes relies upon the legality of the scenarios to oversee the difference in the participants' evaluation of the ethical act based on its legality. Compared to other applicable measures, Emerson et al. (2007, p. 75) elaborated upon the limitations of using vignettes as the main methodology in ethics research: "We are not able to provide one composite (individual) measure of moral development such as the DIT's "P-score," or a reliable aggregated measure of ethical orientation such as the multidimensional ethical scale (MES) [. . .] for comparison across samples."

3.8.2. The Rokeach Value Survey

As a prevalent measure in ethics studies, one can mention the Rokeach value survey (RVS). Rokeach (1968) proposed a model of measuring values using the RVS, which was mainly validated in his studies (Rokeach, 1973). He suggested that values are classified as terminal and instrumental. Whereas terminal values reflect one's ultimate objective to achieve the desired end target, the instrumental values indicate preferable modes of behavior, which can be divided into moral values and competence values. In its original version, the RVS requires the respondents to rate two lists of terminal and instrumental values and prioritize them.

3.8.3. Forsyth's Ethics Position Questionnaire

In addition to the RVS, Forsyth (1980) created the ethics position questionnaire (EPQ), which aims at measuring one's ethical orientation. The instrument enables one to scrutinize ethical differences based on the philosophies of idealism and relativism and therefore have them apply to ethics research (Barnett et al., 1994; Bass et al., 1999; Kleiser et al., 2003; Vitell et al., 2003; Vitell & Paolillo, 2003). It consists of twenty questions, which are aimed at evaluating one's levels of idealism and relativism, and the respondents are required to state their level of agreement with each of the statements. The EPQ scores include the mean scores of their responses to the idealism and relativism statements.

3.8.4. Rest's Defining Issues Test (DIT)

Based on the six stages of Kohlberg's (1969) theory, Rest (1979) created his most highly developed instrument, which is called the defining issues test (DIT). The DIT enables one to examine ethical development, with emphasis on ethical reasoning (Chan & Leung, 2006). It is a self-administered instrument to evaluate moral judgment, which has been used in various disciplines and studies (Chambers, 2011). Moreover, its goal is to assess the individual's default schema to morally interpret actions and situations.

Trevino (1986, p. 606) provided another description of the instrument:

> The DIT is an objective recognition test that is concerned with how people at different developmental stages choose different statements as representing the most important issue in a moral dilemma. Major indices assess the relative importance a subject gives to principled moral considerations and provide an overall index of moral judgment development.

This instrument was validated by Bebeau's writing (2002) in the dental context. The DIT's theoretical basis relies upon the neo-Kohlbergian approach, as one's moral reasoning may exhibit a scale of stages through moral development. Even though the DIT scholars argue that the moral understating is developmental, it is not considered identical to Kohlberg's measure (Gibbs et al., 1982; Rest et al., 1999).

Furthermore, the DIT and its updated version, the DIT-2, have been an integral part of the ethics research in auditing and accounting. Bailey et al. (2010, p. 1) claim that despite the DIT's relative usefulness, some have witnessed its scholastic flaws: "the pioneers and influential thinkers in accounting ethics research feel that the DIT has outlived its usefulness or, worse yet, proven to be flawed as a measure of the ethical judgment of accounting professionals."

In addition, numerous researchers argue that the DIT is not a proper measurement instrument of accountants' or auditors' ethical development. According to Massey (2002, p. 213), the "low internal consistency of the DIT [. . .], it is possible that auditors share some systematic characteristics that call into question the appropriateness of using the DIT." Moreover, Shaub (1997) suggested that ethics researchers should work on developing additional measures that are more enriching and innovative to the scholarly discourse and not necessarily easier to operate. In this regard, in addition to enhancing the vignettes' contents, one should: "develop scenarios that contain an explicit accounting context" (Shaub, 1997, p. 46).

Other scholars such as Bay (2002) raised additional criticism, as her findings showed that DIT-based studies in accounting are mostly partial and requested further analysis. Moreover, Emler et al. (1983) raised a validity obstacle of the instrument due to its alleged correlation with political bias. Another study (Emler & Stace (1999) supports this correlation between the DIT scores and the political position. As a counter-reaction to this notion, the DIT proponents have attempted to undermine the internal validity of these experiments (Thoma et al., 1999). Moreover, Crowson et al. (2007) managed to show that DIT scores and political identification are not significantly correlated in their student-based sample.

Following the DIT critics as a questionable measure of ethical judgment, various alternatives have been offered and will be partially elaborated in this chapter (Doyle et al., 2009; Fisher, 1997; Massey, 2002; Thorne, 2000; Welton et al., 1994).

3.8.5. Multidimensional Ethics Scale Versus the Consumer Ethics Scale

The literature raises various ethical judgments scales, such as the multidimensional ethics scale (MES) (Reidenbach & Robin, 1990) and the consumer ethics scale (CES) (Muncy & Vitell, 1992). The MES was developed by Reidenbach and Robin in 1988 and was enhanced in 1990. As articulated by Emerson et al. (2007, p. 74), the MES: "serves as an alternative methodological approach to the DIT." The need for a multidimensional scale and not a single-item scale was raised since "individuals use more than one rationale in making ethical judgments" (Reidenbach & Robin, 1990, p. 639).

Reidenbach and Robin (1995, p. 160) claim that the MES: "represents the ethical evaluative criteria that individuals use in making an ethical judgement." Various studies have validated the scale's reliability in estimating behavioral intentions in the business sphere (Cohen et al., 1993, 1995, 1996, 2001; McMahon, 2002; Reidenbach et al., 1991). Therefore, the MES is considered a broadly valid and useful measure in the study of ethical judgments (Dunfee, 2006; Babin et al., 2004). Several scholars highlight the advantages of the MES with emphasis on its relatively high consistency (Loo, 2002; Valentine & Barnett, 2007).

The scale includes eight items relating to three elements of business ethics, including moral equity, relativism, and contractualism. In terms of scenarios, the MES contains "at least one scenario-action pair of the researchers' choosing. . . . Each scenario-action pair [. . .] consists of one hypothetical scenario and one possible action that is open to an agent within the scenario" (Skipper & Hyman, 1993, p. 535). To form the scale, the participants are required to assess the scenario-action pairs, which were originally taken from Dornoff and Tankersley (1975). Important to mention, their sales ethics vignettes were used in additional empirical studies (Singhapakdi, 1999; Singhapakdi, Vitell, & Kraft, 1996; Singhapakdi, Vitell, & Franke, 1999; Singhapakdi, Marta et al., 2000).

Nonetheless, the MES was criticized by Skipper and Hyman (1993), and they argued it remains unclear what the scale measures. Moreover, they mentioned that the scale neglects several crucial ethical rationales and that: "the semantic differential items used in the scale seem problematic" (p. 535).

As a response to the vagueness of the measurement, Reidenbach and Robin (1995) claimed that the scale suffers from demand effects, as it restricts the participants' opinion to eight items only. As a result, the participants may perceive the eight preselected opinions as irrelevant to their ethical judgments. Additional criticism was raised by Nguyen et al. (2008, p. 427), who claimed:

> [t]he lack of a well-defined and agreed upon framework for perceiving and dealing with contractualism ethics. As a result, we are unable to assert that the students responded to the moral issues in the MES from a knowledge-based or behavioral intention-based perspective of contractual ethics, thus drawing conclusions about their contractual ethical decisions problematic.

In addition to MES, one can mention the CES (Muncy & Vitell, 1992), which focuses on the consumer perspective as it evaluates ethical judgments on seventeen consumer actions. This method examines the relationship between a consumer's ethical ideology and the ethical perception of controversial consumer conduct. An enhanced and modified CES version was raised in 2005, examining a student sample that included new items. The modified items were categorized into: "(1) downloading/buying counterfeit goods, (2) recycling/environmental awareness, and (3) doing the right thing/doing good" (Vitell & Muncy, 2005, p. 267).

Important to mention, most of the empirical studies of consumers' ethics have addressed the CES, and it has been broadly employed in various cross-cultural studies. Notable examples are Austria (Rawwas, 1996); Indonesia (Lu and Lu, 2009); Ireland (Rawwas, Patzer, & Klassen, 1995; Rawwas, Patzer, & Vitell, 1998); South Africa (Higgs-Kleyn, 1998) and Turkey (Rawwas et al., 2005).

Following the above, it is important to examine the methodological ambiguity arising from the usage of MES and CES. According to Pan and Sparks (2012, p. 87), the usage of different scales in this research field may lead to validity issues, in case there are substantial differences between the measures:

> Because the MES and the CES also differ substantially in their length, wording, and scaling, they might differ in the validity with which they operationalize ethical judgments. If so, the strengths of the correlations produced by these measures could systematically differ from each other.

3.8.6. Additional Ethics Judgment Measures

An additional ethics judgment instrument was offered by Welton et al. (1994), which was adapted to assess the ethical reasoning levels of individuals. It is based upon Rest's DIT but consists of four accounting-related scenarios, dealing with several aspects of the accounting environment. To evaluate the ethical sensitivity, the individual is required to assess the statements by their relevance and prioritize them.

Furthermore, one can note the ethical judgments measure formed by Hunt and Vasquez-Parraga (1993). Their method used a sample of sales and marketing managers and paired different actions and results to measure ethical judgments. Two different vignettes were employed with a single seven-point scale to use the instrument. Their study found that managers' decisions are led primarily by deontological evaluations when forming ethical judgments. The teleological factors, as reflected by the outcomes of the behavior on the organization were ranked only secondarily compared to the deontological evaluations.

Important to mention, this instrument has been used in several studies (Burns & Keicker, 1995; DeConinck & Lewis, 1997). For example, Mengüç (1998) used Hunt and Vasquez-Parraga's (1993) measure while investigating the reactions of Turkish sales managers to allegedly ethical or unethical conduct in sales-related issues. The findings reported that the managers mainly relied upon deontological evaluations, but to some extent on teleological evaluations as well.

Following the term's semantic and methodological ambiguity, Pan and Sparks (2012) overviewed additional measurement instruments of ethical attitudes and ethical perceptions. For instance, Christie et al. (2003) measured the ethical attitude by asking the respondents for a scale of approval or rejection of predetermined behaviors. Likewise, DuPont and Craig (1996) and Honeycutt et al. (2001) provided ethically questionable behaviors and asked the respondents for their approval or rejection with the statements aligned with the particular behavior. Moreover, Dubinsky et al. (2004) measured ethical perceptions by using responses to "questionable sales practices," which were rated according to their appropriateness.

3.8.7. Multi-Item Versus Single-Item Measures

Besides the instruments above, there are further measurement criteria, which are examined in the literature. Pan and Sparks (2012) mentioned that there exists a methodological inconsistency when several studies of ethical judgments use multiple-item measures and others who use single-item measures. It should be noted that single-item scales are considered less reliable, and they may lessen the effect-size estimates.

In comparison, the multiple-item scales are perceived as more reliable, as raised above, and with stronger effects (Babin et al., 2004; Fern & Monroe, 1996; McMahon, 2002; Reidenbach et al., 1991). According to their review:

> While a single standardized measure of ethical judgments may not be necessary or even desirable, testing of ethical decision theories requires valid measures of major constructs. A wide array of study-specific measures could work against this requirement. (Pan & Sparks, 2012, p. 88)

3.8.8. Student and Non-Student Samples

Another important issue to address is the sample type used in EDM study. O'Fallon and Butterfield (2005) recommended using samples, which will properly represent the population. Nonetheless, one may deduce that the larger sample size used contradicts the recommendation to represent the hypothesized population accurately. Whereas the three previous reviews (Ford & Richardson, 1994; Loe et al., 2000; O'Fallon & Butterfield, 2005) showed that 40% of the empirical studies employed a student sample or a combination of students and non-students, Craft (2013) showed a higher percentage of 53%.

Pan and Sparks (2012) reinforced this notion and argued that student samples are more homogenous and tend to provide higher correlations than non-student samples. It is also mentioned that the relatively limited variance of the student sample's similarity augments the odds of statistically significant effects. As a comparison, non-student samples may increase error variance and miscalculate effect sizes (Fern & Monroe, 1996). This notion may possibly indicate higher correlations in student samples than in non-student samples.

Pan and Sparks suggest the differences between student and non-student samples undermine the sample composition, as student samples do not necessarily represent the entire population: "to the extent that student samples inflate effect sizes, researchers should utilize samples that more readily permit generalizability of results" (2012, p. 88).

3.9. Ethical Sensitivity

Following the above, the chapter will elaborate upon the first phase of ethical judgment, known as the stage of ethical sensitivity. It is defined as "the empathic interpretation of a situation by determining who is involved, what actions to take, and what possible reactions and outcomes might ensue" (Naudé & Bornman, 2016, p. 3). Rest (1994) also includes moral awareness under moral sensitivity in his four-component model.

Furthermore, Chambers (2011, p. 24) claims that moral sensitivity signifies an: "awareness that ethical issues are a part of the situation, the skill of identifying when an ethical response is appropriate, or willingness to activate the moral apparatus. Sensitivity is awareness of how our actions affect others."

Nonetheless, Chan and Leung (2006) argue that ethical sensitivity cannot be evaluated in the same way as ethical judgments. Supporting this notion, Rest (1986) found that ethical sensitivity and judgment behave as separable processes and that a wide array of factors may influence ethical sensitivity. Interestingly, empirical evidence suggests that ethical sensitivity is affected by the gender and nationality of the individual.

Following the above, the literature does not distinguish between ethical sensitivity and ethical perception unanimously. For example, Wittmer (2005) separated ethical sensitivity from ethical perception. He argued that while perceiving the ethical aspects of a certain situation, one can demonstrate a lack of importance to an issue as a type of ethical perception. However, it does not exhibit ethical sensitivity. Different than Wittmer, Choi and Perry (2010) do not present any difference between the terms.

3.10. Ethical Sensitivity Measures

As two separate variables, one may suggest a different measurement of ethical sensitivity compared to ethical judgments. Numerous studies have addressed moral sensitivity in accounting (Karcher, 1996; Shaub et al., 1993; Yetmar & Eastman, 2000). A review by Jordan (2007) has elaborated upon the study of moral judgment and its measurement instruments. She claims that Rest's second component of moral judgment received more scholastic attention compared to the other components due to the abundance of reliable measures in the literature.

3.10.1. Shaub's Ethical Sensitivity Measure

For example, Shaub et al. (1993) created an instrument that measures auditors' ethical sensitivity. It consists of an auditing scenario and three ethical issues. To measure the respondent's ethical sensitivity, he or she is required to prioritize the issues. The respondent's recognition of the ethical issues within the scenario represents an absolute measure of ethical sensitivity. Empirically, this instrument has been employed in two studies (Shaub et al., 1993; Shaub, 1997).

Shaub et al. (1993) examined the factors influencing auditors' sensitivity to ethical situations and attempted to outweigh the concept of Rest's DIT.

The findings of the study did not show any support of the influence of the auditor's ethical orientation on his ethical sensitivity. However, there was a positive correlation between ethical sensitivity and age. An additional study examined the effects of auditors' ethical orientation on professional commitment and ethical sensitivity. The findings showed that relativistic auditors were less likely to identify ethical issues in an auditing scenario.

3.10.2. Bebeau's Dental Ethical Sensitivity Test

Furthermore, Bebeau et al. (1985) used the dental ethical sensitivity test (DEST) and evaluated the correlation between ethical sensitivity and DIT. It is considered the most reputable instrument designed to assess students' ability to identify ethical issues in real-life professional scenarios, and other scholars have modified the DEST to apply to different professions. The study used a student sample, where the respondents were asked to imagine themselves in the role of the dentist.

The DEST has been modified to evaluate the student's sensitivity to the distinct needs and interests of others. It consists of audio recordings, to which the student records an immediate verbal response. The findings were considered relatively reliable as they raised a high internal consistency, thus compared to previous research on measuring ethical sensitivity (Bailey et al., 2010).

3.10.3. Additional Measures of Ethical Sensitivity

Another test was formed by Bebeau, alongside the researcher Thoma (2006), and is called the dental ethical reasoning and judgment test (DERJT). It includes five ethical issues in dentistry that evaluate profession-specific intermediate concepts. The respondent is required to rank his or her choice of actions and add his or her justifications and then decide upon the best and worst action choices and justifications. The scores are calculated according to the consistency between one's selected actions and justifications and the judgment of them.

In addition to Bebeau et al. (1985), Wittmer (1992) developed a measure of ethical sensitivity test (EST), aimed at administrative decision-making. Its findings showed a positive correlation between ethical sensitivity and decision outcomes. Moreover, augmented levels of personalized and biased information lead to higher levels of ethical sensitivity in decision-making processes.

Wittmer's study also showed the important role of education in increasing ethical sensitivity. To measure EST, the method uses an actual decision-making scenario, where the respondents had to play a managerial role and face related decisions. Clarkeburn (2002) criticized Wittmer's method since this study employs a semi-structured survey to assess ethical sensitivity, which may lead to distorted results.

Moreover, Clarkeburn (2002) suggested a different test for ethical sensitivity in science (TESS). The study employs unstructured cases to assess tangible ethical sensitivity and not examine its importance on behalf of the respondents. It should be noted that the literature has raised only a moderate correlation between ethical sensitivity and decision-making.

From a different angle, the ethical sensitivity of individuals to ethical issues differs. Prior empirical studies raise ambiguous findings regarding the alleged effect of personal factors on the ethical sensitivity process of professional accountants. Chan and Leung (2006) suggest increasing the research of ethical sensitivity in the accounting profession and its correlation with various personal factors.

Window on Management

This chapter depicts the theoretical foundations and measurement of ethical decision-making, highlighting the leading scholarship of Rest's four-component model, Trevino's person-situation interactionist model, Ferrell and Gresham's model, Hunt and Vitell's general theory of marketing ethics, Dubinsky and Loken's model, Jones's issue contingent model, and Schwartz's ethical decision-making model. In addition, we reviewed the leading definitions of ethical judgment, and scrutinized its notable antecedents, including age, education, gender, and religion. To further comprehend this term, the chapter suggests a brief overview of measurement instruments aimed at evaluating different ethical stages, such as the Rokeach value survey and Rest's defining issues test, and highlights the unique measurement of ethical sensitivity. Since ethical sensitivity becomes a key competency in professional life and an important prerequisite for managing ethical challenges and misconduct in organizations, developing measurement and assessment and education tools should be extended to the field of management. While this is already occurring in management ethics courses, more systematic and empirically based approaches should be applied to sensitize employees to ethical dilemmas. In addition, using empirical tools to identify ethical issues confronted by public service employees can provide managers with information useful for policy and planning purposes.

Chapter 4

Antecedents of Ethical Judgments in the Public Service

One of the major challenges in today's increasingly complex and diverse work environment of public administrators is how the public service should manage and communicate its ethos (i.e., its set of shared values and ethical principles) and characterize its professional identity. The public service ethos is viewed as an important management tool for building the ethical culture of a profession or organization by developing a deep sense of commitment to ethical conduct and pride among professional community members. The introduction of new public management (NPM) reforms has increased the demand for public service ethics to adopt "new" values of accountability, efficiency and effectiveness, incorruptibility, lawfulness, and transparency (Farazmand, 2002; Kaptein & Wempe, 2002; Kernaghan, 2003; Van der Wal & Huberts, 2008). These reforms cover business-oriented themes such as more efficient public management, customer services focus, and application of cost-benefit calculation in the public sector decision-making process leading to the transformation of administrative doctrines (Exworthy & Halford, 1998; Ferlie & Geraghty, 2005; Kirkpatrick et al., 1983; Minogue, 1998; Powell et al., 1999; Rayner et al., 2012).

To further comprehend why public servants engage in unethical behavior, we will briefly overview recent studies examining the antecedents and consequences of ethical judgment in the public service. The scholarly discourse of public sector ethics identifies several antecedents to ethical judgment classified as organizational, environmental, and personal demographic characteristics underlying a wide array of global- and geographic-based trends. However, one can notice the impact of contemporary reforms and geographic-based incidents, which alter the traditional focus of studies on this topic. Whereas a substantial body of research deals with traditional ethical practices such as ethical leadership, gender-based discrimination, and corruption in developing countries, one may observe the outgrowing literature dealing with the ethical impact of big data and the role of civil society in mitigating unethical patterns in developing and developed countries as one.

4.1. Organizational Characteristics

Organizational antecedent variables for ethical decision-making and behavior among public-organization employees often include codes of ethics and ethical leadership.

Codes of ethics set forth values and standards to meet the expectations of employees in the professional community, and shape their professional identity. Codes of ethics are often used as an important management tool for building the ethical culture of a profession or organization by improving the profession's reputation and developing a deep sense of commitment to ethical conduct and pride among professional community members (Beeri et al., 2013; Ireni-Saban, 2015).

According to Richard Stillman, the importance of a code is defined in this way: "A profession requires an ethical code in order that there might be a standard for the very best relations with employer, citizen, the public at large, such as other professional fraternities have to foster" (1979, p. 37). Within public administration, codes of ethics are regarded as an effort to enhance public trust and confidence in public organizations. Such understanding denies holding public servants as ethically neutral professionals apart from the electorate, thereby allowing more room for public administrators to exercise substantial discretion (decision-making power) on their own, discretion that affects people's lives (Svara, 2007).

Drawing on corporate and public sector corruption scandals has led Garcia-Sanchez et al. (2011) to explore the effectiveness of ethics codes in both private and public organizations. Their research has shown that corporate codes positively advance corporate reputation and brand image, and communicate the commitment of the company to ethical behavior. On the other hand, codes of ethics within the public sector have yielded relatively low effects on ethical decision-making and behavior. The researchers conclude that ethics codes without effective implementation mechanisms are weaker in their effect than those supported with them. Consequently, to increase the effectiveness of codes of ethics in public organizations, the public managers must develop a comprehensive framework for effective implementation of codes of ethics in public administration in a way that incorporates strategic methods to improve the implementation of codes of ethics in public administration (i.e., communication, training, education, monitoring, enforcement, leadership by example, and ethical climate) across different stages of the ethical decision-making process (awareness, understanding, implementation, and follow-up).

Given the importance and complexity of implementing and communicating ethics codes, Downe et al. (2016) suggest that

> the success of codes is dependent on the culture of the organization where people naturally do the right thing when faced with dilemmas . . . the role of leaders is crucial as they may be aware that the implementation of an ethics code and can be useful in increasing consciousness of ethical principles and a suitable management tool in nurturing an ethical climate within an organization. (p. 900)

In a study that measured the effectiveness of the public service ethos in strengthening good governance and tackling corruption in Africa, Tanzania was scrutinized as a use case due to its adoption of the public service ethos as a core pillar of the public personnel combating against maladministration patterns. Important to mention, moral corruption in developing countries raises great controversy in terms of ethical practices due to their inherent socio-economic challenges. This notion is highlighted compared to developed countries, whose enhanced conditions enable them to "morally" thrive. The local findings showed the ethical constraints of the public service ethos in Tanzania, under the limited monitoring of public performance and the high frequency of nepotism of public servants. In addition, the ongoing corruption in the Tanzanian public sector had continued to harm the quality of services, which rendered the public service ethos obsolete in the country (Nkyabonaki, 2019).

Additional geographic-based articles overviewed the local ethical framework in the Nigerian public service. Similar to the ethical malpractices in Tanzania, the findings exposed a high frequency of ethical negligence in the local public service due to the lack of integrity and the complex culture of corruption among public servants (Ogbonnaya, 2018). Following the above, the African-based discourse may indicate the local inability to enforce ethical codes of conduct in developing countries, whose main goal is to survive, both economically and socially.

There have been several empirical studies assessing the effects of ethical leadership in government organizations, in particular how enhancing the effectiveness and importance of leadership facilitates ethical behavior and prevents unethical conduct in government organizations (Beeri et al., 2013; Hassan et al., 2013; Huberts et al., 2007).

Ethical leadership is defined in most leadership studies as "the demonstration of normatively appropriate conduct through personal actions and interpersonal relationships, and the promotion of such conduct to followers through two-way communication, reinforcement, and decision-making" (Brown et al., 2005, p. 120). Ethical leadership is associated with moral persons and moral managers (Brown & Treviño, 2006). Moral individuals as ethical leaders tend to be fair and trustworthy, whereas moral managers are leaders who use transactional efforts to hold employees to acting according to ethical standards, including sanctioning unethical behaviors.

Notably, Gan (2018) examined employee moral justification as a cognitive mediating mechanism in the relationship between ethical leadership and unethical employee behavior, and examined employee moral identity as a moderator of this indirect relationship. The study results indicate that leaders are able to control unethical employee behavior by engaging in normatively appropriate behaviors, and by obliging that employees be accountable for the ethical consequences of their behavior and care for others' interests. As for Gan (2018), ethical leadership is defined as "the demonstration of normatively appropriate conduct through individual actions and social relationships, and the promotion of such conduct to followers through two-way communication, reinforcement, and decision-making" (p. 1271). Gan's (2018) research suggests that the behavioral standards for managers and supervisors should be emphasized in organizations to ensure that their behaviors are ethical. Furthermore, it is suggested that the mediating role of moral justification in the relationship between ethical leadership and unethical employee behavior may raise the awareness of managers of organizations to employees' cognitive judgment and should ensure that their employees have low levels of moral justification, which can restrain unethical behavior.

The research of Hassan et al. (2014) examined the consequences of ethical leadership and its correlation to organizational commitment, absenteeism, and willingness to report ethical problems. Findings highlight the role of public managers in encouraging ethical attitudes and behavior of employees. For example, managers who display higher levels of ethical leadership can make ethical behavior more salient and reduce unethical behavior of employees. Subordinates are inclined to report misconduct if the employee has confidence in the organization's management to take corrective action. Moreover, ethical leader behavior was also found to increase organizational commitment, which may reduce turnover, improve job performance, and increase citizenship behavior. Lastly, the study also indicates that ethical leadership could reduce absenteeism. This evidence has important implications in promoting ethical behavior for employees who tend to misuse or abuse sick leave policies.

Some scholars pinpoint the needed creation of a leadership ethos when discussing corruption and ethical leadership, as seen in the Tanzanian public service. The literature highlights the necessity of amplified leadership abilities to enact public policy processes (Bekker & Van Heyningen, 2011; Kołomycew & Kotarba, 2017). On the strategic level, the leadership ethos provides leaders with the ability to gain the public's trust and support and promote participatory decision-making processes. Moreover, effective leadership may include organizational integrity and create long-term value (Kouzes & Posner, 2012; Xu et al., 2016).

In the scholarly framework of ethical ethos, Lewis and Catron (1996) offered four guidelines of a bureaucrat's ethical standard: equality, equity, loyalty, and responsibility. Mustafa (2019) explored the ethics of public service bureaucrats by using the traditional Lewis and Catron indicators and implementing them in public services in Indonesia. Based on these indicators, he assessed a low ethical level of bureaucrats in the local public service. The article raised increasing evidence of discriminatory practices in service delivery in the country due to solid political affiliation, ethnic and religious networks, and the uncertainty of service costs and time. This led to greater rates of corruption, collusion, and nepotism. Moreover, Mustafa suggests enhancing employee welfare in order to augment the responsibilities of the public sector.

In a similar context, an article by Ndalamba and Esau (2020) examined the considerations of public sector leaders about leadership ethos and its inherent critical success factors. The paper elaborated upon leadership ethics and leaders' integrity as a virtue-based ethic, which emphasize the attributes of leadership ethos, including but not limited to vision, virtues, values, and obligations. Therefore, the leader's behavior shall positively reshape and impact the follower's actions. Furthermore, the leadership ethos enables a mutually trusting relationship, recognition of power dynamics in the leadership relationship, effectiveness in reaching the objectives, effectiveness in reaching the objectives, and participatory leadership.

4.2. Moral Entrepreneurship

Recently, the third component of ethical leadership has been introduced, a moral entrepreneur. Moral entrepreneurship complements the two other components of ethical leadership since it emphasizes the creation of new norms and standards that correspond to current technological and economic changes at the global level. Big data and artificial intelligence systems call attention to new ethical issues that challenge prevailing norms. This fact raises issues about the role of ethical leadership and how they can meet the new technological challenges and fill the moral void around new ethical challenges. The public as a whole will benefit if the public officials would comply with what is normatively appropriate and provide an appropriate normative response (Kaptein, 2019).

The era of big data brings significant opportunities and ethical challenges for public leadership, which are currently dealt with by public servants in various jurisdictions and government domains. For example, Andrews (2019) addresses the algorithmic challenges facing public leaders and their attempts to cope with the ethical and public value issues.

In 2018, there were several use cases indicating the unethical malpractices of algorithms leading to racial discrimination and mass profiling, such as the Cambridge Analytica affair and biased facial recognition incidents (Burgess, 2018; Solon & Laughland, 2018). Moreover, the article mentions six algorithmic challenges for public leaders at local, federal, national, and international levels. Among the challenges, Andrews states the ethical and legal implications of algorithmic selection error, algorithmic law-breaking, algorithmic manipulation or gaming, algorithmic brand contamination, and algorithmic unknowns (Andrews, 2019).

According to evidence by the private sector performance, data exploitation can be highly beneficial for organizations, and it is of paramount importance to promote the implementation of big data tools and techniques in the public sector. For example, big data can assist in better budgetary allocation by local governments, thus possibly preventing costly governmental interferences (Almeida & Calistru, 2013; Kim et al., 2014; Malomo & Sena, 2017). However, managing the public sector's large sums of sensitive data represents an inherent challenge, which requires the enhancement of accountability and public administration planning.

Among the ethical challenges, Biancone et al. (2018) analyzed the impact of big data on accountability and transparency and showed that low-quality data inhibits a suitable assessment of the most-needed services to the final users. One of the main insights in the article is the increasing need to enhance data-management processes by public institutions and diminish the costs produced by low-quality data. Therefore, the article suggests the following to promote transparency and accessibility:

> [t]he active participation systems adopted by public administrations in recent years, the free access to the budget data and the decision-making process with the direct convoying of citizens, the big data, geolocation and services, the use of social media for the collection of information and the use of sensors located throughout the city. (Biancone et al., 2018, p. 496)

An additional article suggests augmenting fairness and accountability in the public sector through algorithmically informed public decisions. Current machine learning technologies are used in various public sector IT projects and fulfill the vision of risk-based regulation (Black, 2005). Veale et al. (2018) recommended supporting the tracking of concept drift in secondary data sources and establishing operational transparency tools to identify threats. This can lead to targeting both directors and "street-level bureaucrats" in the public sector.

Moreover, several scholars focus on the social and ethical issues due to AI-powered initiatives in the public sector (Quraishi et al., 2017; Ransbotham et al., 2017). The AI discourse is divided into ethical considerations and implications of AI usage, such as in lethal autonomous weapons and the embedding process of ethical principles into AI platforms (Anderson & Anderson, 2011; Russell, 2015). Important to mention, the spectrum of challenges within AI ethics is vast, including: "AI rulemaking for human behavior, to the compatibility of machine versus human value judgment, to moral dilemmas and AI discrimination" (Wirtz et al., 2019, p. 604).

4.3. Ethical Climate

An ethical climate pertains to how organizational members perceive and value organizational policies, practices, and procedures. Victor and Cullen define ethical climates as "the shared perceptions of what is ethically correct behavior and how ethical issues should be handled" (1988, pp. 51–52). Ethical climate typology and questionnaires are usually used in business ethics studies. However, only a few studies adapted these tools to measure ethical contexts and climates within public organizations (Brower & Shrader, 2000; Maesschalck, 2004; Tsai & Huang, 2008).

Following the study of Gorsira et al. (2018): "[a]n organizational-level predictor of (un)ethical behavior in organizations is the culture or climate of an organization" (p. 3). The study examined whether the ethical climate reduces unethical behavior and whether it affects corruption through individual motives for bribery among high-rank public officials and businesses. Findings show a relationship between the perceived ethical climate of both public and private agencies and corruption. That is, employees who perceive their work environment as more egoistic and less ethical are more predisposed to corruption. However, the relationship was interceded by personal and social norms on corruption. Employees who perceive their workplace as egoistic thus experience weaker personal and social norms to exhort from unethical behavior (Gorsira et al., 2018). Likewise, Lilly et al. (2016) found that "managers working in a positive ethical climate perceived a positive association amongst success and ethical behavior while managers operating in an adverse ethical climate recognized a negative association between achievement and ethical behavior" (p. 34).

Growing concerns with the rise of incidents of corruption in public and private sector organizations have led Mayer et al. (2010) to consider the relationship between ethical leadership, ethical climate, and unethical behavior. The study examined the effect of ethical climate on the relationship between ethical leadership and unethical behavior. The findings suggest that ethical leaders serve as role models for their subordinates by enforcing regulations and codes of conduct. They enhance a positive and ethical work environment so that subordinates will learn how to maintain high ethical standards by learning how to resolve ethical dilemmas and by making ethical decisions.

4.4. Public Service Motivation (PSM)

Since Perry and Wise (1990), in "The Motivational Bases of Public Service," laid out the theoretical foundations of the public service motivation (PSM) construct and offered to make progress in the exploration of its possible positive effect on work-related outcomes in the public sector (Bright, 2005, 2008, 2013; Christensen & Wright, 2011; Coursey et al., 2011; Esteve et al., 2016; Kim, 2012; Quratulain & Khan, 2015; Taylor, 2014; Vandenabeele, 2011). PSM literature has concentrated on cross-sectional and longitudinal analyses to gain important insights to the dynamics of PSM (e.g., Bright, 2005; Christensen & Wright, 2011; Kjeldsen, 2014; Leisink & Steijn, 2009; Moynihan, 2013; Pedersen, 2015; Perry & Hondeghem, 2008; Quratulain & Khan, 2015; Ritz & Brewer, 2013; Vandenabeele, 2011; Wright & Grant, 2010).

The work of Perry and Wise (1990, p. 368) asserts that behavior that appears to be altruistic usually is motivated by a deferral of individual interests, demarcating a line (border) between the public and the private sector: an "individual's predisposition to respond to motives grounded primarily or uniquely in public institutions and organizations." By emphasizing the normative implications of pro-social forms of behavior underlying PSM, Vandenabeele (2007, p. 547) offers that PSM should encompass "[t]he belief, values, and attitudes that go beyond self-interest or organizational interest that concern the interest of a larger political entity and that motivate individuals to act accordingly whenever appropriate."

The contributions of studies and developments on PSM led by Perry and Wise's (1990) categorization of PSM, including affective, rational, and normative types of motives might account for the effects of both normative and behavioral congruence between public servants and the public sector. Affective motives are grounded in individual emotional states such as patriotism or benevolence, rational motives are rooted in the maximization of individual utility, and norm-based motives are driven by the desire to serve the public interest (Perry & Wise, 1990, pp. 368–369). Although we have witnessed a burgeoning exploration of many positive aspects of organizational behavior in the public service associated with PSM, an area not extensively researched in the literature involves how the dynamics of PSM are associated with ethical perceptions (Beeri et al., 2013; Brewer & Selden, 1998; Christensen & Wright, 2018; Downe et al., 2016; Hassen et al., 2014; Lewis & Cho, 2011; Macaulay & Lawton, 2006; Perry & Vandenabeele, 2008; Perry et al., 2014; Ritz et al., 2016; Stazyk & Davis, 2015; Vandenabeele et al., 2018; Wright & Pandey, 2008). PSM scholarship demonstrates that individuals with higher levels of PSM are more likely to join the public service because they value service to society (Brewer & Selden, 1998; Kim, 2006; Pandey & Stazyk, 2008).

Therefore, employees with higher PSM are predicted to exhibit better ethical behavior and decision-making as it matches their core values, which do not prioritize their own self-interest (Wright et al., 2016). Moreover, a large experimental PSM survey held in 2019 had shown that PSM is able to: "[p]romote ethical behavioral intent and suggests that activating public employees' PSM can benefit public sector ethics" (Meyer-Sahling, Mikkelsen & Schuster, 2019, p. 445). Important to mention, recent PSM studies have not shown clear empirical evidence indicating a positive correlation between PSM and ethical behavior, thus requiring additional scholarly scrutiny. Moreover, it is argued that the persistent existence of PSM will depend on the extent to which successive generations of public service workers hold that PSM encourages ethical decision-making and behavior.

4.5. Environmental Antecedents

Even though the topic of corruption mitigation is not considered relatively innovative in the ethical discourse, recent studies have addressed additional aspects relating to the efficiency of civil society and public whistleblowing. The literature raises the emerging need to curb political corruption due to its detrimental socio-economic implications (Gans-Morse et al., 2018). Corruption in the public sector undermines service efficiency and trust in public institutions, thus augmenting government costs and budgets (Abdullah et al., 2018). Empirical evidence suggests that the unethical behavior in the public service is prevalent in both developed and developing countries (Meyer-Sahling, Schuster, & Mikkelsen, 2019). Numerous studies emphasize the civil society-corruption nexus, but little research has dealt with the proper conditions for civil society's anti-corruption effects and successes.

In this regard, Harasymiw (2019) claims that the role of civil society in tackling corruption is highly ambiguous and depends on the geo-political circumstances. As articulated in the article:

> In liberal democracies, where the rule of law generally prevails, a vibrant civil society aids in the control of political corruption due to transparency of government, a competitive party system, and a high degree of press freedom. In post-communist countries, where rule of law is less well established, the relationship between civil society's viability and its role in assisting the anti-corruption struggle is less direct, although still meaningful. (Harasymiw, 2019, p. 304)

> Therefore, one may claim that the regime type impacts the ability of civil society to tackle corruption within the public sector.

Moreover, Villanueva (2019) claims that the power of civil society is limited, and in order to mitigate corruption in the public sector, there must be a combination of civil society, transparency of laws, and predictability of enforcement. Another reference to the citizenry dynamics against corruption rises in the context of public whistleblowing. In this regard, the public employees within the government aspire to fulfill public values and the wide citizenry. Meaning, citizens have a civic duty to expose unethical or illegal practices regarding public employment or services (Su & Ni, 2018).

Other scholars address corruption in the context of partisan favoritism in public procurement. Dávid-Barrett and Fazekas (2019) analyzed the perils and promises of partisan favoritism in Hungary and the United Kingdom, two European countries who have been under the jurisdiction of the European Union by the time the article was written. In Hungary, the widespread politicization of the bureaucracy strengthens partisan favoritism (Fazekas & King, 2019).

Compared to Hungary, corruption risk is significantly lower in the UK and stands at 10% of the market. Nonetheless, the empirical evidence of a certain level of corruption indicates that the UK government is not fully transparent and unbiased. Therefore, the findings undermine the role of the EU in mitigating corruption and exhibit the ambiguous reliance on domestic regulatory implementation (Dávid-Barrett & Fazekas, 2019). Due to the upcoming date of Brexit, this comparison, scrutinizing the functionality of the EU in mitigating inter-state corruption, becomes even more relevant to further research.

From the Asian perspective, one can observe an article discussing anti-corruption measures in public services in Malaysia. Even though there are numerous initiatives to tackle political malpractices in the country, the frequency of corruption is still relatively high. Therefore, the study attempts to scrutinize the correlation between the quality of the governance environment, assessed by the smart governance matrix, and the ability to predict corruption risk. Its findings highlighted the emerging need to enhance the governance environment in public services in the country to assess corruption risk and moderate unethical practices of public personnel (Abdullah et al., 2018). A similar study was conducted in the divisional secretariats in Sri Lanka, which developed a new scale to measure employee perception of ethical leadership behavior in the public service (Wijesekera & Fernando, 2018).

4.6. Personal Antecedents

Recently, scholars have overviewed discrimination in the public sector by using audit studies to research individuals' learning costs in relation to accessing public services. Various studies provided evidence of racial discrimination in voting processes and data requested from traditional public service providers (Costa, 2017; Giulietti et al., 2019, White et al., 2015). In addition, Jilke et al. (2018) analyzed discriminatory practices against ethnic minorities among street-level organizations in Belgian public and private long-term care facilities. Based on the literature, the article claims that: "[a]cts of discrimination are the product of taste-based animosity and not rational-strategic considerations" (p. 427).

In addition, one may notice several studies dealing with gender stereotyping in local political leadership and voter decision-making. The literature raises that female candidates are favored during local elections since various public issues exhibit stereotypic strengths of women (Holman, 2014; Kahn, 1994; Windett, 2014). Nonetheless, research on local policy making demonstrates that tasks related to local political offices require more masculine qualities compared to feminine ones.

According to Bauer (2020), emphasizing masculine stereotypes strengthens the status of Republican female candidates. This notion is consistent with the work of Oliver and Conroy (2018), indicating that female officeholders perceive themselves as possessing masculine qualities and that most entities who participate in the political pipeline tend to have masculine traits (McDermott, 2016). Based on the findings, one may deduce that those female candidates attempting to emphasize their feminine traits are predicted to undergo major obstacles. This may require them to exhibit their masculinity at the local political level. The article strengthens this notion and states that: "Female candidates receive the most positive evaluations when they emphasize masculine rather than feminine qualities" (Bauer, 2020, p. 114).

Following the above, one can mention the outgrowing importance of social equity in the distribution of public services. Sumra (2019) found that fairness, justice, and social equity change among different income level groups, which shows an increasing rate of inequality in Pakistan.

As suggested by the article, it is of paramount importance to implement social equity in the public sector and promote social change in local public organizations (Sumra, 2019).

A study examined the ethical reasoning of Russian public sector employees based on the virtue ethics approach and several chosen parameters such as age, gender, management experience, and field specialization (Ermasova et al., 2018; Farazmand, 2017). Farazmand (2018) suggested enhancing the ethical reasoning of public sector employees by using the education of virtues and justice from an early age. In addition, professional public servants should adopt codes of ethics that will shape administrative and employee practices.

The Russian findings showed substantial differences in ethical reasoning among individuals based on age and field specialization but not at the same level among the other parameters. For example, the article raises: "Respondents who specialized in the areas of technology and computer science seemed to have higher ethical maturity than all other specializations, followed by those specialized in science" (Ermasova et al., 2018, p. 370). To conclude, the impending wave of Baby Boomer retirements combined with the relatively smaller size of the Generation Y workforce entering the public sector raise staggering challenges for diversity management in public organizations manifested in the unique values and attitudes that members from different generational cohorts bring with them to the workplace. Both trends may yield stronger or weaker relationships with ethical judgment than what is currently offered in the literature. Next, we will address the relationship between ethical judgment and the generational cohort in the public service that has yet to receive empirical support.

Window on Management

This chapter provides a brief overview of contemporary studies on antecedents of ethical decision-making and behavior in the public sector. The literature review indicates two main trends in potential explanatory factors for observed differences in public service employees' ethical judgment and behavioral intentions: moral entrepreneurship as a new component of ethical leadership and dimensions of diversity. Thus, this chapter makes an appeal to managers not only to comply with what is considered as normatively appropriate and to encourage employees to comply but also to explore whether there are opportunities to create new ethical norms, to realize these opportunities when possible and desirable, and to get others to adopt these new norms. Managers in the public sector can start by being alert to current or potential moral issues emerging from the introduction of technology in governance and how these ethical issues exist in a moral void within the public service. Next, managers can choose one or more issues that are relevant to their expertise and the public interest so they can develop a new ethical norm on the basis of a vision of how and why the norm contributes to the trust of society and its moral development. Then, managers must communicate this norm and generate support for this new norm among public service employee

Chapter 5

Generational Diversity and Public Service Ethics in Israel

As seen in the previous chapter, the ethical judgment construct occupies prominent theoretical and empirical roles in both public and business ethics literature. Among the antecedents to ethical judgment, in empirical studies that identify age as an antecedent variable for ethical judgment, the age variable frequently appears to be inconsistent with theory and occasionally shows a significant relationship between age and ethical judgments (Chiu, 2003; Pan & Sparks, 2012; Peterson et al., 2001).

Since ethical judgment plays a key role in theories of ethical decision-making and ethical sensitivity in particular, this construct remains an important part of research on ethical decision-making and diversity management. To help resolve inconsistent or contradictory results, this chapter reviews an empirical study to identify generational cohort antecedents instead of age and their moderating role on the relationship between public sector ethos and ethical sensitivity in the public sector in Israel. By drawing on a generational cohort approach, we do not attempt to argue that the generation cohort provides the main antecedent of ethical or unethical perceptions, nor can it be seen as the overruling explanatory feature. Our aim in this study is to draw on the effects of differences between generational cohorts on public service employees' ethical sensitivity that might be conducive to fostering an ethical organizational culture, even after taking several other variables into consideration. That said, generational cohorts target the distinct experience that shapes each generation; age does not utilize the cohort effects arising from distinctive life patterns and values but rather from age and maturation (Ramsey et al., 2007).

Studies on the differences between generational cohorts have put the spotlight on the new challenges for current and future workplace ethics (Benson & Brown, 2011; Cennamo & Gardner, 2008; Cogin, 2012; Costanza et al., 2012; Erickson, 2008; Fullerton & Dixon, 2010; Howe & Strauss, 2000; Lyons & Kuron, 2014; Twenge, 2010; Twenge et al., 2010; Wong et al., 2008). For example, Generation Y sees the workplace as a location of self-realization and values entrepreneurship, teamwork, communication, and collaboration. Simultaneously, Generation Y possesses diffuse boundaries between the workplace and the private sphere in relation to ethical attitudes and values (Paul, 2001; World of Work, 2008). Although these findings are replete in both public and private organizations, they should be of great concern for the public organizations that require employees to promote the public interest (Beeri et al., 2013; Downe et al., 2016; Lawton & Doig, 2005; Macaulay & Lawton, 2006; Stazyk & Davis, 2015). The existing literature on generational differences suggests that generational differences can sometimes be stereotyped negatively or positively; managers and leaders in the public sector must make decisions based on these stereotypes, which may or may not be factual. To this end, the proposed research is an important addition to research on public sector workplace diversity. It ensures that employees at all levels of an organizational hierarchy have the knowledge to engage in ethical decision-making in their daily practice in a way that reduces or eliminates prejudice and stereotype in a diverse environment, and keeps younger employees committed and willing to stay and improve the public service.

Viewing generations as cohorts implies that they are homogenous enough to have meaningful and observable characteristics that can be measurable by scores on attitudinal variables (Lyons & Kuron, 2014). The cohort perspective, along with Walsh's (1995) model of organizational cognition, can be used to provide preliminary insights into the research of public service ethos (PSE) and Generation Y's ethical orientation, in comparison to other generational groups, in making judgments about ethically questionable actions. This chapter suggests that insights into this question focusing on the way this Generation Y cohort approaches ethical issues in the public service should be drawn from PSE scholarship. For the purpose of this research, we define ethical sensitivity as the process of identifying ethical issues and the likelihood of taking into account ethical implications when making choices.

To investigate how generational diversity affects the extent to which successive generations of public service employees hold that public service ethos encourages ethical decision-making and behavior, we first define the construct of ethical sensitivity, public service ethos, and generational cohort. Second, we offer a set of propositions about how each variable influences the perceptions of ethical sensitivity in the public service and examine the effect of the interaction between PSE and generational cohorts on ethical sensitivity among public service employees. Next, we describe the methodology and the findings of the field study. We conclude by considering the implications of our findings for developing further research on the generational cohorts' approach of PSE and public administration ethics for improving the effectiveness of diversity management practices in organizational ethics in the future.

In sum, the proposed research aims to contribute to the scholarship on public service ethics by leveraging generational differences. The study's key objective is to stipulate and measure work-values differences and similarities across generations in the public service given the coming of age of a younger generation and the retirement of an older generation. It implies that understanding of generational diversity in public sector values as they are inducted or socialized into normative attitudes and behaviors may facilitate the development of diversity management practices to address growing challenges spawned by age diversity. The proposed research is of special importance, given the disturbing growth of corruption and ethical misconduct in the public sector in Israel.

The second objective is to uncover the underlying mechanism of PSE by scrutinizing the effects of the three dimensions of PSE and ethical decision-making regarding ethically questionable conduct in the public service across generational cohorts. By focusing on the interaction effect between PSE and generational cohort on ethical sensitivity, rather than on the chosen variables alone, our study aims to contribute to the burgeoning exploration of the dynamic nature of the PSE construct in predicting what forms of ethical attitudes and judgments are associated with the most recent generation to enter the public service. An examination of the sort suggested here will focus on generational differences and their possible effect on public management, providing for informed management strategies to ethical training and code enforcement placed on the agenda of administrative ethics committees. Public managers need to be more proactive than reactive in handling diversity issues involving members of different generations, including ethical issues.

Finally, the following research introduces a scenario-based instrument designed to explore and measure ethical perceptions and judgments of what is ethical or unethical conduct in the public service. The development of a scenario-based instrument to compare reasoning in public organizations will contribute to the literature on research methods in the field of defining issues test (DIT) and will facilitate cross-study comparisons.

5.1. Ethical Sensitivity (ES)

The assessment of the ethicality of a particular course of action is part of an ethical decision-making process. According to Rest (1986), the individual ethical decision-making progress goes through four stages corresponding to distinct psychological processes, including moral sensitivity, moral judgment, moral motivation/intention, and moral character/action.

The first stage concerns identification of an ethical dilemma. This stage is highly important as it involves a moral awareness that a dilemma may affect the well-being of others (Reynolds, 2006). As articulated by Chia and Mee (2000, p. 255): "When individuals recognize the moral dimension of an issue, this recognition has the potential to influence their judgments, intentions, and decisions."

The second stage refers to an ethical judgment. The realization of a situation as a moral dilemma entails an assessment of the expected outcomes to occur in a given situation. Ethical judgment is constituted in part by a person's moral competency, which is associated with Kohlberg's (1969) highest stage of moral development. Normative ethical theory is meant to support ethical judgment by identifying relevant features that help to tip the balance one way or the other in moral judgment. This requires moral reasoning through the possible choices and impending consequences to determine which are ethically sound.

The third stage concerns the intention to act ethically. This stage is based on a person's commitment to act ethically to resolve a moral dilemma. According to Fishbein and Ajzen (1975), intentions play a critical role in linking ethical judgment to action in the ethical decision-making process (Barnett, 2001; Singhapakdi et al., 1996). These intentions, when referring to moral motivation, are the person's intention to make the morally optimal choice and to follow through on that choice.

The last stage considers ethical action/behavior. This stage refers to the implementation of the ethical action. It involves the individual's ability to exhibit moral courage (moral action), that is, to follow through with the moral decision (Jones et al., 2003). Rest's model may present a simplistic link between moral judgment and action, while critics have shown that moral action develops independently of moral judgment and that individuals positioned in constraining environments may act immorally despite their capacity for moral reasoning (White, 1999).

In the ethical decision-making literature, there has been very little research on the first stage. This is partly due to the debate over the need to distinguish the perception of an ethical problem and ethical sensitivity. Cooper (2006) posits that the perception of an ethical problem is the initial stage before ethical reasoning is realized. The importance of this stage lies in the manner in which an individual must first perceive that a given situation has ethical implications. Wittmer (1992, 2005) distinguishes ethical perception from ethical sensitivity, which places more value on the ethical dimensions of an ethical situation.

From a situation-specific approach, ethical sensitivity is often measured using tests of ethical awareness, such as the defining issues test (DIT) based on Rest's four-stage model of ethical decision-making (Rest, Narvaez et al., 1999). The DIT is a questionnaire consisting of twelve situation items on a five-point scale of the importance of ethical issues. According to Clarkeburn (2002, p. 443), the DIT test for ethical sensitivity does not measure subjects' awareness of ethical issues but rather the importance subjects place on them.

In this research, we will not differentiate between ethical perception and ethical sensitivity, partly because we view ethical sensitivity as the perceptual dimension of the initial stage of Rest's (1986) four-stage model of the ethical deliberation process. Ethical sensitivity concerns how ethical situations and practices are recognized and interpreted (O'Fallon & Butterfield, 2005). Ethical sensitivity or awareness of an ethical issue refers to the ability of the decision-maker to perceive situations as involving ethical implications or issues. In the field of public administration, Wittmer's studies on ethical sensitivity (1992, 2000) included public administration students who applied the DIT measure. However, this study did not yield any significant results regarding the ethical perceptions of public servants. Studies on ethical sensitivity integral to the process of moral reasoning in the public sector were conducted by Stewart and Sprinthall (1993) and Lim Choi (2006). Lim Choi and Perry's study (2010) on perceptions of ethical sensitivity in public administration suggests public administrators demonstrate a lower level of ethical sensitivity in situations related to organizational hierarchy. These findings suggest that more research should be devised to identify the situations that public administrators are less inclined to perceive as involving ethical issues, regardless of the importance attached to the issues.

In the present study, we develop a measure of ethical sensitivity (the first stage of Rest's model) based on Walsh's (1995) definition of ethical sensitivity as a knowledge structure. Walsh's model (1995) of ethical sensitivity expands on Rest's first stage, that is, on the recognition of a dilemma given a specific scenario. Walsh introduces the idea of knowledge structure as "a mental template that individuals impose on an information environment to give it form and meaning" (1995, p. 281). Walsh's study addresses the factors that cognitively relate to the organizational environment in which a person lives and works as experiences that contribute to the development of an individual's ethical sensitivity as a knowledge structure.

Walsh's definition of knowledge structure suggests that ethical sensitivity research should be focused on identifying generalized perceptions and beliefs about the relative desirability of various values that result in common work-related expectations. As such, this paper builds on Walsh's knowledge structure to denote the dynamic interaction of public service ethos and ethical sensitivity on the developmental characteristics of the generation cohort.

5.2. Public Service Ethos (PSE)

Conflicting public duties are inherent in serving as a public administrator. A public servant holds direct responsibility for the welfare of the public, responsibility towards a political superior in executing public policies, as well as to his professional association (Cooper & Menzel, 2013; Lewis & Gilman, 2012; Svara, 2007; Witesman & Walters, 2014). The public service ethos comprises shared values, beliefs, and expectations of public servants. As such, an ethos is viewed as an important management tool for building the professional identity of public employees by improving the development of a deep sense of commitment to serve the public interest and pride among public servants (Cooper & Menzel, 2013; Frederickson & Ghere, 2005; Gueras & Garofalo, 2005; Lawton & Doig, 2005; Maesschalck, 2004; Menzel, 2005).

Historically, the construct of public service ethos (PSE) emerged in the United Kingdom during the nineteenth-century civil service reforms. During the last two decades, the public service witnessed a change in its organizational values and practices that marked a shift from the tradition of bureaucracy towards a more "customer-oriented service," associated with economy, efficient and effective allocation of goods, and the quality of public services (Brereton & Temple, 1999; Ferlie & Geraghty, 2005; Hebson et al., 2003; Rayner et al., 2012). New public management (NPM) reforms in the past thirty years have produced a steady stream of new developments and changes, most notably in many OECD (Organization for Economic Cooperation and Development) countries. With this advance in businesslike methods and the introduction of quality management techniques comes the need to take the next step in changing the public service ethos. Driven by NPM reforms, public service ethos embodies values of efficiency, effectiveness, impartiality, accountability, professionalism, honesty, and integrity (Aldrich & Stoker, 2002; Bowman, 2000; Lawton, 1998; Rayner et al., 2010). Therefore, the evolving nature of the public service ethos denies ideas of administration as ethically neutral professionals apart from the electorate, thereby allowing more room for public administrators to exercise substantial discretion (decision-making power) on their own, discretion that affects peoples' lives (Svara, 2007). Public service ethos must bear the distinctive nature of public administration as a profession whose higher commitment and priority are to serve public interests. By identifying the core values and purposes of public administration as a profession, public service ethos provides guidance to help public servants when faced with competing values, loyalties, and interests. Viewed in this way, public service ethos can be used as a mechanism to enhance professional socialization. It can contribute to developing a sense of pride of belonging to a distinctive group or profession in motivating individuals towards a common good (Brown, 2001).

PSE is, therefore, akin to the construct of public service motivation (PSM) as both constructs are based on publicly oriented motives to benefit the commonweal (Perry & Wise, 1990). However, PSE and PSM are based on different theoretical frameworks; PSE is based on philosophical roots, whereas PSM is rooted in psychological theory.

Rayner et al. (2010) developed a measurement tool of PSE construct based on three dimensions—public service belief, public service practice, and public interest:

> **Public Service Belief** encapsulates why individuals are motivated to work for the public services and reflects personal attributes such as altruism, compassion, and sentiments of wanting to make a difference to the lives of others. **Public**

> **Service Practice** is concerned with how organizational values, processes, and practices including accountability, fairness, and probity are perceived to support motivation toward public service. **Public Interest** reflects the ends of a public office in which individuals act in the interests of the common good rather than in their own selfish interests, the interest of particular groups, or other individuals. (Rayner et al., 2010, p. 34)

Since these dimensions are sensitive to new organizational reforms and values, the overarching aim is to analyze the relationship between PSE and ethical perceptions to better respond to new ethical concerns as they arise. Since PSE is utilized in an attempt to develop an ethical context, there is a reason to believe that PSEs that formalize ethical values that are expected by their public organizations should positively influence public servants' professional perceptions of their organizations of what is ethical and unethical conduct and behavior. While this research does not show that PSE can increase the ethical sensitivity of public sector employees, it does aim to support the idea that there is a connection between PSE and ethical sensitivity. Therefore, we expect that higher levels of ethical sensitivity vary with PSE criteria, although these effects are observed for only the three categories of PSE. In accordance with this logic, we hypothesize that:

Hypothesis 1: PSE will affect ethical sensitivity.
To investigate this relationship, we hypothesize the following linkages:

> 1–1. Individuals who hold a high level of public service belief will show a high level of ethical sensitivity.
>
> 1–2. Individuals who hold a high level of public interest will show a high level of ethical sensitivity.
>
> 1–3. Individuals who hold a high level of public service practice will show a high level of ethical sensitivity.

5.3. Generational Cohorts of Generation Y

Generational cohort refers to members of each generation who share life experiences (e.g., entering the education system, entering the workforce, retiring at related age) and constitutive events with the same time period.

These shared experiences beginning in their formative years guide the members of the generational group's attitudes and values. Ramsey et al. (2007, p, 195) refer to cohort analysis with the general proposition that: "A cohort process rather than an aging process tends to explain the differences in ethical judgements."

From this perspective of cohort-bound forms of aging, five categories of generational cohorts are classified in literature[1]: (a) the Traditionalists (also termed Veterans; individuals born between 1922 and 1945); (b) the Baby Boomers (individuals born between 1946 and 1964); (c) Generation Xers (individuals born between 1965 and 1980); (d) Generation Y/Millennials (individuals born between 1979 and 1990); and (e) Generation Z (born between 1991 and 2002) (Zemke et al., 2000).

Although the differences between cohort and age are difficult to sustain in practice, we argue that a generational cohort perspective needs to be distinguished. In terms of social and cultural realities, the Generation Y cohort has grown up with the Internet and the opportunities and challenges of digital technology developments (also defined as the "digital natives") (Shore et al., 2009; Székely & Nagy, 2011). Within the workforce, the cohort of Generation Y marks them out as holding values of teamwork, communication, and collaboration. Furthermore, they are civic-minded, meaning they place a premium on volunteering (Ertas, 2016; Hayes, 2013; Urick, 2012; Wey Smola & Sutton, 2002). It is the combination of exposure to digital technological developments coupled with the Baby Boomer generational cohort nearing transition into retirement, thus paving the way for the workforce's cohort succession (the gradual replacement of the Baby Boomers cohort by Generation Y) that forms the distinct basis for a generational cohort approach to ethics in the public service. The Generation Y cohort's unique experience and characteristics may impact the way this cohort approaches ethical issues in public service. Indeed, recent studies on generational differences provide compelling evidence of work-values differences across generations in the public sector. (Lyons & Kuron, 2014).

This paper aims to examine the interplay between the perceptions of Gen Y public employees' ethical conduct in the public service and PSEs that prescribe specific standards and norms as "ethical" in the public service

---

1. It should be noted that the age range of Generation Y varies across disciplinary research areas. Specifically, the generational cohorts of Generation Y raise substantial debate regarding its age range. Literature defines the beginning of Generation Y as early as 1977 and as late as 1981 and ending as early as 1994 and as late as 2002 (Copeland, 2008; Erickson, 2008).

(Beeri et al., 2013; Downe et al., 2016; Lawton & Doig, 2005; Macaulay & Lawton, 2006). It is also worth pursuing the effects of the generational cohort of Generation Y on the relation between PSE and ethical sensitivity in the public service. Based on the empirical and theoretical findings, we aim to explore the possibility that PSE would interact with generational cohorts of Generation Y and positively affect ethical sensitivity. We, therefore, propose the following additional hypotheses:

Hypothesis 2: Generational cohort will affect ethical sensitivity.

Hypothesis 3: The relationship between generational cohorts of Generation Y and PSE will affect perceived ethical sensitivity. Generation Y with a high level of PSE will be more ethically sensitive than other generations.

5.4. Method

5.4.1. Sample

A brief overview of public administration research on workforce diversity published from 2000 to 2018 revealed 179 articles. Of this number, only 15% addressed age in the workplace, and only 52 examined diversity empirically at the organizational level. These preliminary figures support the claim that the generational difference is one of the dimensions of diversity grossly ignored by researchers in public administration. In addition, preliminary scale development of multiple scenarios of ethical issues was utilized in reviewing public administration ethics studies between 1998–2018 to identify broad areas that are considered as particularly problematic, among which are included: whistleblowing, technical incompetence, ability to communicate ethical misconduct to a manager, conflicts of interest, and personal gain.

The Israeli government is highly centralized, with the central government collecting over 77% of revenues and accounting for over 72% of total expenditures. The public service in Israel at the federal level is composed of 28 primary ministries. These ministries deliver a range of civil services, from national defense to public diplomacy and diaspora affairs. Public expenditures have been concentrated in the defense, education, employment, and health care sectors, while local governments are responsible for secondary schools, local health care, waste management, road maintenance, parks, and local emergency services. Each ministry is run by a minister who is a member of the prime minister's cabinet and a member of the Israeli parliament (the Knesset), though several ministerial positions are often led directly by the prime minister. The HRM system in the central government of Israel is extremely centralized. The fully delegated HRM responsibility to line departments is based on allocation decisions of the budget envelope between payroll and other expenses.[2] The data for this study were collected as part of a large survey of ethical decision-making processes of public employees across Israeli government agencies. Out of 978 valid surveys delivered, a total of 674 responded at a response rate of 68.9%. To increase the generality of the study, we used a cross-sectoral sample in public administration, including the Ministry of Interior, Ministry of Foreign Affairs, Ministry of Defense, Ministry of Finance, Ministry of Education, Ministry of Health, local government agencies, etc. The limitations include the use of a single national setting (Kim & Vandenabeele, 2010; Perry & Hondeghem, 2008). Although the overall sample is cross-sectoral, readers must be cautious not to overgeneralize results as this sample refers to a single national setting (Israel). Indeed, variation in national cultures can affect the ethical sensitivity of individuals (Guillén et al., 2002). Forty-two percent of the respondents were females. Not surprisingly, Baby Boomers had a longer tenure than younger groups as tenure is often collinear with the generation; thus, statistically, it does not make a difference if tenure was omitted from the factor analysis (Ambrose et al., 2008; Hassan et al., 2013; Natarajan & Nagar, 2012).

5.4.2. Measures

We gathered three types of information from each respondent: individual demographics (age, gender, job title, and tenure), individual public service ethos, and individual ethical sensitivity (Table 5.1).

2. See at https://www.gov.il/en/departments/improving-government-service-unit.

Table 5.1. Descriptive Statistics

	N	Mean	SD	Min	Max
1. Perceived Incorruptibility	673	5.29	1.9	1.2	9
2. PSE					
a. Public Sector Belief	674	1.5	0.72	0	2
b. Public Interest	674	1.29	0.7	0	2
c. Public Sector Practice	674	1.51	0.72	0	2
3. Gender (1-male; 0-female)	638	0.44	0.5	0	1
4. Age	662	40.82	8.04	20	60
Generation Y (23–39)	288	0.434	—	0	1
Generation X (40–51)	320	0.48	—	0	1
Baby Boomers (≥52)	54	0.08	—	0	1
5. Tenure	671	14.12	7.83	0	37
6. Job Title	664	2.66	0.6	1	4

5.4.3. Ethical Sensitivity

Due to the changing nature of ethical dilemmas across an organization, research often uses key ethical principles to measure ethical sensitivity rather than the area-specific ethical issue (Trevino, 1986). However, our measure of ethical sensitivity, the dependent variable in this research, concerns how public service employees perceive ethical issues in their organization. Based on this consideration, this study employs a situation-specific measurement so that different situations uphold different perceptions of ethical and unethical conduct. The instrument includes public administration scenarios that are grouped into three categories adopted from Heidenheimer's color-based typology of corruption (Heidenheimer et al., 1989). Heidenheimer's typology (1989, pp. 149–151) classifies various incidents of corrupted officials' behaviors according to violations of public norms and ethical rules by differentiating varying levels of corruption as perceived by the public in color-based categories of black, gray, and white (Van der Wal et al., 2008).

Utilization of ethical dilemmas as a method of measuring an individual's ethical attitude consisted of three phases: 1) twenty-five interviews were conducted with experts and practitioners to identify key ethical problems in public service daily practice; 2) a scenario focus group was held with 40 participants from Israeli public service to further refine the scenarios; 3) a ten-item measure was developed to assess the level of ethical sensitivity. For example, the scenarios from the survey that are grouped to analyze beliefs and attitudes towards what public officials might regard as "rule-bending" actions (white corruption category) include: running private engagements in on-duty hours or using social media at work for personal purposes. The scenarios that are grouped to analyze beliefs and attitudes towards what public officials might regard as "official corruption" actions (black corruption category) include: covering for a colleague who shows up late or altering a time sheet or accepting gifts and hospitality from citizens. The scenarios that are grouped to analyze beliefs and attitudes towards what public officials might regard as "rule-breaking" actions (gray corruption category) include: accepting gifts up to $8.61 (30 shekels) for performing a specific service, accepting discounts from supermarket corporations, arranging an office for a family member, promoting a colleague based on personal relations (showing favoritism), or lying to hide your colleagues' mistakes.

Each item (statement) ranges from 1 (totally disagree) to 9 (totally agree). Respondents can receive a score from 10 (lowest score on all items) to 90 (highest score on all items). The highest score on all items is considered as a high level of ethical sensitivity. Ethical sensitivity is based on a quasi-interval scale that is based on the arrangement of scale degrees according to official corruption-type categories. The reversed scale of perceived incorruptibility coefficient alpha was 0.85, supporting the construct validity.

5.4.4. Public Service Ethos (PSE)

As indicated earlier, public service ethos (PSE) was measured with three categories of public service ethos developed by Rayner et al. (2010), including public service belief, public service practice, and public interest. The three dimensions of public service ethos have a five-point Likert-style response format (1 = strongly disagree to 5 = strongly agree). However, we decided to split the continuous variable, which transforms the scale variable into a three-level group (low, medium, and high) based on our desire to draw inferences about these specific levels of perceptions of PSE and their effect on ethical sensitivity.

5.4.5. Public Sector Belief

Public sector belief was measured with three items of Rayner et al.'s scale (2010) including: "It is important to me that the work I do is considered to be motivated by altruism rather than personal gain," "Making a difference in society means more to me than personal achievements," "I am motivated more by financial reward rather than by making a positive contribution to the lives of individuals." The internal reliability (Cronbach's alpha) of public sector belief was 0.69.

5.4.6. Public Sector Practice

Public sector practice was assessed with three items of Rayner et al.'s scale (2010) including: "Private sector organizations deliver services to the public more efficiently and effectively than public sector organizations," "Adopting private management style is a good way to run the public sector," "There is too much waste in public sector organizations." The Cronbach's alpha was 0.67.

5.4.7. Public Interest

Public interest included three items from Rayner et al.'s scale (2010): "I believe that the public sector should not be concerned with profit," "I believe that the culture of a public sector organization should primarily be concerned with helping clients/citizens," "In general, public service should be provided on the basis of need rather than ability to pay." The Cronbach's alpha was 0.72.

5.4.8. Generational Cohorts of Generation Y

In this study, we conducted a number of analyses to assess the effects of the moderator variable, generational cohorts of Generation Y, on the form or strength of the relationship between an independent and a dependent variable. The effects of the moderator variable also defined interactions because the third variable interacts with the relation between two other variables (Aguinis, 2004). The use of generational cohorts as a moderator allows assessing if an observed relation is different across subgroups. Moderation analysis may allow identifying subgroups in which public service ethos is counterproductive in terms of ethical sensitivity. It is possible that there will be subgroups (generational cohorts) with low PSE that are more inclined than others to unethical attitudes. Without investigation of generational cohorts of Generation Y as a moderating variable, these types of effects would not be observable.

For this study, we offer to take an intra-country generational cohort approach. More specifically, we developed an age-grouping scheme that is consistent with the socioeconomic events experienced by each generation in Israel in shaping its value orientation (see table 5.2):

Table 5.2. Generational Cohort in Israel

Generation	Years of Birth	Age Range	General Characteristics
The Pre-Revival Generation	Before mid-1940s	Older than 80	Grew up in different countries (Jewish Diaspora) and immigrated to Israel at an older age, after its establishment. Many experienced the Holocaust, persecutions, and lack of physical and economic security to a high degree.
The Revival Generation	Between the mid-1940s and the mid-1950s	64–79	After the traumas of the Holocaust and experienced the revival of the Israeli state.
The Recession Generation	1956–1967	52–63	Grew up during a time when the young state could not cope economically with the mass immigration of Jews from all over the world, especially from Europe and the Arab countries.
The Prosperity Generation	1967–1979	40–51	Born after the big victory in the Six-Day War (June 1967) when Israel occupied Syrian, Egyptian, and Jordanian territories. The military victory was followed by economic prosperity.
The Capitalism Generation/ Generation Y	1981–today	Younger than 40	Born into a similar reality and undergo similar processes as the Generation Y counterparts from the US (e.g., consumed similar social media content and experienced similar technological developments), but experienced a dramatic shift from a socialistic economy to a capitalistic one, massive privatization of the public sector, and periods of physical insecurity (wars, suicide bombers, missile attacks, etc.).

Table information derived from Sharabi, M., & Harpaz, I. (2016). Impact of generational differences on work values in the Israeli context. In M. Sharabi (Ed.), *Generational differences in work values and work ethic: An international perspective* (pp. 19–41). Nova Science Publishers.

Results

We applied two-way ANOVA to compare the mean differences between generational cohorts. Specifically, the use of two-way ANOVA reveals whether there is an interaction between the two independent variables (public sector ethos [PSE] and generational cohort) on the dependent variable (ethical sensitivity [ES]) amongst public sector employees. Therefore, in order to provide more concrete implications in studying public service ethics, the interaction effects between these two sets of factors must be further studied. A two-way ANOVA not only analyses the main effects of public service ethos and generational cohort on ethical sensitivity, but also analyses the interaction effects of these two factors on ethical sensitivity.

1. Interaction effects of Public Service Belief and generational cohort on ethical sensitivity

A two-way ANOVA was conducted that examined the effect of generation and public service belief levels on ethical sensitivity (Table 5.3). A statistically significant interaction was found in the model, $F(8,409)=16.81$, $p < 0.001$, indicating that the mean ethical sensitivity score was significantly different within levels of public service belief and across generational groups.

Regarding the generational cohort, Generation Y had a statistically higher score (mean=5.21, SD=0.16) than Generation X (mean=4.67, SD=0.11). Generation Y employees possessed a higher level of ethical sensitivity than Generation X, irrespective of public sector belief. As a result, levels of public sector belief contributed to the interaction between

Table 5.3. ANOVA Ethical Sensitivity by Generation and Public Service Belief

Source	**df**	**Mean Square**	**F**	**Sig.**	**Eta Squared**
Corrected Model	8	51.13	16.81	.00	.17[a]
Intercept	1	6167.09	2027.29	.00	.76
Generation	2	12.18	4.01	.02	.01
PSBelief—3 cat	2	45.13	14.84	.00	.04
generation * PSBelief— 3 cat	4	27.46	9.03	.00	.05
Total	661				

generational groups and ethical sensitivity. Consequently, it was inferred that the difference in ethical sensitivity between Generation Y and Generation X exists only at the lower level of public service belief (Table 5.4). It is likely that younger respondents with higher levels of belief may perceive that the public service is aligned with their values, and therefore they may be more able to recognize ethical issues. Figure 5.1 presents the interaction between generational cohort and public service belief on ethical sensitivity. Baby Boomers showed lower values for ethical sensitivity at medium and higher levels of public service belief. It is possible that for Baby Boomer respondents, who may have longer tenure and/or experience with the public service, values of altruism and intentions to improve the public service are no longer salient for them, whereas younger respondents (Generation X and Generation Y) are still holding values of altruism and commitment to improving the public service. In short, the two groups that hold a high level of ethical sensitivity showed a high level of public service belief (Generation X and Generation Y). Consequently, ethical sensitivity dominates with respect to the high level of public sector belief.

Table 5.4. Descriptive Statistics of Ethical Sensitivity for Generational Groups and Public Service Belief

Age	Public Sector Belief	Mean	SD	N
Gen Yers (23–39)	Low	4.99	4.01	19
	Mid	4.98	1.77	67
	High	5.64	2.05	202
	Total	5.44	1.95	288
Gen Xers (40–51)	Low	3.28	0.61	60
	Mid	4.86	1.34	68
	High	5.86	1.91	192
	Total	5.16	1.90	320
Baby Boomers (≥52)	Low	3.55	1.1	8
	Mid	6.47	1.11	23
	High	4.86	1.34	23
	Total	5.35	1.6	54
Total	Low	3.68	1.03	87
	Mid	5.15	1.6	158
	High	5.69	1.97	417
	Total	5.3	1.9	662

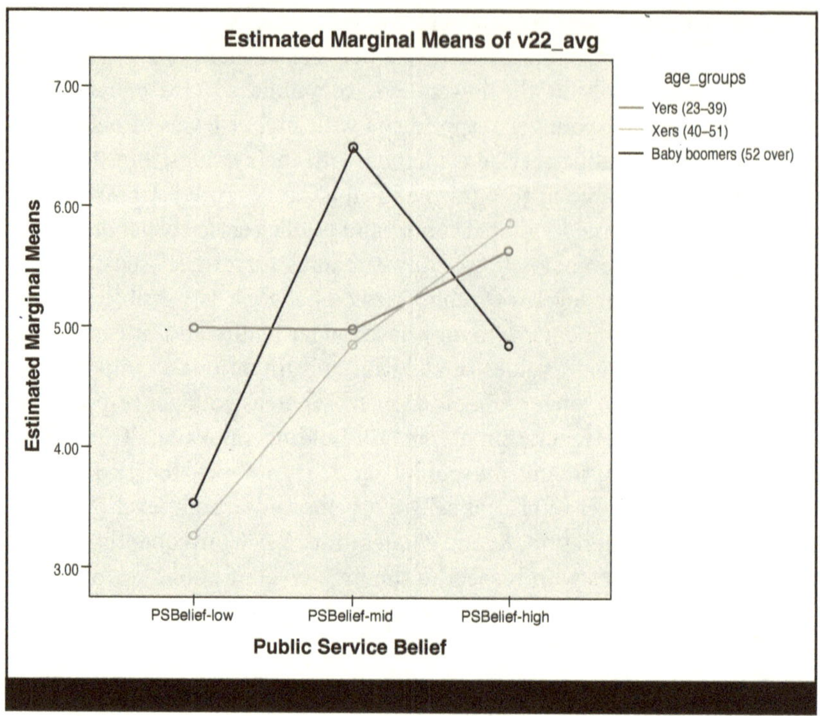

Figure 5.1. Interaction effect of generational cohort and public service belief on ethical sensitivity.

2. Interaction effects of Public Interest and generational cohort on ethical sensitivity

A two-way ANOVA was conducted that examined the effect of generation and public service interest levels on ethical sensitivity (Table 5.5). A statistically significant interaction was found in the model, $F(8,291)=11.32$, $p < 0.05$. Although the model is significant, it found that the generational cohort has no effect on ethical sensitivity while public sector interest has significant effects on ethical sensitivity. At all levels of public interest, the differences between public service employees were significant. There are significant effects between public interest and ethical sensitivity; for example, at a lower level of public interest (mean=6.32, SD=0.23), at a medium level of public interest (mean=5.6, SD=0.16), and for employees with high

Table 5.5. ANOVA Ethical Sensitivity by Generation and Public Service Interest

Source	df	Mean Square	F	Sig.	Partial Eta Squared
Corrected Model	8	36.46	11.32	.00	.12[a]
Intercept	1	9120.92	2830.99	.00	.81
Generation	2	3.37	1.05	.35	.01
Public interest— 3 cat	2	66.69	20.70	.00	.06
generation * Public interest— 3 cat	4	2.61	.81	.52	.01
Total	661				

public interest (mean=4.71, SD=0.14). There are no significant interaction effects between generational cohort and public interest on ethical sensitivity. The striking aspect of the data in Table 5.6 is that public service employees who seem to hold weaker perceptions of the public interest have higher levels of ethical sensitivity. This is an important finding given the fact

Table 5.6. Descriptive Statistics of Ethical Sensitivity for Generational Groups and Public Interest

Age group	Public Interest	Mean	SD	N
Gen Yers (23–39)	Low	4.99	4.01	19
	Mid	4.98	1.77	67
	High	5.64	2.05	202
	Total	5.44	1.05	288
Gen Xers (40–51)	Low	3.28	0.61	60
	Mid	4.86	1.34	68
	High	5.86	1.91	192
	Total	5.16	1.90	320
Baby Boomers (≥52)	Low	3.55	1.1	8
	Mid	6.47	1.11	23
	High	4.86	1.34	23
	Total	5.35	1.6	54
Total	Low	3.68	1.03	87
	Mid	5.15	1.6	158
	High	5.69	1.97	417
	Total	5.3	1.9	662

that the public interest is often criticized as a vague and fluid criterion for defining the boundaries of the public sector while at the same time it is the highest ethical standard for guiding decision-making in the public sector.

3. Interaction effects of **Public Service Practice** and generational cohort on ethical sensitivity

A two-way ANOVA was conducted that examined the effect of generation and public sector practice levels on ethical sensitivity. A statistically significant interaction in the model was found, F(8,293=11.40, $p < 0.001$, indicating that the mean ethical sensitivity score was significantly different within levels of public sector practice and across generational groups (Table 5.7).

The two-way ANOVA results indicate that there is no significant difference in ethical sensitivity across generations. However, employees who have high levels of public service practice show high levels of ethical sensitivity. At a high level of public service practice, the mean ethical sensitivity score stood at 5.69 (SD=0.13), at a medium level of public service practice mean=5.08 (SD=0.22), and at a lower level of public service practice mean=4.34 (SD=0.24). An interesting finding emerges with respect to the interaction effects between public service practice and generational cohort on ethical sensitivity. At a high level of public service

Table 5.7. ANOVA Ethical Sensitivity by Generation and Public Service Practice

Source	**df**	**Mean Square**	**F**	**Sig.**	**Partial Eta Squared**
Corrected Model	8	36.70	11.40	.00	.12[a]
Intercept	1	6250.32	1941.81	.00	.75
Generation	2	9.66	3.0	.05	.01
PSPractice—3 cat	2	44.55	13.84	.00	.04
generation * PSPractice—3 cat	4	16.57	5.15	.00	.03
Total	661				

practice, there are no differences between generational cohorts, while at both medium and low levels of public service practice, the interaction effects of these two factors on ethical sensitivity are significant (Figure 5.2). By drawing on each generation, the interaction effects for Generation Y's ethical sensitivity indicates differences between medium (mean 4.69, SD=0.46) and lower (mean=5.70, SD=0.22) level of public service practice. For Generation X, employees who hold a high perception of public service practice show high levels of ethical sensitivity (Table 5.8). At a higher level of public service practice, the average ethical sensitivity score is 5.74 (SD=0.13), at a medium level of public service practice mean=5.08 (SD=0.22), and at a lower level of public service practice mean=3.47 (SD=0.23).

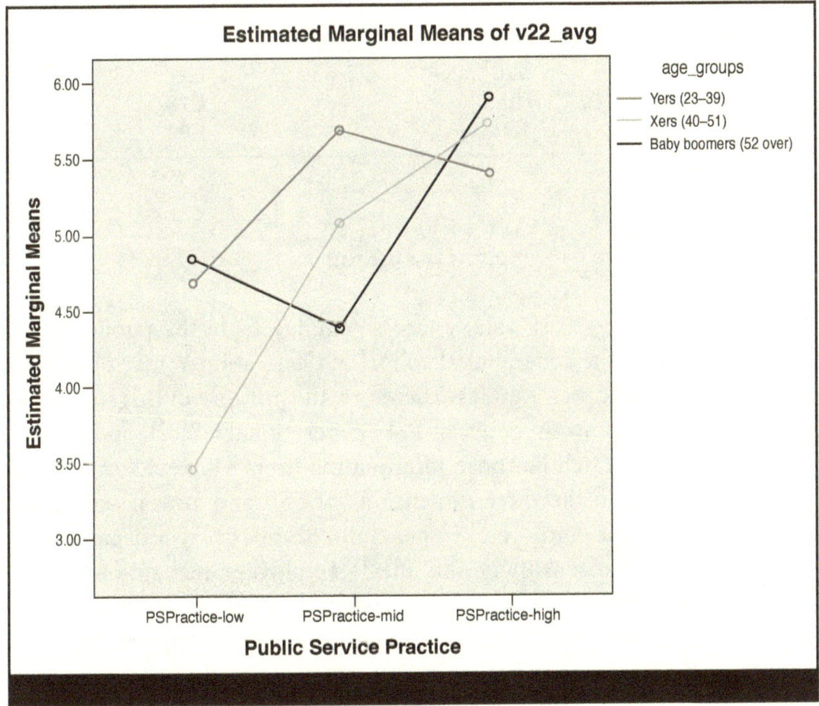

Figure 5.2. Interaction effect of generational cohort and public service practice on ethical sensitivity

Table 5.8. Descriptive Statistics of Ethical Sensitivity for Generational Groups and Public Service Practice

Age group	**Public Interest**	**Mean**	**SD**	**N**
Gen Yers (23–39)	Low	4.69	2.16	15
	Mid	5.70	2.26	69
	High	5.41	1.82	204
	Total	5.44	1.95	288
Gen Xers (40–51)	Low	3.47	0.88	63
	Mid	5.08	1.96	64
	High	5.74	1.79	193
	Total	5.16	1.90	320
Baby Boomers (≥52)	Low	4.85	2.03	14
	Mid	4.39	1.22	10
	High	5.91	1.27	30
	Total	5.35	1.6	54
Total	Low	3.88	1.48	92
	Mid	5.33	2.1	143
	High	5.6	1.78	427
	Total	5.3	1.90	662

5.5. Discussion

Previous research on work values across generations in the public sector has suggested that the generational cohort of Generation Y may pose new challenges for public sector ethics. Therefore, the purpose of this study was to explore the relationship between PSE, generational cohort, and ethical sensitivity. This research has been illuminating in proving evidence of the relationship between the three dimensions of PSE and ethical sensitivity among public sector employees. In general, PSE does play a decisive role in advancing ethical sensitivity and affects employees' perceptions about what is ethically right or wrong. However, this relationship indicates inconsistency regarding the way different generational cohorts perceive the public service ethos and their ability to recognize the ethical content of a situation (ethical sensitivity). On the one hand, inconsistent results were found for the relationship between dimensions of public service interest. These results support claims that the public service interest by itself is not sufficient to affect employees' ethical sensitivity and including employees who demonstrate a high level of public interest can produce mixed results. This further highlights the notion that Gen Y's assessment of what is ethically wrong may not be moderated by the notion of public service interest.

First, the results suggest that employees who are aware of the public service belief possess a higher level of ethical sensitivity. No significant differences were found across generations at higher levels of public service belief. The results suggest that public service belief and generational cohort are likely to influence the level of ethical sensitivity, while the level of public service belief mediates this effect. There is no difference across generational cohorts at a higher level of public service belief. At a lower level of public service belief, Generation Y exhibits a higher level of ethical sensitivity. One may suggest that due to this component of public service ethos, employees perceive a greater degree of "fit" between the public sector values and their own, such as altruism, civic-mindedness, and commitment to benefit the commonweal. This finding is consistent with findings from past research (Székely & Nagy, 2011).

Although we predicted that public service interest affects ethical sensitivity, the results provide no support. It is possible that employees perceive the component of public interest as an ethical double standard. The lack of significant interaction might indicate that employees across generations are still unable to clearly identify this norm as the basis of this agency. This suggests that public organizations interested in developing ethical decision-making among their employees should improve communicating public sector interest as a key ethical norm and communicate its content to their employees. This study provides empirical evidence to support the view that public interest is still a complex, multi-faceted construct interacting as a separable component with ethical sensitivity. Indeed, the findings point to the fact that an employee who demonstrates a high level of public interest may not necessarily be adequate ethical sensitivity. Hence, an employee who possesses a sense of public interest may fail to identify ethical issues as a result of his deficiency in identifying ethical issues (low ethical sensitivity) in the situation that he encountered (Rayner et al., 2010).

This study also implies that the component of public service practice can be a strategic asset for translating management practices into ethical values that reflect a serious commitment to entrepreneurial values that Generation Y prioritizes. Viewed in this way, the result of this study provides evidence to contest the assertion that NPM reform has not violated the public service ethos across generational cohorts (Hebson et al., 2003;

Rayner et al., 2012). Regarding the findings on the component of public service practice, it is suggested that public service ethos can bridge the differences between generational cohorts among public sector employees. In the establishment of ethics education and training programs diverging from the "traditional" frameworks of conducting codes of ethics, it is essential to create a specific professional ethos that upholds the standards of the profession with more emphasis on entrepreneurial and social responsibility values so that this generation of employees can commit themselves to act ethically and effectively in the interest of the public service.

5.6. Limitations and Future Research Directions

Despite the study's findings, several limitations should be raised. First, the study was cross-sectional, which does not allow for studying subjects' attitudes over a long period of time. To separate the effects of generational differences on ethical sensitivity, longitudinal research is required. Second, to strengthen the generalizability of our findings, future studies should examine generational differences in employees' ethical perceptions based on other organizational variables such as sector, department, and ethical leadership, as suggested by Hassen et al. (2014). It is suggested that leaders shape and guide organizational climate and influence employees through their own behaviors, values, and expectations (Hassen et al., 2014).

It is also possible that this sample may be biased due to the fact that it aimed to represent only those employees who are willing to participate or are interested in ethics. Therefore, more research is needed to replicate these results with samples recruited in other ways.

Another challenge lies in the comparison of the PSE construct in various cultural settings. Although cultural differences may influence PSE, it remains the norm to adopt the US PSE categories within democratic cultures.

An additional challenge, which is specific to the cohort-based approach adopted in this study, is the age-period cohort confound. Although some scholars hold that age-related effects might plausibly explain ethical sensitivity, namely maturation, to date, no single methodology enables disentangling these two effects (Krahn & Galambos, 2014).

The ethical sensitivity measure used in the present study was developed from professional ethics-specific scenarios and patterned on Heidenheimer's (Heidenheimer et al., 1989) color-based typology of corruption.

In the area of ethics, measuring perceptions of ethical issues may be one of the major challenges for conducting research. Therefore, more research is needed on measuring ethical sensitivity in the public service, utilizing both quantitative and qualitative data and techniques to improve the ability to measure the spontaneous recognition of ethical issues.

Implications of this study's findings point to the benefits of having Generation Y employees with high levels of public service belief and public service practice. The results of this research will provide valuable insights for public management in fostering effective ethics programs appropriate to socializing Generation Y employees toward public service ethos and ethical decision-making as the values of public service belief (social and altruism-related values) and of public service practice (innovation and entrepreneurialism) claimed to "fit" with values of the generational cohort of Generation Y.

Window on Management

This study examines the interaction effects of public service ethos and generational cohort on ethical sensitivity among public service employees in Israel. Results point to the interaction effects between public service ethos and ethical sensitivity. The link between public service ethos and ethical sensitivity is important because it implies that public service ethos plays a decisive role in advancing ethical sensitivity among public service employees. Existing findings relating three dimensions of public service ethos to levels of ethical sensitivity indicate that public service belief and public service practice dimensions are positively associated with ethical sensitivity across generational cohorts.

By applying a generational cohort approach beyond those resulting from comparisons of organizational-based values, attitudes, and expectations of different generations, the study demonstrated the possibility of different effects of public service ethos on Generation Y and the relationships between PSE and varying levels of ethical sensitivity. Overall, all generational cohorts hold similar levels of ethical sensitivity for both dimensions of public service ethos (public service belief and public service practice), while Millennials reported better fit for public service belief (such as social responsibility and altruism) and values underlying public management practices and reforms. Yet, public sector managers should recognize that the generational characteristics of Generation Y can be a double-edged sword for public organizations. If public sector managers are to foster Millennials' unique civic-minded characteristics in delivering public service, then the standards by which this cohort judges ethical conduct will need to be flexible. Therefore, it might serve public sector organizations to craft ethical training programs for Millennials in ways that allow them to establish their own set of values while being able to identify the "ends" of the public service and eventually possess strict boundaries around conceptions of what is or is not ethical in line with the public service interest dimension.

Therefore, our findings are an important addition to research linking multidimensional measures of public service ethos and the perceived differences in ethical sensitivity between generational cohorts in the public service. More importantly, this link is salient despite the dearth of references to cultural issues and considerations. Specifically, endorsing ethics through management practices based on public service ethos is a potentially useful way to keep younger employees committed and willing to stay and improve public service.

Conclusion

This book has critically and constructively engaged with generational diversity in work-related decisions in the public service. To date, the impending wave of Baby Boomer retirements combined with the relatively smaller size of the Generation Y workforce entering the public sector raise staggering challenges for diversity management in public organizations manifested in the unique values and attitudes that members from different generational cohorts bring with them to the workplace. This book then implies that understanding of generational diversity in public sector values as they are inducted or socialized into normative attitudes and behaviors may facilitate the development of diversity management practices to address growing challenges spawned by age diversity. Reflecting on generational diversity as a central theme in current organizational settings and how to manage its complexity is closely related to Millennials' ethical judgments about acceptable workplace behaviors. Just like the proactive social responsibility strategy of business organizations and corporations, the public sector should employ a proactive ethics strategy through which public organizations can introduce new norms. Therefore, instead of just following current or accepted public service ethos, public managers should lead ethics through generational diversity management.

In the past ten years, the number of Millennials who came to occupy managerial positions has increased significantly (Ernst & Young, 2014), making them highly engaged in decision-making about strategic goals and ethical issues, with some of the most common referring to official corruption, discrimination, health and safety violations, financial issues, and pollution. For this reason, Millennials are now considered to profoundly influence the ethical climate of public organizations. Accordingly, Millennials' ethical reasoning in the workplace is of interest, particularly in times of growing incidents of ethical misconduct.

For the purpose of explaining Millennials' work-related ethical decision-making, we developed a conceptual model, which connects the interaction effects of public service ethos and generational cohort on ethical sensitivity among public service employees. Empirical testing of the proposed conceptual model offered some thought-provoking results. As expected, we found interaction effects between public service ethos and ethical sensitivity. The link between public service ethos and ethical sensitivity is important because it implies that public service ethos plays a decisive role in advancing ethical sensitivity among public service employees. The findings relating three dimensions of public service ethos to levels of ethical sensitivity show that public service belief and public service practice dimensions are positively associated with ethical sensitivity across generational cohorts.

Using generational cohort approach shows that all generational cohorts hold similar levels of ethical sensitivity for both dimensions of public service ethos (public service belief and public service practice), while Millennials reported better fit for public service belief (such as social responsibility and altruism) and values underlying public management practices and reforms. Yet, public sector managers should recognize that the generational characteristics of Generation Y can be a double-edged sword for public organizations. If public sector managers are to foster Millennials' unique civic-minded characteristics in delivering public service, then the standards by which this cohort judges ethical conduct will need to be flexible. Public sector organizations should build ethical training programs for Millennials in ways that allow them to establish their own set of values while meeting the public service interest dimension.

Therefore, our findings are an important addition to research linking multidimensional measures of public service ethos and the perceived differences in ethical sensitivity between generational cohorts in the public service. More importantly, this link is salient despite the dearth of references to cultural issues and considerations. Specifically, endorsing ethics through management practices based on public service ethos is a potentially useful way to keep younger employees committed and willing to stay and improve public service. Furthermore, the study aims to shed light on the burgeoning exploration of the dynamic nature of the public service ethos construct in predicting what forms of ethical attitudes and judgments are associated with the most recent generation to enter the public service. This study also implies that the conceptualization of public service ethos can be a strategic asset for the recruitment and management of the emerging public service (Mayer, 2014).

As described above, the purpose undertaken in this book is to investigate how ethics in public service can be enhanced through critical engagement with generational diversity management. To better understand how public service ethics can benefit from insights into generational diversity, it is useful to sketch a number of distinct steps to allow public managers not only to comply with what is regarded as normatively appropriate and to encourage employees to comply but also to explore whether there are opportunities to develop new ethical norms, to realize these opportunities when possible and desirable, and to get employees to adopt these new norms.

The first step includes the awareness of current or potential moral issues for which an adequate morality has not yet been established. Managing the changing workforce requires the understanding and the appreciation of generational differences if public managers are to build an ethical climate in which Millennials can fulfil and satisfy their personal needs while meeting the public interest. As generational diversity grows in public organizations, workplace age stereotypes conceived as overgeneralized perceptions and expectations of employees based on their generational cohort can lead to age discrimination and negatively impact employees by creating barriers to promotion, satisfaction, performance, and training opportunities. From an ethics management perspective, age stereotypes can distort information processing (e.g., biased judgments that lead to discriminatory behavior during decision-making processes in recruitment, promotion and tenure decisions, and professional identification). Since recent scholarship addresses the content of stereotypes towards generations, public management must attempt to better clarify the characteristics that individuals use to describe generations and how these stereotypes affect public organizations' ethical climate and performance.

Next, public managers can identify one or more competencies and skills of Millennials relevant to tech adoption so they can develop a new ethical norm on the basis of a vision of how and why the norm contributes to a better society and improved public sector performance. Managers must evolve and adapt their processes and ways of working in order to maximize the benefit they receive from Millennials in a fast-paced environment with continuously changing technology. Public administration should facilitate collective debates like roundtables, brainstorming sessions, and idea boards to boost innovative thinking across generations. This strategy of generational diversity management leads to the development of working relationships across all generations and supports the evolution of the Millennial Generation to undertake leadership roles.

The next step would be for public managers to stimulate open communication and encourage sharing. Communication is conceived as a powerful tool for effective leadership. To communicate more effectively within the context of a diverse workforce in which four generations differ in their levels of comfort with technology, public management must keep up to date with technological innovations applied in public administration practices and provide practical and relevant information, co-created with Millennials to meet both public service goals and employees' needs. The objective is to communicate more effectively, engaging different generational cohorts through dialogue to raise ethical issues related to generational-based work values and public sector ethos and seek solutions to ethical dilemmas and concerns to embed ethical decision-making.

Bibliography

Abdullah, W. M. T. W., Ahmad, N. N., & Ariff, A. M. (2018). Combating corruption for sustainable public services in Malaysia: Smart governance matrix and corruption risk assessment. *Journal of Sustainability Science and Management*, 1.

Adecco. (2015). Generation Z vs. Millennials. Retrieved July 20, 2020, from http://pages.adeccousa.com/rs/107-IXF-539/images/generation-z-vs-millennials.pdf

Aguinis, H. (2004). *Regression analysis for categorical moderators*. Guilford Press.

Ahmad, H., & Ibrahim, B. (2015). Leadership and the characteristic of different generational cohort towards job satisfaction. *Procedia–Social and Behavioral Sciences*, *204*, 14–18.

Ajzen, I. (1985). From intentions to actions: A theory of planned behavior. In J. Kuhl & J. Beckmenn (Eds.), *Action control: From cognition to behavior*. (pp. 11–39). Springer.

Ajzen, I. (1989). Attitude structure and behavior. In S. J. Breckler & A. G. Greenwald (Eds.), *Attitude Structure and Function* (pp. 241–274). Lawrence Erlbaum.

Akaah, I. P. (1989). Differences in research ethics judgments between male and female marketing professionals. *Journal of Business Ethics*, *8*(5), 375–381.

Akaah, I. P. (1997). Influence of deontological and teleological factors on research ethics evaluations. *Journal of Business Research*, *39*(2), 71–80.

Aldrich, R., & Stoker, G. (2002). *Advancing a Public Service Ethos*. New Local Government Network.

Alexander, C. S., & Becker, H. J. (1978). The use of vignettes in survey research. *Public opinion quarterly*, *42*(1), 93–104.

Almeida F., & Calistru, C. (2013). The main challenges and issues of big data management. *International Journal of Research Studies in Computing*, *2*(1), 11–20.

Alsop, R. (2008). *The trophy kids grow up: How the millennial generation is shaking up the workplace*. John Wiley & Sons.

Alvesson, M., & Willmott, H. (1996). *Making sense of management: A critical introduction*. SAGE Publications.

Amayah, A. T., & Gedro, J. (2014). Understanding generational diversity: Strategic human resource management and development across the generational divide. *New Horizons in Adult Education & Human Resource Development, 26*(2), 36–48.

Ambrose, M. L., Arnaud, A., & Schminke, M. (2008). Individual moral development and ethical climate: The influence of person-organization fit on job attitudes. *Journal of Business Ethics, 77*(3), 323–333.

Anderson, M., & Anderson, S. L. (Eds.). (2011). *Machine ethics*. Cambridge University Press.

Anderson, M., & Perrin, A. (2017, May 17). Technology use among seniors. Pew Research Center. Retrieved July 20, 2020, from https://www.pewresearch.org/internet/2017/05/17/technology-use-among-seniors/

Andrews, L. (2019). Public administration, public leadership, and the construction of public value in the age of the algorithm and "big data." *Public Administration, 97*(2), 296–310.

Apfelbaum, E. P., Norton, M. I., & Sommers, S. R. (2012). Racial color blindness: Emergence, practice, and implications. *Current Directions in Psychological Sciences, 21*(3), 205–209.

Ashikali, T., & Groeneveld, S. (2015). Diversity management in public organizations and its effect on employees' affective commitment: The role of transformational leadership and the inclusiveness of the organizational culture. *Review of Public Personnel Administration, 35*(2), 146–168.

Avery, D., & McKay, P. (2006). Target practice: An organizational impression management approach to attracting minority and female job applicants. *Personnel Psychology. 59*, 157–187.

Awasthi, V. N. (2008). Managerial decision-making on moral issues and the effects of teaching ethics. *Journal of Business Ethics, 78*(1–2), 207–223.

Babalola, S., & Marques, L. (2013). Integrated approach to workplace diversity through human resource management. *Journal of Social and Development Sciences, 4*(9), 435–445.

Babin, B. J., Griffin, M., & Boles, J. S. (2004). Buyer reactions to ethical beliefs in the retail environment. *Journal of Business Research, 57*(10), 1155–1163.

Bailey, A., & Ngwenyama, O. (2010). Bridging the generation gap in ICT use: Interrogating identity, technology, and interactions in community telecenters. *Information Technology for Development, 16*(1), 62–82.

Bailey, C. D., Scott, I., & Thoma, S. J. (2010). Revitalizing accounting ethics research in the neo-Kohlbergian framework: Putting the DIT into perspective. *Behavioral Research in Accounting, 22*(2), 1–26.

Ball, P., Monaco, G., Schmeling, J., Schartz, H., & Blanck, P. (2005). Disability as diversity in Fortune 100 companies. *Behavioral Sciences and the Law, 23*, 97–121.

Balser, D. B. (1999). *Implementing new employment law: A contested terrain* [Unpublished doctoral dissertation]. Cornell University.

Barnett, T. (2001). Dimensions of moral intensity and ethical decision-making: an empirical study. *Journal of Applied Social Psychology, 31*(5), 1038–1057.

Barnett, T., & Vaicys, C. (2000). The moderating effect of individuals' perceptions of ethical work climate on ethical judgments and behavioral intentions. *Journal of Business Ethics, 27*(4), 351–362.

Barnett, T., & Valentine, S. (2004). Issue contingencies and marketers' recognition of ethical issues, ethical judgments, and behavioral intentions. *Journal of Business Research, 57*(4), 338–346.

Barnett, T., Bass, K., & Brown, G. (1994). Ethical ideology and ethical judgment regarding ethical issues in business. *Journal of Business Ethics, 13*(6), 469–480.

Barnett, T., Bass, K., & Brown, G. (1996). Religiosity, ethical ideology, and intentions to report a peer's wrongdoing. *Journal of Business Ethics, 15*(11), 1161–1174.

Barnett, T., Brown, G., Bass, K., & Hebert, F. J. (1999). *New measures for proposed dimensions of the moral intensity of ethical issues* [Paper presentation]. Academy of Management, Chicago.

Bartley, S. J., Ladd, P. G., & Morris, M. L. (2007). Managing the multigenerational workplace: Answers for managers and trainers. *College & University Professional Association—HR Journal*. 28–34.

Bass, K., Barnett, T., & Brown, G. (1999). Individual difference variables, ethical judgments, and ethical behavioral intentions. Business Ethics Quarterly, 9(2), 183–205.

Bass, B. M., & Riggio, R. E. (2006). *Transformational leadership* (2nd ed.). Psychology Press.

Bass, B. M., & Riggio, R. E. (2014) *Transformational Leadership* (2nd ed.). Routledge.

Bauer, N. M. (2020). Running local: gender stereotyping and female candidates in local elections. *Urban Affairs Review, 56*(1), 96–123.

Baumgärtner, S. E., Weeda, W. D., van der Heijden, L. L., & Huizinga, M. (2014). The relationship between media multitasking and executive function in early adolescents. *The Journal of Early Adolescence, 34*(8), 1120–1144.

Bay, D. (2002). A critical evaluation of the use of the DIT in accounting ethics research. *Critical Perspectives on Accounting, 13*(2), 159–177.

Bebeau, M. J. (2002). The defining issues test and the four component model: Contributions to professional education. *Journal of Moral Education, 31*(3), 271–295.

Bebeau, M. J., Rest, J. R., & Yamoor, C. M. (1985). Measuring dental students' ethical sensitivity. *Journal of Dental Education, 49*(4), 225–235.

Bebeau, M., & Thoma, S. J. (1999). Intermediate concepts and the connection to moral education. *Educational Psychology Review, 11*, 343–360.

Beekun, R. I., Stedham, Y., Yamamura, J. H., & Barghouti, J. A. (2003). Comparing business ethics in Russia and the US. *The International Journal of Human Resource Management, 14*(8), 1333–1349.

Beeri, I., Dayan R., Vigoda-Gadot, E., & Werner, S. B. (2013). Advancing ethics in public organizations: The impact of an ethics program on employees' perceptions and behaviors in a regional council. *Journal of Business Ethics, 112*(1), 59–78.

Bejtkovský, J. (2016). The employees of Baby Boomers generation, Generation X, Generation Y, and Generation Z in selected Czech corporations as conceivers of development and competitiveness in their corporation. *Journal of Competitiveness, 8*(4), 105–123.

Bekker, J. C. O., & Van Heyningen, H. (2011). A strategic leadership model for policy implementation. *African Journal of Public Affairs, 4*(1), 23–36.

Bell, M. P. (2012). *Diversity in organizations.* South-Western Publishing Co.

Bengtson, V. L., Furlong, M. J., & Laufer, R. S. (1983). Time, aging, and the continuity of social structure: Themes and issues in generational analysis. *Journal of Social Issues, 39*(4), 45–71.

Benimadhu, P. P., & Wright, R. (1991). Employment equity: Impact of the legislation. *Canadian Business Review, 18*(2), 22–25.

Bennett, S., Maton, K., & Kervin, L. (2008). The "digital natives" debate: A critical review of the evidence. *British Journal of Educational Technology, 39,* 775–786.

Benson, J., & Brown, M. (2011). Generations at work: Are there differences and do they matter? *The International Journal of Human Resource Management, 22*(9), 1843–1865.

Berg, N., & Lien, D. (2002). Measuring the effect of sexual orientation on income: evidence of discrimination. *Contemporary Economic Policy, 20,* 394–414.

Betters-Reed, B. L., & Moore, L. L. (1992). Managing diversity: Focusing on women and the whitewash dilemma. In U. Sekaran & F. T. L. Leong (Eds.), *Women power: Managing times of demographic turbulence* (pp. 31–58). SAGE Publications.

Biancone, P., Secinaro, S., & Brescia, V. (2018). The innovation of local public-sector companies: Processing big data for transparency and accountability. *African Journal of Business Management, 12*(15), 486–500.

Bilimoria, D. (2006). The relationship between women corporate directors and women corporate officers. *Journal of Managerial Issues, 18*(1), 47–61.

Black, J. (2005). The emergence of risk-based regulation and the new public risk management in the United Kingdom. *Public Law,* 510–546.

Blandford, J. M. (2003). The nexus of sexual orientation and gender in the determination of earnings. *Industrial and Labor Relations Review, 56,* 622–642.

Blasi, A. (1980). Bridging moral cognition and moral action: A critical review of the literature. *Psychological Bulletin, 88*(1), 1–45.

Blau, F. D., & Khan, L. M. (2006). The U.S. gender pay gap in the 1990s: Slowing convergence. *Industrial and Labor Relations Review, 60*(1), 45–66.

Bleijenbergh, I., Peters, P., & Poutsma, E. (2010). Diversity management beyond the business case. *Equality, Diversity and Inclusion, 29*(5), 413–421.

Bolin, G., & Westlund, O. (2009). Mobile generations: The role of mobile technology in the shaping of Swedish media generations. *International Journal of Communication, 3,* 108–124.

Bolton, R. N., Parasuraman, A., Hoefnagels, A., Migchels, N., Kabadayi, S., Gruber, T., Loureiro, Y. K., & Solnet, D. (2013). Understanding Generation Y and their use of social media: A review and research agenda. *Journal of Service Management, 24*(3), 245–267.

Bose, C. E. (2012). Intersectionality and global gender inequality. *Gender & Society, 26,* 67–72.

Bose, S. (2017). *Surprising stats on every generation's social media habits* [Infographic]. Retrieved July 20, 2020, from https://smallbiztrends.com/2017/03/social-media-usage-by-age.html

Bowen, D. E., & Ostroff, C. (2004). Understanding HRM–firm performance linkages: The role of the "strength" of the HRM system. *Academy of Management Review, 29,* 203–221.

Bowman, J. (2000). Towards a professional ethos: From regulatory to reflective codes. *International Review of Administrative, 66,* 6773–6787.

Boyle, B. A. (2000). The impact of customer characteristics and moral philosophies on ethical judgments of salespeople. *Journal of Business Ethics, 23*(3), 249–267.

Bozeman, B., & Feeney, M. K. (2009). Public management mentoring a three-tier model. *Review of Public Personnel Administration, 29,* 134–157.

Brah, A. & Phoenix, A. (2013). Ain't I a woman? Revisiting intersectionality. *Journal of International Women's Studies, 5*(3), 75–86.

Brereton, M., & Temple, M. (1999). The new public service ethos: An ethical environment for governance. *Public Administration, 77*(3), 455–474.

Brewer, G. A., & Selden, S. C. (1998). Whistle blowers in the federal civil service: New evidence of the public service ethic. *Journal of Public Administration Research and Theory, 8*(3), 413–439.

Bright, L. (2005). Public employees with high levels of public service motivation. Who are they, where are they, and what do they want? *Review of Public Personnel Administration, 25*(2), 138–154.

Bright, L. (2008). Does public service motivation really make a difference on the job satisfaction and turnover intentions of public employees? *American Review of Public Administration, 38,* 149–166.

Bright, L. (2013). Where does public service motivation count the most in government work environments? A preliminary empirical investigation and hypotheses. *Public Personnel Management, 42*(1), 5–26.

Bright, L., & Graham, C. B. (2015). Why does interest in government careers decline among public affairs graduate students? *Journal of Public Affairs Education, 21*(4), 575–594.

Brower, H. H., & Shrader, C. B. (2000). Moral reasoning and ethical climate: Not-for-profit vs. for-profit boards of directors. *Journal of Business Ethics, 26,* 147–167.

Brown, C. L. (1998). Sexual orientation and labor economics. *Feminist Economics, 4,* 89–95.

Brown, D. S. (2001). *The Managerial Ethic and Productivity Improvement.* Routledge.

Brown, I., De Rijk, K., Patel, K., Twum-Ampofo, Y., & Van Belle, J. P. (2006, July 16–18). *T-commerce: An investigation of non-adoption in South Africa* [conference proceedings]. Conference on Information Science, Technology and Management (CISTM), Chandigarh, India.

Brown, M. E., & Treviño, L. K. (2006). Ethical leadership: A review and future directions. *The Leadership Quarterly, 17*(6), 595–616.

Brown, M. E., Treviño, L. K., & Harrison, D. A. (2005). Ethical leadership: A social learning perspective for construct development and testing. *Organizational Behavior and Human Decision Processes, 97,* 117–134.

Bucar, B., Glas, M., & Hisrich, R. D. (2003). Ethics and entrepreneurs: An international comparative study. *Journal of Business Venturing, 18*(2), 261–281.

Buheji, M. (2019). Alleviation of generation gap through socio-economic issues involvement. *Review of European Studies, 11,* 12–20.

Bullen, M., Morgan, T., & Qayyum, A. (2011). Digital learners in higher education: Generation is not the issue. *Canadian Journal of Learning and Technology, 37.* Retrieved July 20, 2020, from https://cjlt.ca/index.php/cjlt/article/view/26364

Burgess, M. (2018). Facial recognition tech used by UK police is making a ton of mistakes. *Wired UK, 4.* https://www.wired.co.uk/article/face-recognition-police-uk-south-wales-met-notting-hill-carnival

Burgess, R. (2011). Harnessing the power of your intergenerational workforce. *The Alabama CPA Magazine,* June, 8–9.

Burke, R. J. (2015). Managing an aging and multi-generational workforce: Challenges and opportunities. In R. J. Burke, C. Cooper, & A. S. Antoniou (Eds.), *The Multi-generational and aging workforce* (pp. 3–38). Edward Elgar Publishing.

Burn, R. B. (1979). *The self concept in theory, measurement, development, and behavior.* Longman Inc.

Burns, J. O., & Kiecker, P. (1995). Tax practitioner ethics: An empirical investigation of organizational consequences. *The Journal of the American Taxation Association, 17*(2), 20.

Buttner, E. H., Lowe, K. B., & Billings-Harris, L. (2010). Diversity climate impact on employee of color outcomes: Does justice matter? *Career Development International, 15*(3), 239–258.

Cahill, T. F., & Sedrak, M. (2012). Leading a multigenerational workforce: Strategies for attracting and retaining millennials. *Frontiers of Health Services Management, 29*(1), 3–15.

Callanan, G. A., Rotenberry, P. F., Perri, D. F., & Oehlers, P. (2010). Contextual factors as moderators of the effect of employee ethical ideology on ethical decision-making. *International Journal of Management, 27*(1), 52.

Casey, C. (2002). *Critical analysis of organizations: Theory, practice and revitalization*. SAGE Publications.

Caskey, M. M. (2003). Using parent–student pairs for Internet instruction. *Journal of Research on Technology in Education, 34*(3), 304–317.

Cassell, C. (2001). The business case and the management of diversity. In M. Davidson & R. Burke (Eds.), *Women in management: Current research issues* (Vol. II). SAGE Publications.

Cekada, T. L. (2012). Training a multigenerational workforce.: Understanding key needs & learning styles. *Professional Safety, 57*(3), 40–44.

Cennamo, L., & Gardner, D. (2008). Generational differences in work values, outcomes and person–organization values fit. *Journal of Managerial Psychology, 23*, 891–906.

Chambers, D. W. (2011). Developing a self-scoring comprehensive instrument to measure Rest's four-component model of moral behavior: The moral skills inventory. *Journal of Dental Education, 75*(1), 23–35.

Chan, S. Y., & Leung, P. (2006). The effects of accounting students' ethical reasoning and personal factors on their ethical sensitivity. *Managerial Auditing Journal, 21*(4), 436–457.

Chatman, J. A., & Flynn, F. J. (2001). The influence of demographic heterogeneity on the emergence and consequences of cooperative norms in work teams. *Academy of Management Journal, 44*, 956–974.

Chi, C. G., Maier, T. A., & Gursoy, D. (2013). Employees' perceptions of younger and older managers by generation and job category. *International Journal of Hospitality Management, 34*, 42–50.

Chia, A., & Mee, L. S. (2000). The effects of issue characteristics on the recognition of moral issues. *Journal of Business Ethics, 27*(3), 255–269.

Chitiga, M., Chogugudza, P., & Chitiga, T. (2011) Teaching outside one's comfort zone: Helping diverse Millennials succeed. *Faculty Working Papers from the School of Education* (pp. 18–30). Fayetteville State University.

Chiu, R. K. (2003). Ethical judgment and whistleblowing intention: Examining the moderating role of locus of control. *Journal of Business Ethics, 43*(1/2), 65–74.

Chiu, R., & Erdener, C. (2003). The ethics of peer reporting in Chinese societies: Evidence from Hong Kong and Shanghai. *International Journal of Human Resource Management, 14*(2), 335–353.

Cho, Y. J., & Lewis, G. B. (2012). Turnover intention and turnover behavior: Implications for retaining federal employees. *Review of Public Personnel Administration, 32*, 4–23.

Choi, D. L., & Perry, J. L. (2010). Developing a tool to measure ethical sensitivity in public administration and its application. *International Review of Public Administration, 14*(3), 1–12.

Choi, S., & Rainey, H. G. (2010). Managing diversity in U.S. federal agencies: Effects of diversity and diversity management on employee perceptions of organizational performance. *Public Administration Review, 70*, 109–121.

Christensen, R. K., & Wright. B. E. (2011). The effects of public service motivation on job choice decisions: Disentangling the contributions of person–organization fit and person–job fit. *Journal of Public Administration Research and Theory, 21*(4), 723–743.

Christensen, R. K., & Wright, B. E. (2018). Public service motivation and ethical behavior: Evidence from three experiments. *Journal of Behavioral Public Administration, 1*(1), 1–8.

Christie, P. M. J., Kwon, I. W. G., Stoeberl, P. A., & Baumhart, R. (2003). A cross-cultural comparison of ethical attitudes of business managers: India, Korea and the United States. *Journal of Business Ethics, 46*(3), 263–287.

Chuang, Y, Church, R., & Ophir, R. (2011). Taking sides: The interactive influences of institutional mechanisms on the adoption of same-sex partner health benefits by Fortune 500 corporations, 1990–2003. *Organization Science, 22*, 190–209.

Chun, J. J., George, L., & Young, S. (2013). Intersectionality as a social movement strategy: Asian immigrant women advocates. *Signs, 38*(4), 917–940.

Chung, J. E., Park, N., Wang, H., Fulk, J., & McLaughlin, M. (2010). Age differences in perceptions of online community participation among non-users: An extension of the technology acceptance model. *Computers in Human Behavior, 26*(6), 1674–1684.

Church, A. H., & Rotolo, C. T. (2013). How are top companies assessing their high potentials and senior executives? A talent management benchmark study. *Consulting Psychology Journal: Practice & Research, 65*, 199–223.

Clark, J. W. (1966). *Religion and the moral standards of American businessmen.* South-Western Publishing Co.

Clark, J. W., & Dawson, L. E. (1996). Personal religiousness and ethical judgements: An empirical analysis. *Journal of Business Ethics, 15*(3), 359–372.

Clarkeburn, H. (2002). A test for ethical sensitivity in science. *Journal of Moral Education, 31*(4), 439–453.

Cleveland, J. N. & Lim, A. S. (2007). Employee age and performance in organizations. In K. S. Schultz & G. A. Adams (Eds.), *Aging and work in the 21st century* (pp. 109–138). Lawrence Erlbaum Associates.

Cogin, J. (2012). Are generational differences in work values fact or fiction? Multi-country evidence and implications. *The International Journal of Human Resource Management, 23*, 2268–2294.

Cohen, J. C., Fowler, M., Vladimir, E., Medenica, E. V., & Rogowski, C. J. (2018). *Millennials and technology: An overview of usage, news consumption, the future of work, and public policy.* GenForward.

Cohen, J. R., & Bennie, N. M. (2006). The applicability of a contingent factors model to accounting ethics research. *Journal of Business Ethics, 68*(1), 1–18.

Cohen, J. R., Pant, L. W., & Sharp, D. J. (1993). A validation and extension of a multidimensional ethics scale. *Journal of Business Ethics, 12*, 13–26.

Cohen, J. R., Pant, L. W., & Sharp, D. J. (1995). An international comparison of moral constructs underlying auditors' ethical judgments. *Research on Accounting Ethics, 1*(2), 165–181.

Cohen, J. R., Pant, L. W., & Sharp, D. J. (1996). Measuring the ethical awareness and ethical orientation of Canadian auditors. *Behavioral Research in Accounting, 8*, 98–119.

Cohen, J. R., Pant, L. W., & Sharp, D. J. (1998). The effect of gender and academic discipline diversity on the ethical evaluations, ethical intentions and ethical orientation of potential public accounting recruits. *Accounting Horizons, 12*(3), 250.

Cohen, J. R., Pant, L. W., & Sharp, D. J. (2001). An examination of differences in ethical decision-making between Canadian business students and accounting professionals. *Journal of Business Ethics, 30*(4), 319–336.

Cooke, F. L., & Saini, D. S. (2010). Diversity management in India: A study of organizations in different ownership forms and industrial sectors. *Human Resource Management, 49*(3), 477–500.

Cooper, T. L. (2006). *The responsible administrator: An approach to ethics for the administrative role* (4th ed.). Jossey-Bass.

Cooper, T. L., & Menzel, D. (Eds.). (2013). *Achieving ethical competence for public service leadership*. M. E. Sharpe.

Copeland, C. W. (2008). *The federal workforce: Characteristics and trends* (RL34685). Retrieved from https://digitalcommons.ilr.cornell.edu/key_workplace/551/

Cornwell, C., & Kellough, J. E. (1994). Women and minorities in federal government agencies: Examining new evidence from panel data. *Public Administration Review, 54*(3), 265–270.

Costa, M. (2017). How responsive are political elites? A meta-analysis of experiments on public officials. *Journal of Experimental Political Science, 4*(3), 241–254.

Costanza, D. P., Badger, J. M., Fraser, R. L., Severt, J. B., & Gade, P. A. (2012). Generational differences in work-related attitudes: A meta-analysis. *Journal of Business and Psychology, 27*, 375–394.

Coulter, J. S., & Faulkner, D. C. (2014). The multigenerational workforce. *Professional Case Management, 19*, 46–51.

Coursey, D., Brudney, J. J., Littlepage, L., & Perry, J. (2011). Does public sector motivation matter in volunteering domain choices? A test of functional theory. *Review of Public Personnel Administration, 31*(1), 48–66.

Cox, T., Jr. (1991). The multicultural organization. *Executive, 5*(2), 34–47.

Cox, T., Lobel, S. A., & McLeod, P. L. (1991). Effects of ethnic group cultural differences on cooperative and competitive behavior on a group task. *Academy of Management Journal, 4*, 827–847.

Craft, J. L. (2013). A review of the empirical ethical decision-making literature: 2004–2011. *Journal of Business Ethics, 117*(2), 221–259.

Cross, T. (1988). Services to minority populations: Cultural competence continuum. *Focal Point, 30*(1), 1–4.

Crowson, H. M., DeBacker, T. K., & Thoma, S. J. (2007). Are DIT score empirically distinct from measures of political identification and intellectual ability? A test using post-9/11 data. *British Journal of Developmental Psychology, 25*(2), 197–211.

Cunningham, G. B. (2009). The moderating effect of diversity strategy on the relationship between racial diversity and organizational performance. *Journal of Applied Social Psychology, 39*(6), 1445–1460.

Cushing, G. M. (2019). Multi-generational workforce strategies for 21st century managers. Retrieved from https://firescholars.seu.edu/coe/45

Cutler, N. E., & Bengtson, V. L. (1974). Age and political alienation: Maturation, generation and period effects. *The Annals of the American Academy of Political and Social Science, 415*(1), 160–175.

Czaja, S. J., Charness, N., Fisk, A. D., Hertzog, C., Nair, S. N., Rogers, W. A., & Sharit, J. (2006). Factors predicting the use of technology: Findings from the Center for Research and Education on Aging and Technology Enhancement (CREATE). *Psychology and Aging, 21*(2), 333–352.

Dahlin, K. B., Weingart, L. R., & Hinds, P. J. (2005). Team diversity and information use. *Academy of Management Journal, 48*(6), 1107–1123.

Dalton, K. M. (2012). Bridging the digital divide and guiding the Millennial Generation's research and analysis. *Barry Law Review, 18*, 167.

Dass, P., & Parker, B. (1999). Strategies for managing human resource diversity: From resistance to learning. *Academy of Management Executive, 13*(2), 68–80.

Dávid-Barrett, E., & Fazekas, M. (2019). Grand corruption and government change: an analysis of partisan favoritism in public procurement. *European Journal on Criminal Policy and Research, 26*(4), 411–430.

Davis, M. A., Andersen, M. G., & Curtis, M. B. (2001). Measuring ethical ideology in business ethics: A critical analysis of the ethics position questionnaire. *Journal of Business Ethics, 32*(1), 35–53.

Dawis, R. V. (1980). Personnel assessment from the perspective of the theory of work adjustment. *Public Personnel Management Journal, 9*(4), 268–273.

Dawis, R. V. (2005). The Minnesota theory of work adjustment. In S. D. Brown and R. W. Lent (Eds.), *Career development and counseling: Putting theory and research to work* (pp. 3–23). John Wiley & Sons, Inc.

Day, N. E., & Schoenrade, P. (2000). The relationship among reported disclosure of sexual orientation, anti-discrimination policies, top management support and work attitudes of gay and lesbian employees. *Personnel Review, 29*(3), 346–363.

DeConinck, J. B., & Lewis, W. F. (1997). The influence of deontological and teleological considerations and ethical climate on sales managers' intentions to reward or punish sales force behavior. *Journal of Business Ethics, 16*(5), 497–506.

Deshpande, S. P. (1997). Managers' perception of proper ethical conduct: The effect of sex, age, and level of education. *Journal of Business Ethics, 16*(1), 79–85.

DiMaggio, P., & Hargittai, E. (2001). From the digital divide to "digital inequality": studying Internet use as penetration increases. Working Paper Series (15) Princeton University, Center for Arts and Cultural Policy Studies. Retrieved July 15, 2020, from http://www.princeton.edu/culturalpolicy/workpap/WP15%20%20DiMaggio+Hargittai.pdf

Dimock, M. (2019). Defining generations: Where Millennials end and Generation Z begins. Pew Research Center. Retrieved July 15, 2020, from https://www.pewresearch.org/fact-tank/2019/01/17/where-millennials-end-and-generation-z-begins/

Dobbin, F., Sutton, J. R., Meyer, J. W., & Scott, W. R. (1993). Equal employment opportunity law and the construction of internal labor markets. *American Journal of Sociology, 99*, 396–427.

DOMO. (2015). Millennials and mobile technology: Adjusting to a mobile-first world. Retrieved July 15, 2020, from https://web-assets.domo.com/blog/wp-content/uploads/2015/08/r02_domo_millennials_report.pdf

Dornoff, R. J., & Tankersley, C. B. (1975). Perceptual differences in market transactions: A source of consumer frustration. *Journal of Consumer Affairs, 9*(1), 97–103.

Downe, J., Cowell, R., & Morgan, K. (2016). What determines ethical behavior in public organizations: Is it rules or leadership? *Public Administration Review, 76*(6), 898–909.

Downs, H. (2019). Bridging the gap: How the generations communicate. *Concordia Journal of Communication Research, 6*(1), 6.

Doyle, E., Frecknall-Hughes, J., & Summers, B. (2009). Research methods in taxation ethics: Developing the defining issues test (DIT) for a tax-specific scenario. *Journal of Business Ethics, 88*(1), 35–52.

Dubinsky, A. J., & Loken, B. (1989). Analyzing ethical decision-making in marketing. *Journal of Business Research, 19*(2), 83–107.

Dubinsky, A. J., Nataraajan, R., & Huang, W. Y. (2004). The influence of moral philosophy on retail salespeople's ethical perceptions. *Journal of Consumer Affairs, 38*(2), 297–319.

Dunfee, T. W. (2006). A critical perspective of integrative social contracts theory: Recurring criticisms and next generation research topics. *Journal of Business Ethics, 68*(3), 303–328.

DuPont, A. M., & Craig, J. S. (1996). Does management experience change the ethical perceptions of retail professionals: A comparison of the ethical perceptions of current students with those of recent graduates? *Journal of Business Ethics, 15*(8), 815–826.

Dwyer, R. J. (2009). Prepare for the impact of the multi-generational workforce! *Transforming Government: People, Process, and Policy, 3*(2), 101–110.

E&Y. (2015). What if the next big disruptor isn't a what but a who? Gen Z is connected, informed and ready for business. EY. Retrieved July 20, 2020, from https://assets.ey.com/content/dam/ey-sites/ey-com/en_gl/topics/digital/ey-rise-of-gen-z-new-challenge-for-retailers.pdf

Earley, P. C., & Mosakowski, E. (2000). Creating hybrid team cultures: An empirical test of transnational team functioning. *Academy of Management Journal, 43*, 26–49.

Ede, F. O., Panigrahi, B., Stuart, J., & Calcich, S. (2000). Ethics in small minority businesses. *Journal of Business Ethics, 26*(2), 133–146.

Edmunds, J., & Turner, B. S. (2005). Global generations: social change in the twentieth century. *The British Journal of Sociology, 56*(4), 559–577.

Einolf, C. (2016). Millennials and public service motivation: Findings from a survey of master's degree students. *Public Administration Quarterly, 40*(3), 429–457.

Eisner, S. P. (2005). Managing Generation Y. *SAM Advanced Management Journal, 70*(4), 4.

Elder, G. H. (2018). *Children of the Great Depression*. Routledge.

Ellemers, N., & Jetten, J. (2013). The many ways to be marginal in a group. *Personality and Social Psychology Review, 17*(1), 3–21.

Ellis, J., & Riggle, E. D. B. (1995). The relation of job satisfaction and degree of openness about one's sexual orientation for lesbians and gay men. *Journal of Homosexuality, 30*, 75–85.

Ely, R. J. (2004). A field study of group diversity, participation in diversity education programs, and performance. *Journal of Organizational Behavior, 25*, 755–780.

Ely, R. J., & Thomas, D. A. (2001). Cultural diversity at work: The effects of diversity perspectives on work group processes and outcomes. *Administrative Science Quarterly, 46*, 229–273.

Emerson, T. L., & Conroy, S. J. (2004). Have ethical attitudes changed? An intertemporal comparison of the ethical perceptions of college students in 1985 and 2001. *Journal of Business Ethics, 50*(2), 167–176.

Emerson, T. L., Conroy, S. J., & Stanley, C. W. (2007). Ethical attitudes of accountants: Recent evidence from a practitioners' survey. *Journal of Business Ethics, 71*(1), 73–87.

Emler, N., Renwick, S., & Malone, B. (1983). The relationship between moral reasoning and political orientation. *Journal of Personality and Social Psychology, 45*(5), 1073.

Emler, N., & Stace, K. (1999). What does principled versus conventional moral reasoning convey to others about the politics and psychology of the reasoner? *European Journal of Social Psychology, 29*(4), 455–468.

Emler, N., Tarry, H., & St. James, A. (2007). Principled moral reasoning and reputation. *Journal of Research in Personality, 41*, 76–89.

Erffmeyer, R. C., Keillor, B. D., & LeClair, D. T. (1999). An empirical investigation of Japanese consumer ethics. *Journal of Business Ethics, 18*(1), 35–50.

Ergeneli, A., & Arıkan, S. (2002). Gender differences in ethical perceptions of salespeople: An empirical examination in Turkey. *Journal of Business Ethics, 40*(3), 247–260.

Erickson, T. J. (2008). *Plugged in: The Generation Y guide to thriving at work.* Harvard Business Press.

Ermasova, N., Clark, D., Nguyen, L., & Ermasov, S. (2018). Russian public sector employees' reasoning of ethical behavior: An empirical study. *International Journal of Public Administration, 41*(5–6), 357–376.

Ernst & Young LLP. 2014. Younger managers rise in the rank. Retrieved from: www.ey.com/US/en/Issues/Talent-management/Talent-Survey-The-generational-management-shift

Ertas, N. (2016). Millennials and volunteering: Sector differences and implications for public service motivation theory. *Public Administration Quarterly, 40*(3), 412–428.

Espinoza, C., Ukleja, M., & Rusch, C. (2010). Managing the Millennials: Discover the core competencies for managing today's workforce. John Wiley & Sons.

Esteve, M., Urbig, D., van Witteloostuijn, A., & Boyne, G. (2016). Prosocial behavior and public service motivation. *Public Administration Review, 76*(1), 177–187.

Ethical judgments and intentions: A multinational study of marketing professionals. *Business Ethics, 77*(4), 417–430.

Ethics Resource Center. (2012). *Inside the mind of a whistleblower: A supplemental report of the 2011 national business ethics survey.* Retrieved from http://www.whistleblowers.org/storage/documents/ethicsresourcecentersuvery.pdf

Eweje, G., & Brunton, M. (2010). Ethical perceptions of business students in a New Zealand university: do gender, age and work experience matter? *Business Ethics: A European Review, 19*(1), 95–111.

Exworthy, M., & Halford, S. (Eds.). (1998). *Professionals and the new managerialism.* Open University.

Facer, K., & Furlong, R. (2001) Beyond the myth of the "cyberkid": Young people at the margins of the information revolution. *Journal of Youth Studies, 4*(4), 451–469.

Farazmand, A. (2002). Administrative ethics and professional competence: Accountability and performance under globalization. *International Review of Administrative Sciences, 68*(1), 127–143.

Farazmand, A. (2017). Ethics and accountability in the age of predatory globalization: An impossibility theorem. In C. Jurkiewicz & R. Giacalone (Eds.), *Radical thoughts on ethical leadership.* (pp. 199–220). Information Age Publishing Inc.

Fazekas, M., & King, L. P. (2019). Perils of development funding? The tale of EU funds and grand corruption in Central and Eastern Europe. *Regulation & Governance, 13*(3), 405–430.

Ferlie, E., & Geraghty, K. J. (2005). Professionals in public services organizations: Implications for public sector "reforming." In E. Ferlie, L. E. Lynn, & C. Pollitt (Eds.), *The Oxford Handbook of Public Management* (pp. 422–445). Oxford University Press.

Fern, E. F., & Monroe, K. B. (1996). Effect-size estimates: Issues and problems in interpretation. *Journal of Consumer Research, 23*(2), 89–105.

Fernandez, S., Resh, W. G., Moldogaziev, T., & Oberfield, Z. W. (2015). Assessing the past and promise of the federal employee viewpoint survey for public management research: A research synthesis. *Public Administration Review, 75*(3), 382–394.

Ferrell, O. C., & Gresham, L. G. (1985). A contingency framework for understanding ethical decision-making in marketing. *Journal of Marketing, 49*(3), 87–96.

Ferri-Reed, J. (2013). Quality, conflict, and communication across the generations. *Journal for Quality and Participation, 35*(4), 12–14.

Fishbein, M., & Ajzen, I. (1975). *Belief, attitude, intention and behavior: An introduction to theory and research.* Addison-Wiley Publishing Company.

Fisher, D. G. (1997). Assessing taxpayer moral reasoning: The development of an objective measure. In L. A. Ponemon (Ed.), *Research on accounting ethics* (Vol. 3, pp. 41–71). JAI Press.

Flory, S. M., Phillips, T. J., Jr., Reidenbach, R. E., & Robin, D. P. (1993). A reply to "a comment on a multidimensional analysis of selected ethical issues in accounting." *Accounting Review, 68*, 417–421.

Foldy, E. G. (2002). "Managing" diversity: Identity and power in organizations. In I. Aaltio & A. Mills (Eds.), *Gender, Identity and the Culture of Organizations.* Routledge.

Foldy, E. G. (2004). Learning from diversity: A theoretical exploration. *Public Administration Review, 64*, 529–538.

Ford, R. C., & Richardson, W. D. (1994). Ethical decision-making: A review of the empirical literature. *Journal of Business Ethics, 13*(3), 205–221.

Forrester Research. (2006). North American Consumer Technology Adoption Study (NACTAS). Retrieved July 20, 2020, from https://www.forrester.com/press-newsroom/forrester-research-the-state-of-consumer-technology-adoption/

Forsyth, D. R. (1980). A taxonomy of ethical ideologies. *Journal of Personality and Social Psychology, 39*(1), 175.

Forte, A. (2004). Business ethics: A study of the moral reasoning of selected business managers and the influence of organizational ethical climate. *Journal of Business Ethics, 51*(2), 167–173.

Fraone, J., Hartmann, D., & McNally, K. (2008). The multi-generational workforce: Management implications and strategies for collaboration. Boston, MA, Retrieved July 20, 2020, from https://www.academia.edu/5459278/The_Multi_Generational_Workforce_Management_Implications_and_Strategies_for_Collaboration_Boston_College_Center_for_Work_and_Family_Executive_Briefing_Series

Frederickson, G. (Ed.). (1993) *Ethics and public administration*, M. E. Sharpe.

Frederickson, G. H., & Ghere, R. K. (2005). *Ethics in Public Management*. M. E. Sharpe.

Frink, D. D., Robinson, R. R., Reithel, B., Arthur, M. M., Ammeter, A. A., Ferris, G. R., Kaplan, D. M., & Morrisette, H. S. (2003). Gender demography and organizational performance: A two study investigation with convergence. *Group Organization Management, 28*(1), 127–147.

Fritzsche, D. J., & Becker, H. (1983). Ethical behavior of marketing managers. *Journal of Business Ethics, 2*(4), 291–299.

Fritzsche, D. J., & Becker, H. (1984). Linking management behavior to ethical philosophy—An empirical investigation. *Academy of Management Journal, 27*(1), 166–175.

Fullerton, A. S., & Dixon, J. C. (2010). Generational conflict or methodological artifact? Reconsidering the relationship between age and policy attitudes in the US, 1984–2008. *Public Opinion Quarterly, 74*(4), 643–673.

Fullerton, S., Kerch, K. B., & Dodge, H. R. (1996). Consumer ethics: An assessment of individual behavior in the market place. *Journal of Business Ethics, 15*(7), 805–814.

Furlong, A. (2016). The changing landscape of youth and young adulthood. In A. Furlong (Ed.), *Handbook of Youth and Young Adulthood* (2nd ed., pp. 3–11). Routledge.

Gafni, R., & Geri, N. (2013, February). Generation Y versus Generation X: Differences in smartphone adaptation. In *Learning in the technological era: Proceedings of the Chais conference on instructional technologies research* (pp. 18–23).

Gan, C. (2018). Ethical leadership and unethical employee behavior: A moderated mediation model. *Social Behavior & Personality: An International Journal, 46*(8), 1271–1284.

Gans-Morse, J., Borges, M., Makarin, A., Mannah-Blankson, T., Nickow, A., & Zhang, D. (2018). Reducing bureaucratic corruption: Interdisciplinary perspectives on what works. *World Development, 105*, 171–188.

Garcia-Sanchez, I. M., Rodriguez-Dominguez, L., & Gallego-Alvarez, I. (2011). Effectiveness of ethics codes in the public sphere: Are they useful in controlling corruption? *International Journal of Public Administration, 34*(3), 190–195.

Gazley, B., Chang, W. K., & Bingham, L. B. (2010). Board diversity, stakeholder representation, and collaborative performance in community mediation centers. *Public Administration Review, 70*(4), 610–620.

Gelfand, M. J., Erez, M., & Aycan, Z. (2007). Cross-cultural organizational behavior. *Annual Review of Psychology, 58*(1), 479–514.

Gelso, B. R., & Peterson, J. M. (2005). The influence of ethical attitudes on the demand for environmental recreation: Incorporating lexicographic preferences. *Ecological Economics, 53*(1), 35–45.

Gentile, M. (1994). *Differences that work: Organizational excellence through diversity.* Harvard Business Press.

Giarla, V. (2019). *Generational social media: How social media influences the online and in-person relationships of Gen X, Gen Y and Gen Z.* [Honors Thesis, Salem State University].

Gibbs, J. C., Widaman, K. F., & Colby, A. (1982). *Social intelligence: Measuring the development of sociomoral reflection.* Prentice-Hall.

Gilleard, C., & Higgs, P. (2005). *Contexts of ageing: Class, cohort and community.* Cambridge Polity Press.

Giulietti, C., Tonin, M., & Vlassopoulos, M. (2019). Racial discrimination in local public services: A field experiment in the United States. *Journal of the European Economic Association, 17*(1), 165–204.

Glass, A. (2007). Understanding generational differences for competitive success. *Industrial and Commercial Training, 39*(2), 98–103.

Gordon, K. (2014). Marketing to Millennials. *ANGUS Journal*, 48–49.

Gorsira, M., Steg, L., Denkers, A., & Huisman, W. (2018). Corruption in organizations: Ethical climate and individual motives. *Administrative Sciences, 8*(1), 4–22.

Gould-Williams, J., & Davies, F. (2005). Using social exchange theory to predict the effects of HRM practice on employee outcomes: An analysis of public sector workers. *Public Management Review, 7*, 1–24.

Grabosky, P. N., & Rosenbloom, D. H. (1975). Racial and ethnic integration in the federal service. *Social Science Quarterly, 56*(1), 71–84.

Green, D. (2008). Knowledge management for a postmodern workforce: Rethinking leadership styles in the public sector. *Journal of Strategic Leadership, 1*(1), 16–24.

Groeneveld, S. (2011). Diversity and employee turnover in the Dutch public sector. Does diversity management make a difference? *International Journal of Public Sector Management, 24*, 594–612.

Groeneveld, S., & Van de Walle, S. (2010). A contingency approach to representative bureaucracy: Power, equal opportunities and diversity. *International Review of Administrative Sciences, 76*, 239–258.

Groeneveld, S., & Verbeek, S. (2012). Diversity policies in public and private sector organizations. An empirical comparison of incidence and effectiveness. *Review of Public Personnel Administration, 32*, 353–381.

Gueras, D., & Garofalo, C. (2005). *Practical Ethics in Public Administration* (2nd ed.). Management Concepts.

Guillén, M., Melé, D., & Murphy, P. (2002). European vs. American approaches to institutionalization of business ethics: The Spanish case. *Business Ethics: A European Review, 11*(2), 167–178.

Gumpert, G., & Cathcart, R. (1985). Media grammars, generations, and media gaps. *Critical Studies in Media Communication, 2*, 23–35.

Gursoy, D., Chi, C. G.-Q., & Karadag, E. (2013). Generational differences in work values and attitudes among frontline and service contact employees. *International Journal of Hospitality Management, 32*, 40–48.

Gursoy, D., Maier, T. A., & Chi, C. G. (2008). Generational differences: An examination of work values and generational gaps in the hospitality workforce. *International Journal of Hospitality Management, 27*(3), 448–458.

Haeger, D. L., & Lingham, T. (2014). A trend toward work–life fusion: A multi-generational shift in technology use at work. *Technological Forecasting and Social Change, 89*, 316–325.

Hammill, G. (2005). Mixing and managing four generations of employees. *FDU Magazine Online* Winter/Spring. Retrieved from http://www.fdu.edu/newspubs/magazine/05ws/generations.htm

Hankivsky, O., & Renee, C. (2011). Intersectionality and public policy: Some lessons from existing models. *Political Research Quarterly, 64*(1), 217–229.

Hannam, S. E., & Yordi, B. (2011). *Engaging a multi-generational workforce: Practical advice for government managers*. IBM Center for the Business of Government.

Haq, R. (2004). International perspectives on workplace diversity. In M. Stockdale & F. J. Crosby (Eds.), *The psychology and management of workplace diversity* (pp. 31–51). Blackwell.

Harasymiw, B. (2019). Civil society as an anti-corruption actor in post-Euromaidan Ukraine. *Canadian Slavonic Papers, 61*(3), 288–320.

Harber, J. G. (2011). *Generations in the workplace: Similarities and differences* (Paper 1255), [Electronic Theses and Dissertations, East Tennessee State University].

Harcourt, M., Lam, H., & Harcourt, S. (2005). Discriminatory practices in hiring: institutional and rational economic practices. *International Journal of Human Resource Management, 16*(11), 2113–2132.

Hargittai, E. (2010). Digital Na(t)ives? Variation in internet skills and uses among members of the "Net Generation." *Sociological Inquiry, 80*, 92–113.

Hargittai, E., Fullerton, L., Menchen-Trevino, E., & Thomas, K. Y. (2010). Trust online: Young adults' evaluation of web content. *International Journal of Communication, 4*, 27.

Hargittai, E., and Hinnart, A. (2008) Digital inequality: Differences in young adults use of the Internet. *Communication Research, 35*(5), 602–621.

Harris, J. R. (1991). Ethical values and decision processes of business and non-business students: A four-group study. *The Journal of Legal Studies Education, 9*, 215–230.

Harrison, D. A., Price, K. H., Gavin, J. H., & Florey, A. T. (2002). Time, teams, and task performance: Changing effects of surface- and deep-level diversity on group functioning. *Academy of Management Journal, 45*, 1029–1045.

Harrison, R. (1973). Choosing the depth of organizational intervention. In F. Kast & J. Rosenzweig (Eds.), *Contingency views of organization and management* (pp. 238–254). Social Research Associates Inc.

Hartikainen, O., & Torstila, S. (2004). Job-related ethical judgment in the finance profession. *Journal of Applied Finance, 14*(1), 62–76.

Hassan, S., Mahsud, R., Yukl, G., & Prussia, G. E. (2013). Ethical and empowering leadership. *Journal of Managerial Psychology, 28*(2), 133–146.

Hassen, S., Wright, B. E., & Yuki, G. (2014). Does ethical leadership matter in government? Effects on organizational commitment, absenteeism, and willingness to report ethical problems. *Public Administration Review, 74*(3), 333–343.

Hayes, B. R. (2013). The implications of multigenerational differences within the workforce. *Research Papers. Paper 407*, 1–48. Retrieved from https://opensiuc.lib.siu.edu/cgi/viewcontent.cgi?article=1521&context=gs_rp

Hayibor, S., & Wasieleski, D. M. (2009). Effects of the use of the availability heuristic on ethical decision-making in organizations. *Journal of Business Ethics, 84*(1), 151–165.

Hays-Thomas, R. (2004). Why now? The contemporary focus on managing diversity. In M. Stockdale & F. J. Crosby (Eds.), *The psychology and management of workplace diversity* (pp. 3–30). Blackwell.

Hebson, G., Grimshaw, D., & Marchington, M. (2003). PPPs and the changing public sector ethos: Case study evidence from the health and local authority sectors. *Work, Employment and Society, 17*(3), 481–501.

Heidenheimer, A. J., Johnston, M., & Levine, V. T. (Eds.). (1989). *Political Corruption: A Handbook.* Transaction Publishers.

Helsper, E. J., & Eynon, R. (2010). Digital natives: Where is the evidence? *British Educational Research Journal, 36*, 503–520.

Hendricks, J. M., & Cope, V. C. (2012). Generational diversity. What nurse managers need to know. *Journal of Advanced Nursing, 69*(3), 717–725.

Herek, G. M. (1990). The context of anti-gay violence: Notes on cultural and psychological heterosexism. *Journal of Interpersonal Violence, 5*, 316–333.

Herington, C., & Weaven, S. (2008). Improving consistency for DIT results using cluster analysis. *Journal of Business Ethics, 80*(3), 499–514.

Herndon, N. C., Fraedrich, J. P., & Yeh, Q. J. (2001). An investigation of moral values and the ethical content of the corporate culture: Taiwanese versus US sales people. *Journal of Business Ethics, 30*(1), 73–85.

Herring, C. (2009). Does diversity pay? Race, gender, and the business case for diversity. *American Sociological Review, 74*(2), 208–224.

Heskett, J. (2007) How will Millennials manage? Working knowledge newsletter. Retrieved July 20, 2020, from https://hbswk.hbs.edu/item/how-will-millennials-manage

Higgs-Kleyn, N. H. (1998). Unethical consumer behavior: An exploratory investigation. *Management Dynamics, 7*(1), 35–52.

Hill, R. (2002). Managing across generations in the 21st century: Important lessons from the ivory trenches. *Journal of Management Enquiry, 11*(1), 60–72.

Ho, J. A. (2010). Ethical perception: Are differences between ethnic groups situation dependent? *Business Ethics: A European Review, 19*(2), 154–182.

Holman, M. R. (2014). *Women in politics in the American city*. Temple University Press.

Holzer, H., & Neumark, D. (2000). What does affirmative action do? *Industrial & Labor Relations Review, 53*, 240–271.

Homan, A., Van Knippenberg, D., Van Kleef, G., & De Dreu, C. (2007). Bridging faultlines by valuing diversity: Diversity beliefs, information elaboration, and performance in diverse work groups. *Journal of Applied Psychology, 92*(5), 1189–1199.

Honeycutt, E. D., Glassman, M., Zugelder, M. T., & Karande, K. (2001). Determinants of ethical behavior: A study of autosalespeople. *Journal of Business Ethics, 32*(1), 69–79.

Horwitz, S. K. (2005). The compositional impact of team diversity on performance: Theoretical considerations. *Human Resource Development Review, 4*(2), 219–245.

Howe, N., & Strauss, W. (2000). *Millennials rising: The next great generation*. Random House.

Huberts, L. L., Kaptein, M. M., & Lasthuizen, K. K. (2007). A study of the impact of three leadership styles on integrity violations committed by police officers. *Policing: An International Journal of Police Strategies & Management, 30*(4), 587–607.

Hunt, S. D., & Vasquez-Parraga, A. Z. (1993). Organizational consequences, marketing ethics, and salesforce supervision. *Journal of Marketing Research, 30*(1), 78–90.

Hunt, S. D., & Vitell, S. J. (1986). A general theory of marketing ethics. *Journal of Macromarketing, 6*(1), 5–16.

Hunt, S. D., & Vitell, S. J. (1993). The general theory of marketing ethics: A retrospective and revision. *Ethics in Marketing, 26*, 775–784.

Hunt, S. D., and Vitell, S. J. (2005). Personal moral codes and the Hunt-Vitell theory of ethics: Why do people's ethical judgments differ? In R. A. Peterson & O. C. Ferrell (Eds.), *Business ethics: New challenges for business schools and corporate leaders* (pp. 18–37). M. E. Sharpe Inc.

Hunt, S. D., & Vitell, S. J. (2006). The general theory of marketing ethics: A revision and three questions. *Journal of Macromarketing, 26*(2), 143–153.

Igel, C., & Urquhart, V. (2012). Generation Z, meet cooperative learning: Properly implemented cooperative learning strategies can increase student engagement and achievement. *Middle School Journal, 43*(4), 16–21.

Infeld, D. L., & Adams, W. C. (2011). MPA and MPP students: Twins, siblings, or distant cousins? *Journal of Public Affairs Education, 17*(2), 277–303.

IPSOS MORI (July 2018). Beyond binary. The lives and choices of Generation Z. Retrieved July 20, 2020, from https://www.ipsos.com/it-it/beyond-binary-lives-and-choices-generation-z.

Ireni-Saban, L. (2015). Understanding the obligations of codes of ethics. In J. Perry and R. Christensen (Eds.), *Handbook of Public Administration* (3rd ed.). Jossey-Bass.

Ismail, S., & Ghazali, N. A. M. (2011). Ethical ideology and ethical judgments of accounting practitioners in Malaysia. *Gadjah Mada International Journal of Business, 13*(2), 107–123.

Ivancevich, J. M., & Gilbert, J. A. (2000). Diversity management. Time for a new approach. *Public Personnel Management, 29*(1), 75–92.

Jackson, S. E., & Joshi, A. (2004). Diversity in a social context: a multi-attribute, multi-level analysis of team diversity and sales performance. *Journal of Organizational Behavior,* 25, 675–702.

Jackson, S. E., Joshi, A., & Erhardt, N. L. 2003. Recent research on team and organizational diversity: SWOT analysis and implications. *Journal of Management*, 29, 801–830.

Jain, H. C., Horwitz, F., & Wilkin, C. L. (2012). Employment equity in Canada South Africa: A comparative review. *International Journal of Human Resource Management*, 23(1), 1–17.

Jamie, B. (2018). *The care and feeding of your young employee: A manager's guide to Millennials and Gen Z.* Create Space Independent Publishing Platform.

Jansen, W. S., Otten, S., & Van der Zee, K. I. (2015). Being part of diversity. The effects of an all-inclusive multicultural diversity approach on majority members' perceived inclusion and support for organizational diversity efforts. *Group Processes & Intergroup Relations, 18*, 817–832.

Jehn, K. A., & Bezrukova, K. (2004). A field study of group diversity, workgroup context, and performance. *Journal of Organizational Behavior, 25*, 703–729.

Jehn, K. A., Northcraft, G., & Neale, M. (1999). Why differences make a difference: A field study of diversity, conflict, and performance in workgroups. *Administrative Science Quarterly, 44*(4), 741–763.

Jenkins, J. (2008). Strategies for managing talent in a multigenerational workforce. *Employment Relations Today, 34*(4), 19–26.

Jenkins, J. (2019). Leading the four generations at work. Retrieved from: https://www.amanet.org/articles/leading-the-four-generations-at-work/

Jilke, S., Van Dooren, W., & Rys, S. (2018). Discrimination and administrative burden in public service markets: Does a public–private difference exist? *Journal of Public Administration Research and Theory, 28*(3), 423–439.

Johnson, C. E. (2009). *Meeting the ethical challenges of leadership: Casting light or shadow*. SAGE Publications.

Johnson, M., & Johnson, L. (2010). *Generations, Inc.* AMACOM.

Jones, D., Pringle, J. K., & Shepherd, D. (2000). Managing diversity meets Aotearoa/New Zealand. *Personnel Review, 29*(3), 364–380.

Jones, J. L., & Middleton, K. L. (2007). Ethical decision-making by consumers: The roles of product harm and consumer vulnerability. *Journal of Business Ethics, 70*(3), 247–264.

Jones, J., Massey, D. W., & Thorne, L. (2003). Auditors' ethical reasoning: Insights from past research and implications for the future. *Journal of Accounting Literature, 22*, 45–103.

Jones, T. M. (1991). Ethical decision-making by individuals in organizations: An issue-contingent model. *Academy of Management Review, 16*(2), 366–395.

Jordan, J. (2007). Taking the first step toward a moral action: A review of moral sensitivity measurement across domains. *The Journal of Genetic Psychology, 168*(3), 323–359.

Joshi, A., Dencker, J. C., & Franz, G. (2011). Generations in organizations. *Research in Organizational Behavior, 31*, 177–205.

Kahn, K. F. (1994). Does gender make a difference? An experimental examination of sex stereotypes and press patterns in statewide campaigns. *American Journal of Political Science, 38*(1), 162–195.

Kamenou, N., Netto, G., & Fearfull, A. (2013). Ethnic minority women in the Scottish labour market: Employers' perceptions. *British Journal of Management, 24*(3), 398–413.

Kamp, A., & Hagedorn-Rasmussen, P. (2004). Diversity management in a Danish context: Towards a multicultural or segregated working life? *Economic and Industrial Democracy, 25*(4), 535–554.

Kane, S. (2010). *Generation Y*. Retrieved July 15, 2020, from: http://legalcareers.about.com/od/practicetips/a/GenerationY.htm

Kaptein, M. (2019). The moral entrepreneur: A new component of ethical leadership. *Journal of Business Ethics, 156*(4), 1135–1150.

Kaptein, M., & Wempe, J. F. D. B. (2002). *The balanced company: A theory of corporate integrity*. Oxford University Press.

Karacaer, S., Gohar, R., Aygün, M., & Sayin, C. (2009). Effects of personal values on auditor's ethical decisions: A comparison of Pakistani and Turkish professional auditors. *Journal of Business Ethics, 88*(1), 53–64.

Karafantis, D. M., Pierre-Louis, J., & Lewandowski, G. W. J. (2010). A comparison of the multicultural and colorblind perspectives on the intergroup attitudes of college students. *Journal of Human Behavior in the Social Environment, 20*(5), 688–710.

Karakowsky, L., McBey, K., & Chuang, Y. (2004). Perceptions of team performance: The impact of group composition and task-based cues. *Journal of Managerial Psychology, 19*(5), 506–525.

Karcher, J. N. (1996). Auditors' ability to discern the presence of ethical problems. *Journal of Business Ethics, 15*(10), 1033–1050.

Kast, F., & Rosenzweig, J. (1973). Contingency views of organization and management. *The Academy of Management Review, 3*(3), 413–427.

Kearney, E., & Gebert, D. (2009). Managing diversity and enhancing team outcomes: The promise of transformational leadership. *Journal of Applied Psychology, 94*, 77–89.

Kellough, J. E. (1990). Federal agencies and affirmative action for Blacks and women. *Social Science Quarterly, 77*(1), 83–92.

Kellough, J. E., & Naff, K. C. (2004). Responding to a wake-up call: An examination of federal agency diversity management programs. *Administration & Society, 36*, 62–90.

Kernaghan, K. (2003). Integrating values into public service: The values statement as centerpiece. *Public Administration Review, 63*(6), 711–719.

Kidwell, J. M., Stevens, R. E., & Bethke, A. L. (1987). Differences in ethical perceptions between male and female managers: Myth or reality? *Journal of Business Ethics, 6*(6), 489–493.

Kim, G. H., Trimi, S., & Chung, J. H. (2014). Big-data applications in the government sector. *Communications of the ACM, 57*(3), 78–85.

Kim, S. (2006). Public service motivation and organizational citizenship behavior in Korea. *International Journal of Manpower, 27*(8), 722–740.

Kim, S. (2012). Does person-organization fit matter in the public sector? Testing the mediating effect of person-organization fit in the relationship between public service motivation and work attitudes. *Public Administration Review, 72*, 830–840.

Kim, S., & Vandenabeele, W. (2010). A strategy for building public service motivation research internationally. *Public Administration Review, 70*, 701–709.

Kim, Y. (2003). Ethical standards and ideology among Korean public relations practitioners. *Journal of Business Ethics, 42*(3), 209–223.

Kimbrough, A. M., Guadagno, R. E., Muscanell, N. L., & Dill, J. (2013). Gender differences in mediated communication: Women connect more than do men. *Computers in Human Behavior, 29*(3), 896–900.

Kirby, E. L., & Harter, L. M. (2003). Speaking the language of the bottom line: The metaphor of "Managing Diversity." *Journal of Business Communication, 40*(1), 28–49.

Kirchmeyer, C., & Cohen, A. (1992). Multicultural groups: their performance and reactions with constructive conflict. *Group & Organization Management, 17*, 153–170.

Kirkman, B. L., Tesluk, P. E., & Rosen, B. (2004). The impact of demographic heterogeneity and team leader-team member demographic fit on team empowerment and effectiveness. *Group and Organization Management, 29*, 334–368.

Kirkpatrick, S., Gelatt, C. D., & Vecchi, M. P. (1983) *Science, New Series, 220*(4598), 671–680.

Kjeldsen, A. M. (2014). Dynamics of public service motivation: Attraction-selection and socialization in the production and regulation of social services. *Public Administration Review, 74*(1), 101–112.

Klawitter, M. M., & Flatt, V. (1998). The effects of state and local antidiscrimination policies on earnings for gays and lesbians. *Journal of Policy Analysis and Management, 17*, 658–686.

Kleiser, S. B., Sivadas, E., Kellaris, J. J., & Dahlstrom, R. F. (2003). Ethical ideologies: Efficient assessment and influence on ethical judgments of marketing practices. *Psychology & Marketing, 20*(1), 1–21.

Kochan, T. A., Bezrukova, K., Ely, R., Jackson, S., Joshi, A., Jehn, K. E., Leonard, Levine, D., & Thomas, D. (2003). The effects of diversity on business performance. *Human Resource Management, 42*(1), 3–21.

Kohlberg, L. (1964). Development of moral character and moral ideology. In M. L. Hoffman & L. W. Hoffman (Eds.), *Review of child development research.* (pp. 383–432). Russell Sage Foundation.

Kohlberg, L. (1969). Stages and sequences: the cognitive development approach to socialization. In D. A. Goslin (Ed.), *Handbook of socialization theory and research* (pp. 346–480). Rand McNally.

Kohlberg, L. (1981). *Essays in moral development: The philosophy of moral development*, Harper and Row.

Kohlberg, L., & Candee, D. (1984). The relationship of moral judgment to moral action. In W. M. Kurtines & J. L. Gewirtz (Eds.), *Morality, moral behaviour and moral development* (pp. 52–72). Wiley.

Kolodinsky, J., Cranwell, M., & Rowe, E. (2002). Bridging the generation gap across the digital divide: Teens teaching internet skills to senior citizens. *Journal of Extension, 40*(3).

Kołomycew, A., & Kotarba, B. (2017). Leadership style, political interest and rationality of municipal executive bodies in the implementation of public policies: The case of Poland. *Challenges of the Future, 2*(8), 121–136.

Konrad, A. (2003). Defining the domain of workplace diversity scholarship. *Group and Organization Management, 28*(1), 4–17.

Konrad, A. M., & Linnehan, F. (1995). Formalized HRM structures: Coordinating equal employment opportunity or concealing organizational practices? *Academy of Management Journal, 38*, 787–820.

Kooij, D. T., Jansen, P. G., Dikkers, J. S., & De Lange, A. H. (2010). The influence of age on the associations between HR practices and both affective commitment and job satisfaction: A meta analysis. *Journal of Organizational Behavior, 31*, 1111–1136.

Kossek, E. E., Lobel, S. A., & Brown, A. J. (2005). Human resource strategies to manage workforce diversity. In A. M. Konrad, P. Prasad, & J. K. Pringle (Eds.), *Handbook of workplace diversity*. SAGE Publications.

Koutropolulos, A. (2011). Digital natives: Ten years after. *Journal of Online Learning and Teaching*, 7. Retrieved July 20, 2020, from http://jolt.merlot.org/vol7no4/koutropoulos_1211.htm

Kouzes, J. M., & Posner, B. Z. (2012). *The leadership challenge: How to make extraordinary things happen in organizations*. Jossey-Bass.

Krahn, H. J., & Galambos, N. L. (2014). Work values and beliefs of "Generation X" and "Generation Y." *Journal of Youth Studies, 17*, 92–112.

Kravitz, D. A. (2003). More women in the workplace: Is there a payoff in firm performance? *Academy of Management Perspectives, 17*, 148–149.

Kuhl, J. S. (2014). Investing in Millennials for the future of your organization. *Leader to Leader, 2014*(71), 25–30.

Kulkarni, M., & Lengnick-Hall, M. L. (2011). Socialization of people with disabilities in the workplace. *Human Resource Management, 50*(4), 521–540.

Kupperschmidt, B. R. (2000). Multigeneration employees: strategies for effective management. *The Health Care Manager, 19*, 65–76.

Laczniak, G. R., & Inderrieden, E. J. (1987). The influence of stated organizational concern upon ethical decision-making. *Journal of Business Ethics,* 6(4), 297–307.

Lancaster, L. C., & Stillman, D. (2003). *When generations collide: Who they are, why they clash, how to solve the generational puzzle at work*. Harper Business.

Landry, R., Moyes, G. D., & Cortes, A. C. (2004). Ethical perceptions among Hispanic students: Differences by major and gender. *Journal of Education for Business, 80*(2), 102–108.

Lanier, K. (2017). 5 things HR professionals need to know about Generation Z: Thought leaders share their views on the HR profession and its direction for the future. *Strategic HR Review, 16*(6), 288–290.

Lapoint, P. A., & Liprie-Spence, A. (2017). Employee engagement: Generational differences in the workforce. *Journal of Organizational Psychology, 17*(5).

Latan, H., Jabbour, C. J. C., & de Sousa Jabbour, A. B. L. (2019). Ethical awareness, ethical judgment and whistleblowing: A moderated mediation analysis. *Journal of Business Ethics, 155*(1), 289–304.

Lawton, A. 1998. *Ethical Management for the public services*. Open University Press.

Lawton, A., & Doig, A. (2005). Researching ethics for public service organizations: The view from Europe. *Public Integrity, 8*(1), 11–33.

Lee, C., & Farh, J. (2004). Joint effects of group efficacy and gender diversity on group cohesion and performance. *Applied Psychology: An International Review*, *53*(1), 136–154.

Leisink, P., & Steijn, B. (2009). Public service motivation and job performance of public sector employees in the Netherlands. *International Review of Administrative Sciences*, *75*(1), 53–78.

Leitsch, D. L. (2004). Differences in the perceptions of moral intensity in the moral decision process: An empirical examination of accounting students. *Journal of Business Ethics*, *53*(3), 313–323.

Leitsch, D. L. (2006). Using dimensions of moral intensity to predict ethical decision-making in accounting. *Accounting Education: An International Journal*, *15*(2), 135–149.

Lenhart, A., Purcell, K., Smith, A., & Zickuhr, K. (2010). Social media & mobile internet use among teens and young adults. *Pew Research Center.* Available at: https://www.researchgate.net/publication/286376855_Social_Media_Mobile_Internet_Use_Among_Teens_and_Young_Adults

Leopold, R., & Moore, J. (2019). *Benefits offerings for a multigenerational workforce.* Available at: https://www.lockton.com/whitepapers/Benefits_offerings_for_a_multigenerational_workforce_Leopold_Moore.pdf

Leung, L. (2013). Generational differences in content generation in social media: The roles of the gratifications sought and of narcissism. *Computers in Human Behavior*, *29*(3), 997–1006.

Levin, A. M., Dato-on, M. C., & Rhee, K. (2004). Money for nothing and hits for free: The ethics of downloading music from peer-to-peer web sites. *Journal of Marketing Theory and Practice*, *12*(1), 48–60.

Levin, S., Matthews, M., Guimond, S., Sidanius, J., Pratto, F., Kteily, N., Pitpitan, V. E., & Dover, T. (2012). Assimilation, multiculturalism, and colorblindness: Mediated and moderated relationships between social dominance orientation and prejudice. *Journal of Experimental Social Psychology*, *48*(1), 207–212.

Lewis, C. W., & Catron, B. L. (1996). Professional standards and ethics. *Handbook of Public Administration*, *2*, 699–712.

Lewis, C. W., & Gilman, S. C. (2012). *The ethics challenge in public service.* Jossey-Bass.

Lewis, G. B. (1996). Gender integration of occupations in the federal civil service: Extent and effects on male-female earnings. *Industrial and Labor Relations Review*, *49*(3), 472–483.

Lewis, G. B., & Allee, C. L. (1992). The impact of disabilities on federal career success. *Public Administration Review*, *52*(4), 389–397.

Lewis, G. B., & Cho, Y. J. (2011). The aging of the state government workforce: Trends and implications. *The American Review of Public Administration*, *41*(1), 48–60.

LifeCourse website (established by Strauss and Howe). Retrieved from: https://www.lifecourse.com/about/method/phases.html

Lilly, J., Duffy, J. A., & WIpawayangkool, K. (2016). The impact of ethical climate on organizational trust and the role of business performance: If business performance increases, does ethical climate still matter? *Journal of Behavioral & Applied Management, 17*(1), 33–49.

Lim Choi, D. (2006). Moral reasoning in public service: Individual, organizational, and societal determinants. *International Review of Public Administration, 11*(1), 35–45.

Lim Choi, D., & Perry, J. L. (2010). Developing a tool to measure ethical sensitivity in public administration and its application. *International Review of Public Administration, 14*(3), 1–12.

Linnes, C., & Metcalf, B. (2017). iGeneration and their acceptance of technology. *International Journal of Management & Information Systems* (*IJMIS*), *21*(2), 11–26.

Litt, E. (2013). Measuring users' internet skills: A review of past assessments and a look toward the future. *New Media & Society, 15*, 612–630.

Livingstone, S., & Helsper, E. (2007). Gradations in digital inclusion: Children, young people and the digital divide. *New Media & Society, 9*, 671–696.

Livingstone, S. (2003). Children's use of the internet: Reflections on the emerging research agenda. *New Media & Society, 5*(2), 147–166.

Loden, M., & Rosener, J. B. (1991). *Workforce America!: Managing employee diversity as a vital resource*. McGraw-Hill.

Loe, T. W., Ferrell, L., & Mansfield, P. (2000). A review of empirical studies assessing ethical decision-making in business. *Journal of Business Ethics, 25*(3), 185–204.

Lofquist, L., & Dawis, R. V. (1969). *Adjustment to work*. Appleton Century Crofts.

Longenecker, J. G., McKinney, J. A., & Moore, C. W. (1989). Ethics in small business. *Journal of Small Business Management, 27*(1), 27–31.

Loo, R. (2001). Encouraging classroom discussion of ethical dilemmas in research management: Three vignettes. *Teaching Business Ethics, 5*, 195–212.

Loo, R. (2002). Tackling ethical dilemmas in project management using vignettes. *International Journal of Project Management, 20*(7), 489–495.

Lorsch, J. (1973). Introduction to the structural design of organizations. In F. Kast & J. Rosenzweig (Eds.), *Contingency views of organization and management* (pp. 179–194). Social Research Associates Inc.

Lovell, A. (1997). Some thoughts on Kohlberg's hierarchy of moral reasoning and its relevance for accounting theories of control. *Accounting Education, 6*(2), 147–162.

Lozano, J. F., & Escrich, T. (2017). Cultural diversity in business: A critical reflection on the ideology of tolerance. *Journal of Business Ethics, 142*(4), 679–696.

Lu, L-J., & Lu, C-J. (2009). Moral philosophy, materialism and consumer ethics: An exploratory study in Indonesia. *Journal of Business Ethics, 94*, 193–210.

Luppicini, R. (2005). A systems definition of educational technology in society. *Educational Technology and Society, 8*(3), 103–109.

Luthans, F., & Stewart, T. (1977). A general contingency theory of management. *Academy of Management Review, 2*(2), 181–195.

Lyons, M., LaVelle, K., & Smith, D. (2017). Gen Z rising. Accenture. Retrieved July 20, 2020, from https://www.accenture.com/_acnmedia/pdf-50/accenture-strategy-workforce-gen-z-rising-pov.pdf

Lyons, S. T., & Schweitzer, L. (2017). A qualitative exploration of generational identity: Making sense of young and old in the context of today's workplace. *Work, Aging and Retirement, 3*(2), 209–224.

Lyons, S., & Kuron, L. (2014). Generational differences in the workplace: A review of the evidence and directions for future research. *Journal of Organizational Behavior, 35*(1), 139–157.

Macaulay, M., & Lawton, A. (2006). From virtue to competence: Changing the principles of public service. *Public Administration Review, 66*(5), 702–710.

Madden, C. (2017). *Hello Gen Z: Engaging the generation of post-Millennials.* Hello Clarity.

Madden, M. (2010). Older adults and social media. Pew Research Center. Retrieved July 20, 2020, from https://www.pewinternet.org/2010/08/27/older-adults-and-social-media/

Maesschalck, J. (2004). The impact of new public management reforms on public servants' ethics: Towards a theory. *Public Administration, 82*, 465–489.

Maier, T. A. (2011). Hospitality leadership implications: Multigenerational perceptions of dissatisfaction and intent to leave. *Journal of Human Resources in Hospitality & Tourism, 10*(4), 354–371.

Malloy, E. (2012). Gen Y, and on to Z. *Foreign Service Journal, 89*(10), 28–41.

Malo, M. A., & Pagán, R. (2012). Wage differentials and disability across Europe: Discrimination and/or lower productivity. *International Labour Review, 151*(1–2), 43–60.

Malomo, F., & Sena, V. (2017). Data intelligence for local government? Assessing the benefits and barriers to use of big data in the public sector. *Policy & Internet, 9*(1), 7–27.

Mannheim, K. (1952). The problem of generation. In *Essays on the sociology of knowledge* (pp. 276–320). Routledge.

Mannix, E., & Neale, M. A. (2005). What differences make a difference? *Psychological Science in the Public Interest, 6*, 31–55.

Marques, P. A., & Azevedo-Pereira, J. (2009). Ethical ideology and ethical judgments in the Portuguese accounting profession. *Journal of Business Ethics, 86*(2), 227–242.

Marta, J., Singhapakdi, A., & Kraft, K. (2008). Personal characteristics underlying ethical decisions in marketing situations: A survey of small business managers. *Journal of Small Business Management, 46*(4), 589–606.

Martin, C. A. (2005). From high maintenance to high productivity: What managers need to know about Generation Y. *Industrial and Commercial Training, 37*(1), 39–44.

Martin, C., and Tulgan, B. (2006). Managing the generation mix (2nd ed.) (HRD Press). https://downloads.hrdpressonline.com/files/7320080417162646.pdf

Massey, D. (2002). The importance of context in investigating auditors' moral abilities. *Research on Accounting Ethics, 8*(2), 195–247.

Mavin, S., Grandy, G., & Williams, J. (2014). Experiences of women elite leaders doing gender: Intra-gender micro-violence between women. *British Journal of Management, 25*(3), 439–455.

Mayer, D., Kuenzi, M., & Greenbaum, R. (2010). Examining the link between ethical leadership and employee misconduct: The mediating role of ethical climate. *Journal of Business Ethics, 95*, 7–16.

Mayer, G. (2014). *Selected characteristics of private and public sector workers.* Congressional Research Service.

McCormick, K. (2007). The evolution of workplace diversity. State Bar of Texas. Available at: http://www.texasbarcle.com/Materials/Events/6369/4079_01.pdf

McCourt, D. M. (2012). The "problem of generations" revisited: Karl Mannheim and the sociology of knowledge in international relations. In *Theory and application of the "generation" in international relations and politics* (pp. 47–70). Palgrave Macmillan.

McCourt, W. (2001). Moving the public management debate forward: A contingency approach. In W. McCourt & M. Minogue (Eds.), *The internationalization of public management: Reinventing the third world state.* Edward Elgar.

McDermott, M. L. (2016). *Masculinity, femininity, and American political behavior.* Oxford University Press.

McGrandle, J. (2017). Understanding diversity management in the public sector: A case for contingency theory. *International Journal of Public Administration, 40*(6), 526–537.

McKay, P. A., Avery, D. R., & Morris, M. A. (2008). Mean racial-ethnic differences in employee sales performance: The moderating role of diversity climate. *Personnel Psychology, 61*(2), 349–374.

McKay, P. F., & Avery, D. R. (2006). What has race got to do with it? Unraveling the role of racioethnicity in job seekers' reactions to site visits. *Personnel Psychology, 59*, 395–429.

McKay, P. F., & McDaniel, C. (2006). A reexamination of Black-White differences in work performance: More data, more moderators. *Journal of Applied Psychology, 91*(3), 538–554.

McKinnon, R. (2010). An ageing workforce and strategic human resource management: Staffing challenges for social security administrations. *International Social Security Review*, *63*(3–4), 91–113.

McLeod, P. L., Lobel, S., & Cox, T. H. (1996). Ethnic diversity and creativity in small groups. *Small Group Research*, *27*(2), 248–264.

McMahon, J. M. (2002). *An analysis of the factor structure of the multidimensional ethics scale and a perceived moral intensity scale, and the effect of moral intensity on ethical judgment* [Doctoral dissertation, Virginia Tech].

Meehan, M. (2016). The next generation: What matters to Gen We. Retrieved July 20, 2020, from https://www.forbes.com/sites/marymeehan/2016/08/11/the-next-generation-what-matters-to-gen-we/?sh=bf41c6373500

Meier, K. J. (1975). Representative bureaucracy: An empirical analysis. *The American Political Science Review*, *69*(2), 526–542.

Meier, K. J., & Nigro, L. G. (1976). Representative bureaucracy and policy preferences: A study in the attitudes of federal executives. *Public Administration Review*, *36*(4), 458–469.

Meister, J. C., & Willyerd, K. (2010). *The 2020 workplace*. Harper Collins Publishers.

Mencl, J., & Lester, S. W. (2014). More alike than different: What generations value and how the values affect employee workplace perceptions. *Journal of Leadership & Organizational Studies*, *21*, 257–272.

Mengüç, B. (1998). Organizational consequences, marketing ethics and salesforce supervision: Further empirical evidence. *Journal of Business Ethics*, *17*(4), 333–352.

Menzel, D. C. (2005). Research on ethics and integrity in governance. *Public Integrity*, *7*, 147–168.

Meriac, J. P., Woehr, D. J., & Banister, C. (2010). Generational differences in work ethic: An examination of measurement equivalence across three cohorts. *Journal of Business and Psychology*, *25*(2), 315–324.

Merritt, S. (1991). Marketing ethics and education: Some empirical findings. *Journal of Business Ethics*, *10*(8), 625–632.

Meyer-Sahling, J. H., Mikkelsen, K. S., & Schuster, C. (2019). The causal effect of public service motivation on ethical behavior in the public sector: Evidence from a large-scale survey experiment. *Journal of Public Administration Research and Theory*, *29*(3), 445–459.

Meyer-Sahling, J. H., Schuster, C., & Mikkelsen, S. (2019). *Civil service management in developing countries: What works? Evidence from a survey with 23,000 civil servants in Africa, Asia, Eastern Europe and Latin America.* London: Report prepared for the UK-Department for International Development (DFID).

Milakovich, M. E., & Gordon, G. J. (2012). *Public administration in America.* Wadsworth Publishing Company.

Milliken, F., & Martins, L. (1996). Searching for common threads: Understanding the multiple effects of diversity in organizational groups. *Academy of Management Review, 21*, 402–433.

Minogue, M. (1998). Changing the state: Concepts and practice in the reform of the public sector. In M. Minogue, C. Polidano, & D. Hulme (Eds.), *Beyond the new public management: Changing ideas and practices in governance* (pp. 17–37). Edward Elgar.

Molyneux, G., & Teixeira, R. (2010). The generation gap on government: Why and how the Millennial Generation is the most pro-government generation and what this means for our future. In C. f. A. Progress (Ed.), *Center for American Progress*. Center for American Progress.

Mondres, T. (2019). How Generation Z is changing financial services: Move over, Millennials. The next rising generation is here. *ABA Banking Journal*, 24–28.

Mor Barak, M. E. (2005). *Managing diversity: Toward a globally inclusive workplace*. SAGE Publications.

Morris, S. A., & McDonald, R. A. (1995). The role of moral intensity in moral judgments: An empirical investigation. *Journal of Business Ethics, 14*(9), 715–726.

Morrison, A. M. (1992). *The new leaders: Guidelines on leadership diversity in America* (Jossey-Bass Management Series). Jossey-Bass.

Morrison, M., Lumby, J., & Sood, K. (2006). Diversity and diversity management: Messages from recent research. *Educational Management Administration & Leadership, 34*(3), 277–295.

Moynihan, D. P. (2013). Does public service motivation lead to budget maximization? Evidence from an experiment. *International Public Management Journal, 16*(2), 179–196.

Mudrack, P. E., & Mason, E. S. (2013a). Dilemmas, conspiracies, and Sophie's choice: Vignette themes and ethical judgments. *Journal of Business Ethics, 118*(3), 639–653.

Mudrack, P. E., & Mason, E. S. (2013b). Ethical judgments: What do we know, where do we go? *Journal of Business Ethics, 115*(3), 575–597.

Mulgan, G. (2014). Innovation in the public sector: How can public organizations better create, improve and adapt? NESTA. Available at: https://media.nesta.org.uk/documents/innovation_in_the_public_sector-_how_can_public_organisations_better_create_improve_and_adapt_0.pdf

Muncy, J. A., & Vitell, S. J. (1992). Consumer ethics: An investigation of the ethical beliefs of the final consumer. *Journal of Business Research, 24*, 297–311.

Mustafa, D. (2019). Bureaucratic ethics in public services case study: Office of the National Land Agency of North Luwu Regency. *International Journal of Mechanical Engineering and Technology, 10*(3).

Nachmias, D., & Rosenbloom, D. H. (1973). Measuring bureaucratic representation and integration. *Public Administration Review, 33*(6), 590–597.

Naff, K. C., & Kellough, J. E. (2003). Ensuring employment equity: Are federal diversity programs making a difference? *International Journal of Public Administration, 26*(12), 1307–1336.

Natarajan, N. K., & Nagar, D. (2012). Effect of service tenure on value congruence—A case of public sector employees. *Indian Journal of Industrial Relations, 47*(4), 717–723.

National Research Group. (2020). 20/20 vision for mobile video: Outlook for a new era of mobile-first experiences. Available at: https://assets.ctfassets.net/inb32lme5009/7KVjeLgGJwFbDuIl1nApP1/546a821d454f37bab305912ea7f3c1a7/2020_Vision_for_Mobile_Video_WhitePaper_KSA.pdf

Naudé, A., & Bornman, J. (2016). Ethical Sensitivity—A multidisciplinary approach. *Humanities and Social Sciences, 4*(2), 1.

Ndalamba, K., & Esau, M. (2020). An exploratory study into the understandings and awareness of leadership ethos and its inherent critical success factors by public sector officials in the Department of Trade and Industry (DTI) and the Ministry of the National Economy (ECONAT). *International Journal of Public Administration, 43*(1), 60–72.

Newton, C. (2019). People older than 65 share the most fake news, a new study finds. Retrieved July 20, 2020, from https://www.theverge.com/2019/1/9/18174631/old-people-fake-newsfacebook-share-nyu-princeton

Nguyen, N. T., Basuray, M. T., Smith, W. P., Kopka, D., & McCulloh, D. (2008). Moral issues and gender differences in ethical judgment using Reidenbach and Robin's (1990) multidimensional ethics scale: Implications in teaching of business ethics. *Journal of Business Ethics, 77*(4), 417–430.

Nishii, L. H., Lepak, D. P., & Schneider, B. (2008). Employee attributions of the "why" of HR practices: Their effects on employee attitudes and behaviors, and customer satisfaction. *Personnel Psychology, 61*, 503–545.

Nkomo, S. M., & Cox, T., Jr. (1999). Diverse identities in organizations. In S. Clegg, C. Hardy, & W. Nord (Eds.). *Managing organizations: Current issues* (pp. 88–106). SAGE Publications.

Nkyabonaki, J. (2019). Effectiveness of the public service code of ethics in controlling corrupt behavior in the public service: Opinion from the grassroots at Toangoma Ward-Temeke Municipal Council. *Journal of Asian and African Studies, 54*(8), 1195–1212.

Norman-Major, K., & Gooden, S. T. (2012). *Culture competency for public administrators*. M. E. Sharpe.

Northouse, P. G. (2016). *Leadership: Theory and practice* (7th ed.). SAGE Publications.

O'Fallon, M. J., & Butterfield, K. D. (2005). A review of the empirical ethical decision-making literature: 1996–2003. *Journal of Business Ethics, 59*(4), 375–413.

O'Reilly, C. A., Caldwell, D. F., & Barnett, W. P. (1989). Work group demography, social integration, and turnover. *Administrative Science Quarterly, 34*(1), 21–37.

OBSERVER. Retrieved July 20, 2020, from https://observer.com/2017/06/social-media-isas-harmful-as-alcohol-and-drugs-for-millennials/

Oksman, V., & Turtiainen, J. (2004). Mobile communication as a social stage: Meanings of mobile communication in everyday life among teenagers in Finland. *New media & society*, *6*(3), 319–339.

Ogbonnaya, D. C. (2018). Revisiting ethics and values in Nigerian public service. *ASPL International Journal of Management Sciences*, *7*(1), 33–42.

Oliver, S., & Conroy, M. (2018). Tough enough for the job? How masculinity predicts recruitment of city council members. *American Politics Research*, *46*(6), 1094–1122.

Olson, E. E., & Eoyang, G. H. (2001). *Facilitating organization change: Lessons from complexity science.* Jossey-Bass/Pfeiffer.

Olson, K. E., O'Brien, M. A., Rogers, W. A, & Charness, N. (2011). Diffusion of technology: Frequency of use for younger and older adults. *Ageing International*, *36*, 123–145.

Ozturk, M. B., & Rumens, N. (2014). Gay male academics in UK business and management schools: Negotiating heteronormativities in everyday work life. *British Journal of Management*, *25*(3), 503–517.

Pan, Y., & Sparks, J. R. (2012). Predictors, consequence, and measurement of ethical judgments: Review and meta-analysis. *Journal of Business Research*, *65*(1), 84–91.

Pandey, S. K., & Stazyk, E. C. (2008). Antecedents and correlates of public service motivation. *Motivation in public management: The call of public service* (pp. 101–117). Oxford University Press.

Park, J., & Gursoy, D. (2012). Generation effects on work engagement among US hotel employees. *International Journal of Hospitality Management*, *31*(4), 1195–1202.

Parry, E. (2014). *Generational diversity at work: New research perspectives*. Routledge.

Parry, E., & Urwin, P. (2011). Generational differences in work values: A review of theory and evidence. *International Journal of Management Reviews*, *13*, 79–96.

Pate, J., Beaumont, P., & Stewart, S. (2007). Trust in senior management in the public sector. *Employee Relations*, *29*(5), 458–468.

Patil, V. (2013). From patriarchy to intersectionality: A transnational feminist assessment of how far we've really come. *Signs*, *38*(4), 847–867.

Patterson, C. K. (2007). The impact of generational diversity in the workplace. *Diversity Factor*, *15*(3), 17–22.

Paul, P. (2001). Getting inside Generation Y. *American Demographics*, *23*(9), 42–49.

Paz, J. C. (2004). Navigators and castaways in cyberspace. In M. Bonilla & G. Cliché (Eds.), *Internet and society in Latin America and the Caribbean* (pp. 147–192). Southbound and IDRC Books.

Pedersen, M. J. (2015). Activating the forces of public service motivation: Evidence from a low-intensity randomized survey experiment. *Public Administration Review*, *75*(5), 734–746.

Pedhazur, E., & Schmelkin, L. (1991). *Measurement, design, and analysis: an integrated approach*. Lawrence Erlbaum Associates.

Pelled, L. H., Ledford, G. E., & Mohrman, S. A. (1999). Demographic dissimilarity and workplace inclusion. *Journal of Management Studies, 36*, 1013–1031.

Perry, J. L., & Hondeghem, A. (2008). Directions for future theory and research. *Motivation in public management: The call of public service* (pp. 294–313). Oxford University Press.

Perry, J. L., & Vandenabeele, W. (2008). The behavioral dynamics of public service motivation. *Motivation in public management: The call of public service* (pp. 56–79). Oxford University Press.

Perry, J. L., & Wise, L. R. (1990). The motivational bases of public service. *Public Administration Review, 50*(3), 367–373.

Perry, J. L., Brudney, J. L., Coursey, D., & Littlepage, L. (2008). What drives morally committed citizens? A study of the antecedents of public service motivation. *Public Administration Review, 68*(3), 445–458.

Perry, J. L., de Graaf, G., van der Wal, Z., & van Montfort, C. (2014). Returning to our roots: "Good government" evolves to "good governance." *Public Administration Review, 74*(1), 27–28.

Peterson, D., Rhoads, A., & Vaught, B. C. (2001). Ethical beliefs of business professionals: A study of gender, age and external factors. *Journal of Business Ethics, 31*(3), 225–232.

Pew Research Center. (2010). Generations 2010: What different generations do online. Available at: https://www.pewresearch.org/internet/2010/12/16/generations-2010-what-different-generations-do-online/

Pilcher, J. (1994). Mannheim's sociology of generations: An undervalued legacy. *British Journal of Sociology, 45*, 481–495.

Pili, D. A. D., Valderrma, S., & Wycoco C. H. (2018). Managing a multi-generational workforce in the BSP. *Bangko Sentral Review*. Available at https://www.bsp.gov.ph/Media_And_Research/Publications/BS2018_05.pdf

Pitts, D. W. (2006). Modeling the impact of diversity management. *Review of Public Personnel Administration, 26*(3), 245–268.

Pitts, D. W. (2009). Diversity management, job satisfaction, and performance: Evidence from U.S. federal agencies. *Public Administration Review, 69*(2), 328–338.

Pitts, D. W., Hicklin, A. K., Hawes, D. P., & Melton, E. (2010). What drives the implementation of diversity management programs? Evidence from public organizations. *Journal of Public Administration Research and Theory, 20*, 867–886.

Plaut, V. C., Garnett, F. G., Buffardi, L. E., & Sanchez-Burks, J. (2011). "What about me?" Perceptions of exclusion and whites' reactions to multiculturalism. *Journal of Personality and Social Psychology, 101*(2), 337–353.

Pless, N., & Maak, T. (2004). Building an inclusive diversity culture: Principles, processes and practice. *Journal of Business Ethics, 54*, 129–147.

Podsiadlowski, A., Gröschke , D., Kogler, M., Springer, C., & Van der Zee, K. I. (2013). Managing a culturally diverse workforce: Diversity perspectives in organizations. *International Journal of Intercultural Relations, 37*(2), 159–175.

Ponemon, L. (1993). Can ethics be taught in accounting? *Journal of Accounting Education, 11*, 185–209.

Ponemon, L. (1995). The objectivity of accountants' litigation support judgments. *The Accounting Review, 70*(3), 467–488.

Ponemon, L. A., & Gabhart, D. R. (1994). Ethical reasoning research in the accounting and auditing professions. In J. R. Rest, and D. Narvaez (Eds.), *Moral development in the professions: Psychology and applied ethics* (pp. 113–132). Psychology Press.

Powell, M. J., Brock, D. M., & Hinings, C. R. (1999). The changing professional. In D. M. Brock, C. R. Hinings, & M. J. Powell (Eds.), *Restructuring the professional: Accounting health care and law*. Routledge.

PPT Solutions. (2018). Bridging the generational gap: Millennial vs. Gen Z CX expectations. Retrieved August 15, 2020, from http://www.musemc.com/wp-content/uploads/2018/07/PPTArticle_GenerationalGap.pdf

Pratt, J., Plamping, D., & Gordon, P. (2007). *Distinctive characteristics of public sector organizations and the implications for leadership* [Working paper]. Centre for Innovation in Health Management, University of Leeds.

Prensky, M. (2001a). Digital natives, digital immigrants, part II: Do they really think differently? *On the Horizon, 9*(5), 1–6. Retrieved from https://www.marcprensky.com/writing/Prensky%20-%20Digital%20Natives,%20Digital%20Immigrants%20-%20Part2.pdf

PricewaterhouseCoopers. (2016). Bridging the generation gap. What directors need to know about managing a multi-generational workforce. Retrieved July 28, 2020, from http://www.pwc.com/ca/en/research-insights/directorconnect/publications/millennials-bridging-generationalgap.html

Priem, R., & Butler, J. (2001). Is the resource-based "view" a useful perspective for strategic management research? *Academy of Management Review, 26*(1), 22–40.

Pugh, D. S., Hickson, D. J., & Hinings, C. R. (1973). An empirical taxonomy of structures in work organizations. In F. Kast & J. Rosenzweig (Eds.), *Contingency views of organization and management* (pp. 195–212). Social Research Associates Inc.

Pugh, D. S., Dietz, J., Brief, A. P., & Wiley, J. W. (2008). Looking inside and out: The impact of employee and community demographic composition on organizational diversity climate. *Journal of Applied Psychology, 93*, 1422–1428.

Purcell, K., Brenner, J., & Rainie, L. (2012) Search engine use 2012. Pew Research Center's Internet and American Life Project. https://www.pewresearch.org/internet/wp-content/uploads/sites/9/media/Files/Reports/2012/PIP_Search_Engine_Use_2012.pdf

Purhonen, S. (2016). Generations on paper: Bourdieu and the critique of "generationalism." *Social Science Information, 55*(1), 94–114.

Quraishi, F. F., Wajid, S. A., & Dhiman, P. (2017). Social and ethical impact of artificial intelligence on public: A case study of university students. *International Journal of Scientific Research in Science, Engineering and Technology, 3*(8), 463–467.

Quratulain, S., & Khan, A. K. (2015). How does employees' public service motivation get affected? A conditional process analysis of the effects of person–job fit and work pressure. *Public Personnel Management, 44*(2), 266–289.

Radtke, R. R. (2000). The effects of gender and setting on accountants' ethically sensitive decisions. *Journal of Business Ethics, 24*(4), 299–312.

Raffel, J. A. (2009). Looking forward: A response to the ASPA task force report on educating for excellence in the MPA. *Journal of Public Affairs Education, 15*(2), 135–144.

Ragins, B. R., & Cornwell, J. M. (2001). Pink triangles: antecedents and consequences of perceived workplace discrimination against gay and lesbian employees. *Journal of Applied Psychology, 86*, 1244–1261.

Ragins, B. R., & Wiethoff, C. (2005). Understanding heterosexism at work: the straight problem. In R. L. Dipboye & A. Colella (Eds.), *Discrimination at work: The psychological and organizational bases* (pp. 177–201). Lawrence Erlbaum Associates.

Ramsey, R. P., Marshall, G. W., Johnston, M. W., & Deeter-Schmelz, D. R. (2007). Ethical ideologies and older consumer perceptions of unethical sales tactics. *Journal of Business Ethics, 70*(2), 191–207.

Ransbotham, S., Kiron, D., Gerbert, P., & Reeves, M. (2017). Reshaping business with artificial intelligence: Closing the gap between ambition and action. *MIT Sloan Management Review, 59*(1), 1–17.

Rao, T. (2017). *Social media is as harmful as alcohol and drugs for Millennials.* The Conversation. https://theconversation.com/social-media-is-as-harmful-as-alcohol-and-drugs-for-millennials-78418

Rattan, A., & Ambady, N. (2013). Diversity ideologies and intergroup relations: An examination of colorblindness and multiculturalism. *European Journal of Social Psychology, 43*(1), 12–21.

Rau, B. L., & Hyland, M. M. (2003). Corporate teamwork and diversity statements in college recruitment brochure framing workforce diversity. *Humans Relations, 66*(2), 271–294.

Rawwas, M. Y. (1996). Consumer ethics: An empirical investigation of the ethical beliefs of Austrian consumers. *Journal of Business Ethics, 15*(9), 1009–1019.

Rawwas, M. Y. A., Patzer, G. J., & Vitell, S. J. (1998). A cross-cultural investigation of the ethical values of consumers: The potential effect of civil war and civil disruption. *Journal of Business Ethics, 17*(4), 435–448.

Rawwas, M. Y. A., Patzer, G. L., & Klassen, M. L. (1995). Consumer ethics in cross-cultural settings: Entrepreneurial implications. *European Journal of Marketing, 29*(7), 62–78.

Rawwas, M. Y. A., Swaidan, S., & Oyman, M. (2005). Consumer ethics: A cross-cultural study of the ethical beliefs of Turkish and American consumers. *Journal of Business Ethics, 57*, 183–195.

Rayner J., Lawton, A., & Williams, H. (2012). Organizational citizenship behavior and the public service ethos: Whither the organization. *Journal of Business Ethics, 106*(2), 117–130.

Rayner, J., Williams, H. M., Lawton, A., & Allinson, C. W. (2010). Public service ethos: Developing a generic measure. *Journal of Public Administration Research and Theory, 21*(1), 27–51.

Reidenbach, R. E., & Robin, D. P. (1988). Some initial steps toward improving the measurement of ethical evaluations of marketing activities. *Journal of Business Ethics, 7*(11), 871–879.

Reidenbach, R. E., & Robin, D. P. (1990). Toward the development of a multidimensional scale for improving evaluations of business ethics. *Journal of Business Ethics, 9*(8), 639–653.

Reidenbach, R. E., & Robin, D. P. (1995). A response to "on measuring ethical judgments." *Journal of Business Ethics, 14*(2), 159–162.

Reidenbach, R. E., Robin, D. P., & Dawson, L. (1991). An application and extension of a multidimensional ethics scale to selected marketing practices and marketing groups. *Journal of the Academy of Marketing Science, 19*(2), 83–92.

Reither, E. N., Hauser, R. M., & Yang, Y. (2009). Do birth cohorts matter? Age-period cohort analyses of the obesity epidemic in the United States. *Social Science & Medicine, 69*(10), 1439–1448.

Rejc, A. (2004). Toward contingency theory of performance measurement. *Journal for East European Management Studies, 9*(3), 243–264.

Ren, L. R., Paetzold, R. L., & Colella, A. (2008). A meta-analysis of experimental studies on the effects of disability on human resource judgments. *Human Resource Management Review, 18*(3), 191–203.

Rest, J. R. (1979). *Development in judging moral issues.* University of Minnesota Press.

Rest, J. R. (1983). Morality. In J. Flavell & E. Markman (Eds.), *Handbook of child psychology* (4th ed., Vol. III, pp. 556–629). Wiley.

Rest, J. R. (1986). *Moral development: Advances in research and theory.* Praeger Publishers.

Rest, J. R. (1994). Background: Theory and research. In J. R. Rest & D. Narvaez (Eds.), *Moral development in the professions: Psychology and applied ethics* (pp.1–26). Lawrence Erlbaum.

Rest, J. R., Thoma, S. J., & Bebeau, M. J. (1999). *Postconventional moral thinking: A neo-Kohlbergian approach*. Psychology Press.

Rest, J., Narvaez, D., Bebeau, M., & Thoma, S. (1999). A neo-Kohlbergian approach: The DIT and schema theory. *Educational Psychology Review, 11*(4), 291–324.

Rest, J., Thoma, S., & Edwards, L. (1997). Designing and validating a measure of moral judgment: Stage preference and stage consistency approaches. *Journal of Educational Psychology, 89*(1), 5.

Reynolds, S. (2006). Moral awareness and ethical predispositions: Investigating the role of individual differences in the recognition of moral issues. *Journal of Applied Psychology, 91*, 233–243.

Riccucci, N. (2002). *Managing diversity in public sector workforces*. Westview Press.

Rice, M. F. (2001). The need for teaching diversity and representativeness in university public administration education and professional public service training programmes in sub-Saharan Africa. In *Managing Diversity in the Civil Service* (pp. 99–110). IOS Press.

Rice, M. F. (2004). Organizational culture, social equity, and diversity: Teaching public administration education in the postmodern era. *Journal of Public Affairs Education, 10*(2), 143–154.

Ritz, A., & Brewer, G. A. (2013). Does societal culture affect public service motivation? Evidence of sub-national differences in Switzerland. *International Public Management Journal, 16*(2), 224–251.

Ritz, A., Brewer, G. A., & Neumann, O. (2016). Public service motivation: A systematic literature review and outlook. *Public Administration Review, 76*(3), 414–426.

Robbins, S. (2013). *Organizational behavior* (15th ed.). Prentice Hall Inc.

Roberson, Q. M. (2006). Disentangling the meanings of diversity and inclusion in organizations. *Group & Organization Management, 31*, 212–236.

Roberson, Q. M., & Park, H. J. (2007). Examining the link between diversity and firm performance: The effects of diversity reputation and leader racial diversity. *Group & Organization Management, 32*, 548–568.

Roberson, Q. M., & Stevens, C. K. (2006). Making sense of diversity in the workplace: Organizational justice and language abstraction in employees' accounts of diversity-related incidents. *Journal of Applied Psychology, 91*, 379–391.

Robin, D. P., Reidenbach, R. E., & Babin, B. J. (1997). The nature, measurement, and stability of ethical judgments in the workplace. *Psychological Reports, 80*, 563–580.

Robin, D., & Babin, L. (1997). Making sense of the research on gender and ethics in business: A critical analysis and extension. *Business Ethics Quarterly, 7*(4), 61–90.

Rokeach, M. (1968). A theory of organization and change within value-attitude systems. *Journal of Social Issues, 24*(1), 13–33.

Rokeach, M. (1973). *The nature of human values*. Free press.

Roman, R., & Colle, R. (2002). *Creating a participatory telecentre enterprise* [Paper presentation]. International Association for Media and Communication Research, Barcelona.

Rosenbloom, D. (1977). *Federal equal employment opportunity: Politics and public personnel administration*. Praeger Publishers.

Rotolo, T., & Wilson, J. (2004). What happened to the "long civic generation"? Explaining cohort differences in volunteerism. *Social Forces, 82*(3), 1091–1121.

Russell, S. (2015). Take a stand on AI weapons. *Nature, 521*(7553), 415–416.

Ryan, C. S., Hunt, J. S., Weible, J. A., Peterson, C. R., & Casas, J. F. (2007). Multicultural and colorblind ideology, stereotypes, and ethnocentrism among Black and White Americans. *Group Processes and Intergroup Relations, 10*, 617–637.

Sabharwal, M. I., Hijal-Moghrabi, I., & Royster, M. (2014). Preparing future public servants: Role of diversity in public administration, *Public Administration Quarterly, 38*, 206–245.

Sarwono, S. S., & Armstrong, R. W. (2001). Microcultural differences and perceived ethical problems: An international business perspective. *Journal of Business Ethics, 30*(1), 41–56.

Sauser, W. I., Jr., & Sims, R. R. (Eds.). (2013). *Managing human resources for the Millennial Generation*. IAP.

Sawyerr, O., Strauss, J., & Yan, J. (2005). Individual value structure and diversity attitudes: The moderating effects of age, gender, race, and religiosity. *Journal of Managerial Psychology, 20*(6), 498–521.

Schepers, D. H. (2003). Machiavellianism, profit, and the dimensions of ethical judgment: A study of impact. *Journal of Business Ethics, 42*(4), 339–352.

Schnittker, J., Freese, J., & Powell, B. (2003). Who are feminists and what do they believe? The role of generations. *American Sociological Review, 68*(4), 607–622.

Schur, L., Kruse, D., & Blanck, P. (2005). Corporate culture and the employment of persons with disabilities. *Behavioral Sciences and the Law, 23*, 3–20.

Schur, L., Kruse, D., Blasi, J., & Blanck, P. (2009). Is disability disabling in all workplaces? Workplace disparities and corporate culture. *Industrial Relations, 48*(3), 381–410.

Schwartz, M. S. (2016). Ethical decision-making theory: An integrated approach. *Journal of Business Ethics, 139*(4), 755–776.

Schwepker, C. H. (1999). Understanding salespeople's intention to behave unethically: The effects of perceived competitive intensity, cognitive moral development and moral judgment. *Journal of Business Ethics, 21*(4), 303–316.

Scott, W. R. (1995). *Institutions and organizations*. SAGE Publications.

Seemiller, M., & Grace, M. (2018). *Generation Z: A century in the making*. Routledge.

Seitel, S. (2005). Generational competence. Update column WFC resources. Retrieved July 20, 2020, from http://www.workfamily.com/Work-life Clearinghouse/UpDates/ud0015.htm

Serwinek, P. J. (1992). Demographic & related differences in ethical views among small businesses. *Journal of Business Ethics, 11*(7), 555–566.

Shafer, W. E. (2008). Ethical climate in Chinese CPA firms. *Accounting, Organizations and Society, 33*(7–8), 825–835.

Shafer, W. E., Morris, R. E., & Ketchand, A. A. (2001). Effects of personal values on auditors' ethical decisions. *Accounting, Auditing & Accountability Journal, 14*(3), 254–277.

Sharabi, M., & Harpaz, I. (2016). Impact of generational differences on work values in the Israeli context. In M. Sharabi (Ed.), *Generational differences in work values and work ethic: An international perspective* (pp. 19–41). Nova Science Publishers.

Shaub, M. K. (1997). Commentary on the relationship between an individual's values and perceptions of moral intensity: An empirical study. *Behavioral Research in Accounting, 9*, 41–49.

Shaub, M. K., Finn, D. W., & Munter, P. (1993). The effects of auditors' ethical orientation on commitment and ethical sensitivity. *Behavioral Research in Accounting, 5*(1), 145–169.

Sherman, R. (2014). Leading Generation Y nurses. *Nurse Leader, 12*(3), 28–50.

Shore, L. M., Chung-Herrera, B. G., Dean, M. A., Ehrhart, K. H., Jung, D. I., Randel, A. E., & Singh, G. (2009). Diversity in organizations: Where are we now and where are we going? *Human Resource Management Review, 19*(2), 117–133.

Sikula, A., Sr., & Costa, A. D. (1994). Are age and ethics related? *The Journal of Psychology, 128*(6), 659–665.

Singhapakdi, A. (1999). Perceived importance of ethics and ethical decisions in marketing. *Journal of Business Research, 45*(1), 89–99.

Singhapakdi, A., Marta, J. K., Rallapalli, K. C., & Rao, C. P. (2000). Toward an understanding of religiousness and marketing ethics: An empirical study. *Journal of Business Ethics, 27*(4), 305–319.

Singhapakdi, A., Vitell, S. J., & Franke, G. R. (1999). Antecedents, consequences, and mediating effects of perceived moral intensity and personal moral philosophies. *Journal of the Academy of Marketing Science, 27*(1), 19–36.

Singhapakdi, A., Vitell, S. J., & Kraft, K. L. (1996). Moral intensity and ethical decision-making of marketing professionals. *Journal of Business Research, 36*(3), 245–255.

Skipper, R., & Hyman, M. R. (1993). On measuring ethical judgments. *Journal of Business Ethics, 12*(7), 535–545.

Smith, K. G., Smith, K. A., Olian, J. D., Sims, H. P., O'Bannon, D. P., & Scully, J. A. (1994). Top management team demography and process: The role of social integration and communication. *Administrative Science Quarterly*, *39*(3), 412–438.

Smith, P. B. (2000). Changes in the generation gap 1972–1998: GSS social change report (Vol. 43). National Opinion Research Center, University of Chicago.

Smola, K., & Sutton, C. (2002). Generational differences: Revisiting generational work values for the new millennium. *Journal of Organizational Behavior*, *23*(4), 363–382.

Society for Human Resource Management. (2012). *Introduction to the human resources discipline of diversity*. Society for Human Resource Management. Retrieved March 14, 2019, from http://www.shrm.org/diversity

Solon, O., & Laughland, O. (2018). Cambridge Analytica closing after Facebook data harvesting scandal. *The Guardian*, at https://www.theguardian.com/uk-news/2018/may/02/cambridge-analytica-closing-down-after-facebook-row-reports-say

Sparks, J. R., & Pan, Y. (2010). Ethical judgments in business ethics research: Definition, and research agenda. *Journal of Business Ethics*, *91*(3), 405–418.

Spicer, A., Dunfee, T. W., & Bailey, W. J. (2004). Does national context matter in ethical decision-making? An empirical test of integrative social contracts theory. *Academy of Management Journal*, *47*(4), 610–620.

Srivastava, S. K., & Barmola, K. C. (2012). Role of motivation in higher productivity. *Management Insight*, *7*(1), 88–99.

Stanga, K. G., & Turpen, R. A. (1991). Ethical judgments on selected accounting issues: An empirical study. *Journal of Business Ethics*, *10*(10), 739–747.

Stanley, D. (2010). Multigenerational workforce issues and their implications for leadership in nursing. *Journal of Nursing Management*, *18*(7), 846–852.

Stazyk, E. C., & Davis, R. S. (2015). Taking the "high road": Does public service motivation alter ethical decision making processes? *Public Administration*, *93*(3), 627–645.

Steele, B., & Acuff, J. (Eds.). (2012). *Theory and application of the "generation" in international relations and politics*. Palgrave Macmillan.

Steenhaut, S., & Van Kenhove, P. (2006). An empirical investigation of the relationships among a consumer's personal values, ethical ideology and ethical beliefs. *Journal of Business Ethics*, *64*(2), 137–155.

Stefaniak, A., & Vetter, C. (2007). *Black hole or window of opportunity? Understanding the generation gap in today's workplace*. Center for Public Policy and Administration, The University of Utah.

Sterns, H. L., and Doverspike, D. (1989), Aging and the retraining and learning process in organizations. In I. Goldstein & R. Katzel (Eds.), *Training and development in work organizations* (pp. 229–332). Jossey-Bass.

Stevens, F. G., Plaut, V. C., & Sanchez-Burks, J. (2008). Unlocking the benefits of diversity: All-inclusive multiculturalism and positive organizational change. *Journal of Applied Behavioral Science*, *44*(1), 116–133.

Stevenson, T. H., & Bodkin, C. D. (1998). A cross-national comparison of university students' perceptions regarding the ethics and acceptability of sales practices. *Journal of Business Ethics, 17*(1), 45–55.

Stewart, D. W., & Sprinthall, N. A. (1993). The impact of demographic, professional and organizational variables and domain on the moral reasoning of public administrators. In H. George Frederickson (Ed.), *Ethics and public administration* (pp. 205–219). M. E. Sharpe.

Stillman, R. J. (1979). *The rise of the city manager: A public professional in local government.* University of New Mexico Press.

Strachan, G., Burgess, J., & Sullivan, A. (2004). Affirmative action or managing diversity: What is the future of equal opportunity policies in organizations? *Women in Management Review, 19,* 196–204.

Strauss, W., & Howe, N. (1991) *Generations. The history of America's future.* William Morrow & Co.

Strauss, W., & Howe, N. (1997). *The fourth turning: An American prophecy.* Three Rivers Press.

Su, X., & Ni, X. (2018). Citizens on patrol: Understanding public whistleblowing against government corruption. *Journal of Public Administration Research and Theory, 28*(3), 406–422.

Sujansky, J. G., & Ferri-Reed, J. (2009). *Keeping the Millennials.* John Wiley & Sons.

Sullivan, S. E., Forret, M. L., Carraher, S. M., & Mainiero, L. A. (2009). Using the kaleidoscope career model to examine generational differences in work attitudes. *Career Development International, 14*(3), 284–302.

Sumra, K. (2019). Social equity in public administration: Fairness, justice and equity, tools for social change. *Pakistan Administrative Review, 3*(1), 1–15.

Svara, J. H. (2007). *The ethics primer for public administrators in government and nonprofit organizations.* Jones & Bartlett Publishers.

Swaidan, Z., Vitell, S. J., & Rawwas, M. Y. (2003). Consumer ethics: Determinants of ethical beliefs of African Americans. *Journal of Business Ethics, 46*(2), 175–186.

Székely, L., & Nagy, A. (2011). Online youth work and eYouth—A guide to the world of the digital natives. *Children and Youth Services Review, 33,* 2186–2197.

Taylor, J. (2014). Public service motivation, relational job design, and job satisfaction in local government. *Public Administration, 92*(4), 902–918.

Thoma, S. J. (2006). Research on the defining issues test. In *Handbook of moral development* (pp. 85–110). Psychology Press.

Thoma, S. J., Bebeau, M., & Bolland, A. (2008). The role of moral judgment in context-specific professional decision-making. In F. K. Oser & W. Veugelers (Eds.), *Global citizenship development and sources of moral values* (pp.147–160). Sense Publishers.

Thoma, S. J., Narvaez, D., Rest, J., & Derryberry, P. (1999). Does moral judgment development reduce to political attitudes or verbal ability? Evidence using the defining issues test. *Educational Psychology Review, 11*(4), 325–341.

Thomas, D. T., & Ely, R. J. (1996). Making differences matter. A new paradigm for managing diversity. *Harvard Business Review*, *74*(5), 1–13.

Thomas, R. R., Jr. (1990). From affirmative action to affirming diversity. *Harvard Business Review*, *68*(2), 107–117.

Thompson, C. A. (2017). Leading a multigenerational workforce in the public sector [Doctoral dissertation, Walden University].

Thorne, L. (2000). The development of two measures to assess accountants' prescriptive and deliberative moral reasoning. *Behavioral Research in Accounting*, *12*, 139.

Tolbize, A. (2008). Generational differences in the workplace. *Research and Training Center on Community Living*, *5*(2), 1–21.

Towner, T., & Lego Munoz, C. (2016). Boomers versus Millennials: Online media influence on media performance and candidate evaluations. *Social Sciences*, *5*(4), 56.

Trevino, L. K. (1986). Ethical decision making in organizations: A person-situation interactionist model. *Academy of Management Review*, *11*(3), 601–617.

Tsai, M. T., & Huang, C. C. (2008). The relationship among ethical climate types, facets of job satisfaction, and the three components of organizational commitment: A study of nurses in Taiwan. *Journal of Business Ethics*, *80*(3), 565–581.

Tsalikis, J., & Nwachukwu, O. (1988). Cross-cultural business ethics: Ethical beliefs difference between blacks and whites. *Journal of Business Ethics*, *7*(10), 745–754.

Twenge, J. M. (2010). A review of the empirical evidence on generational differences in work attitudes. *Journal of Business and Psychology*, *25*, 201–210.

Twenge, J., Campbell, S., Hoffman, B., & Lance, C. (2010). Generational differences in work values: Leisure and extrinsic values increasing, social and intrinsic values decreasing. *Journal of Management*, *36*(5), 1117–1142.

Urick, M. J. (2012). Exploring generational identity: A multiparadigm approach. *Journal of Business Diversity*, *12*, 103–115.

Urick, M. J. (2017). The aging of the sandwich generation. *Generations*, *41*(3), 72–76.

Urquhart, C., Lehmann, H., & Myers, M. D. (2012). Putting the "theory" back into grounded theory: Guidelines for grounded theory studies in information systems. *Information and Software Technology*, *54*(5), 479–500.

Valentine, S. R., & Rittenburg, T. L. (2004). Spanish and American business professionals' ethical evaluations in global situations. *Journal of Business Ethics*, *51*(1), 1–14.

Valentine, S. R., & Rittenburg, T. L. (2007). The ethical decision-making of men and women executives in international business situations. *Journal of Business Ethics*, *71*(2), 125–134.

Valentine, S., & Barnett, T. (2007). Perceived organizational ethics and the ethical decisions of sales and marketing personnel. *Journal of Personal Selling & Sales Management*, *27*(4), 373–388.

Van der Kaay, C. D., & Young, W. (2012). Age-related differences in technology usage among community college faculty. *Community College Journal of Research and Practice, 36*(8), 570–579.

Van der Wal, Z., & Huberts, L. (2008). Value solidity in government and business: Results of an empirical study on public and private sector organizational values. *The American Review of Public Administration, 38*(3), 264–285.

Van der Wal, Z., De Graaf, D., & Lasthuizen, K. (2008). What's valued most? A comparative empirical study on the differences and similarities between the organizational values of the public and private sector. *Public Administration, 86*(2), 465–482.

Van Hoye, G., & Lievens, F. (2003). The effects of sexual orientation on hirability ratings: An experimental study. *Journal of Business and Psychology, 18*, 15–30.

van Knippenberg, D., De Dreu, C. K. W., & Homan, C. (2004). Work group diversity and group performance: An integrative model and research agenda. *Journal of Applied Psychology, 89*, 1008–1022.

Van Volkom, M., Stapley, J. C., & Amaturo, V. (2014). Revisiting the digital divide: Generational differences in technology use in everyday life. *North American Journal of Psychology, 16*(3), 557–574.

Vandegrift, D. (2016). "We don't have any limits": Russian young adult life narratives through a social generations lens. *Journal of Youth Studies, 19*(2), 221–236.

Vandenabeele, W. (2007). Toward a theory of public service motivation: An institutional approach. *Public Management Review, 9*(4), 545–556.

Vandenabeele, W. (2011). Who wants to deliver public service? Do institutional antecedents of public service motivation provide an answer? *Review of Public Personnel Administration, 31*(1), 87–107.

Vandenabeele, W., Ritz, A., & Neumann, O. (2018). Public service motivation: State of the art and conceptual cleanup. In E. Ongaro & S. Van Thiel (Eds.), *The Palgrave Handbook of Public Administration and Management in Europe* (pp. 261–278). Palgrave Macmillan.

Vaterlaus, J. M., Jones, R. M., & Tulane, S. (2015). Perceived differences in knowledge about interactive technology between young adults and their parents. *Cyberpsychology: Journal of Psychosocial Research on Cyberspace, 9*(4).

Veale, M., Van Kleek, M., & Binns, R. (2018, April). *Fairness and accountability design needs for algorithmic support in high-stakes public sector decision-making* [Conference proceedings (pp. 1–14)]. *Chi Conference on Human Factors in Computing Systems.*

Verkuyten, M. (2005). Ethnic group identification and group evaluation among minority and majority groups: Testing the multiculturalism hypothesis. *Journal of Personality and Social Psychology, 88*, 121–138.

Victor, B., & Cullen, J. B. (1988). The organizational bases of ethical work climates. *Administrative Science Quarterly, 33*(1), 101–125.

Villanueva, P. A. G. (2019). Why civil society cannot battle it all alone: The roles of civil society environment, transparent laws and quality of public administration in political corruption mitigation. *International Journal of Public Administration*, *43*(2), 1–10.

Vitell, S. J., Bakir, A., Paolillo, J. G., Hidalgo, E. R., Al-Khatib, J., & Rawwas, M. Y. (2003). Ethical judgments and intentions: A multinational study of marketing professionals. *Business Ethics a European Review*, *12*(2), 151–)171.

Vitell, S. J., Bing, M. N., Davison, H. K., Ammeter, A. P., Garner, B. L., & Novicevic, M. M. (2009). Religiosity and moral identity: The mediating role of self-control. *Journal of Business Ethics*, *88*(4), 601–613.

Vitell, S. J., & Muncy, J. (2005). The Muncy–Vitell consumer ethics scale: A modification and application. *Journal of Business Ethics*, *62*(3), 267–275.

Vitell, S. J., & Paolillo, J. G. (2003). Consumer ethics: The role of religiosity. *Journal of Business Ethics*, *46*(2), 151–162.

Vitell, S. J., Paolillo, J. G., & Singh, J. J. (2005). Religiosity and consumer ethics. *Journal of Business Ethics*, *57*(2), 175–181.

Vogels, E. A. (2019). Millennials stand out for their technology use, but older generations also embrace digital life. Pew Research Center. Retrieved July 20, 2020, from https://www.pewresearch.org/fact-tank/2019/09/09/us-generations-technology-use/

Wade-Benzoni, K. A. (2002). A golden rule over time: Reciprocity in intergenerational allocation decisions. *Academy of Management Journal*, *45*(5), 1011–1028.

Wyatt-Nichol, H., & Antwi-Boasiako, K. (2008). Diversity across the curriculum: Perceptions and practices, *Journal of Public Affairs Education*, *14*(1), 79–90.

Waldrop, J. S., & Grawich, M. (2011). Millennials—Who are they, really? *Organizational Health Initiative*, 1–3.

Walker, S. K., Dworkin, J., & Connell, J. (2011). Variation in parent use of information and communications technology: Does quantity matter? *Family and Consumer Sciences Research Journal*, *40*(2), 106–119.

Walsh, J. P. (1995). Managerial and organizational cognition: Notes from a trip down memory lane. *Organizational Science*, *6*, 280–321.

Wang, P., & Schwarz, J. L. (2010). Stock price reactions to GLBT nondiscrimination policies. *Human Resource Management*, *49*(2), 195–216.

Warner, L. R., & Shields, S. A. (2013). The intersections of sexuality, gender, and race: Identity research at the crossroads. *Sex Roles*, *68*, 803–810.

Watson, H. (2010). *The multigenerational workforce: Strategies for managing four generations* [Honors thesis, Texas State University—San Marcos].

Watson, W., Kumar, K., & Michaelsen, L. (1993). Cultural diversity's impact on interaction process and performance: Comparing homogenous and diverse task groups. *Academy of Management Journal*, *36*, 590–602.

Webber, S. S., & Donahue, L. M. (2001). Impact of highly and less job-related diversity on work group cohesion and performance: A meta-analysis. *Journal of Management*, *27*, 141–162.

Weeks, W. A., Moore, C. W., McKinney, J. A., & Longenecker, J. G. (1999). The effects of gender and career stage on ethical judgment. *Journal of Business Ethics, 20*(4), 301–313.

Weigand, R. A. (2007). Organizational diversity, profits and returns in U.S. firms. *Problems & Perspectives in Management, 5*(3), 69–83.

Welton, R. E., Lagrone, R. M., & Davis, J. R. (1994). Promoting the moral development of accounting graduate students: An instructional design and assessment. *Accounting Education, 3*(1), 35–50.

Wey Smola, K., & Sutton, C. D. (2002). Generational differences: Revisiting generational work values for the new millennium. *Journal of Organizational Behavior, 23*(4), 363–382.

White, A. R., Nathan, N. L., & Faller, J. K. (2015). What do I need to vote? Bureaucratic discretion and discrimination by local election officials. *American Political Science Review, 109*(1), 129–142.

White, R. D., Jr. (1999). Are women more ethical? Recent findings on the effects of gender upon moral development. *Journal of Public Administration Research and Theory, 3*, 459–471.

Wiedmer, T. (2015). Generations do differ: Best practices in leading Traditionalists, Boomers, and Generations X, Y, and Z. *Delta Kappa Gamma Bulletin, 82*(1), 51–58.

Wiersema, M. F., & Bantel, K. A. (1992). Top management team demography and corporate strategic change. *Academy of Management Journal, 35*(1), 91–121.

Wijesekera, A. T., & Fernando, R. L. S. (2018). Ethical leadership measures for public service in Sri Lanka. *International Business Research, 11*(7), 106–119.

Williams, A. (2015). Move over, Millennials, here comes Generation Z. *The New York Times. 18*, 1–7. Retrieved from https://www.nytimes.com/2015/09/20/fashion/move-over-millennials-here-comes-generation-z.html

Williams, K. C., Page, R. A., Petrosky, A. R., & Hernandez, E. H. (2010). Multi-generational marketing: Descriptions, characteristics, lifestyles, and attitudes. *The Journal of Applied Business and Economics, 11*(2), 21.

Williams, K. Y., & O'Reilly, C. A. (1998). Demography and diversity in organizations: A review of 40 years of research. *Research in Organizational Behavior, 20*, 77–140.

Williams, S., Beard, J., & Tanner, M. (2011). Coping with Millennials on campus. *BizEd, 10*(4), 42–49.

Windett, J. H. (2014). Gendered campaign strategies in US elections. *American Politics Research, 42*(4), 628–655.

Wirtz, B. W., Weyerer, J. C., & Geyer, C. (2019). Artificial intelligence and the public sector—Applications and challenges. *International Journal of Public Administration, 42*(7), 596–615.

Wise, L. R., & Tschirhart, M. (2000). Examining empirical evidence on diversity effects: How useful is diversity research for public-sector managers? *Public Administration Review, 60*(5), 386–394.

Wisniewski, M. A. (2010). Leadership and the Millennials: Transforming today's technological teens into tomorrow's leaders. *Journal of Leadership Education, 9*(1), 53–68.

Witesman, E., & Walters, L. (2014). Public service values: A new approach to the study of motivation in the public sphere. *Public Administration, 92*(2), 375–405.

Wittmer, D. (1992). Ethical sensitivity and managerial decision-making: An experiment, *Journal of Public Administration Research and Theory. 2*(4), 443–462.

Wittmer, D. (2000). Ethical sensitivity in management decisions: Developing and testing a perceptual measure among management and professional student groups. *Teaching Business Ethics, 4*(2), 181–205.

Wittmer, D. (2005). Developing a behavioral model for ethical decision making in organizations: Conceptual and empirical research. In H. G. Frederiskson & R. K. Ghere (Eds.), *Ethics in Public Management* (pp. 49–69). M. E. Sharpe.

Wolsko, C., Park, B., Judd, C. M., & Wittenbrink, B. (2000). Interethnic ideology in advertising: A social psychological perspective. In J. D. Williams, W. Lee, & C. Haugtvedt (Eds.), *Diversity in advertising* (pp. 75–92). Erlbaum.

Wong, M., Gardiner, E., Lang, W., & Coulon, L. (2008). Generational differences in personality and motivation: Do they exist and what are the implications for the workplace? *Journal of Managerial Psychology, 23*, 878–890.

Wood, S. (2005). Spanning the generation gap in the workplace. *Journal (American Water Works Association), 97*(5), 86–97.

Woodhams, C., & Corby, S. (2007). Then and now: Disability legislation and employers' practices in the UK. *British Journal of Industrial Relations, 45*, 556–580.

Wooten, L. P. (2008). Guest editor's note: Breaking barriers in organizations for the purpose of inclusiveness. *Human Resource Management, 47*(2), 191–197.

World of Work Survey. (2008). *The Randstad USA world of work*. Retrieved from https://www.equiposytalento.com/contenido/download/estudios/2008WorldofWork.pdf

Wright, B. E., & Grant, A. M. (2010). Unanswered questions about public service motivation: Designing research to address key issues of emergence and effects. *Public Administration Review, 70*(5), 691–700.

Wright, B. E., Hassan, S., & Park, J. (2016). Does a public service ethic encourage ethical behavior? Public service motivation, ethical leadership and the willingness to report ethical problems. *Public Administration, 94*(3), 647–663.

Wright, B. E., & Pandey, S. K. (2008). Public service motivation and the assumption of person—Organization fit: Testing the mediating effect of value congruence. *Administration & Society, 40*(5), 502–521.

Wright, P. M., & Nishii, L. H. (2007). *Strategic HRM and organizational behavior: Integrating multiple levels of analysis* [CAHRS Working Paper Series]. Center for Advanced Human Resource Studies. Retrieved from http://digitalcommons.ilr.cornell.edu/cahrswp/468

Wright, P., Ferris, S. P., Hiller, J. S., & Kroll, M. (1995). Competitiveness through management of diversity: Effects on stock price valuation. *Academy of Management Journal, 38*, 272–287.

Wyatt-Nichol, H., Brown, S., & Haynes, W. (2011). Social class and socioeconomic status: Relevance and inclusion in MPA–MPP programs. *Journal of Public Affairs Education, 77*(2), 187–208.

Xu, F., Caldwell, C., & Anderson, V. (2016). Moral implications of leadership—transformative insights. *International Journal of Business and Social Research, 3*(6), 75–85.

Yang, Y., & Konrad, A. M. (2011). Understanding diversity management practices: Implications of institutional theory and resource-based theory. *Group & Organization Management, 36*(1), 6–38.

Yang, Z. V. (2019, August). *Generation gap and its impact on the public sector* [Master's thesis, California State University]. http://scholarworks.csun.edu/handle/10211.3/212959

Yang. S. M., & Guy, M. E. (2006). GenXers versus Boomers: Work motivators and management implications. *Public Performance & Management Review, 29*, 267–284.

Yetmar, S. A., & Eastman, K. K. (2000). Tax practitioners' ethical sensitivity: A model and empirical examination. *Journal of Business Ethics, 26*(4), 271–288.

Yu, H. C., & Miller, P. (2003). The generation gap and cultural influence: A Taiwan empirical investigation. *Cross Cultural Management: An International Journal, 10*(3), 23–41.

Zemke, R., Raines C., & Filipczak, B. (2013). *Generations at work: Managing the clash of Veterans, Boomers, Xers and Nexters in your workplace.* Amacom Books.

Zickuhr, K., & Madden, M. (2012). *Older adults and internet use.* Pew Research Center's Internet and American Life Project. Retrieved July 20, 2020, from https://www.pewresearch.org/internet/2012/06/06/older-adults-and-internet-use/

Zickuhr, K. (2010). Generations 2010. *Pew Research Center.* Available at: https://www.pewresearch.org/internet/2010/12/16/generations-2010/

Zopiatis, A. A., & Krambia-Kapardis, M. (2008). Ethical behavior of tertiary education students in Cyprus. *Journal of Business Ethics, 81*(3), 647–663.

Index

active participation systems, 117
Acuff, J., 31–32
affirmative action, 14, 15
age, 30–31, 125, 138t; discrimination based on, 13–15. *See also specific generations*
Ajzen, I., 93, 128
all-inclusive multiculturalism (AIM), 21, 27
Alsop, R., 1, 58, 59
altruism, 119, 149
Alvesson, M., 16
Antwi-Boasiako, K., 12
archetypes, generational, 42–48, 49
artificial intelligence (AI), 117
Avery, D., 24–25

Baby Boom Generation (1943–1960), 54, 143t; Gen Y and, 46, 123; retirement of, 51, 151
Bailey, A., 102
Barnett, T., 87–88, 91
Bauer, N. M., 122
Bebeau, M. J., 87; dental ethical sensitivity test of, 102, 109
Beekun, R. I., 99
Biancone, P., 117
Bolton, R. N., 68
Bornman, J., 107
Bose, C. E., 11
Bourdieu, Pierre, 39
Boyle, R. N., 97
Brown, M. E., 114
Buffett, Warren, 57
Burgess, R., 59
Butterfield, K. D., 93, 106

Categorization-Elaboration Model (CEM), 17
Catron, B. L., 115
CEMEX Corporation, 27
CES (consumer ethics scale), 103–105
Chambers, D. W., 107
Chan, S. Y., 108, 110
Chia, C. G., 128
Chitiga, M., 47
Cho, Y. J., 76
Christie, P. M. J., 106
Clarkeburn, H., 110
Cleveland, J. N., 30
cognitive moral development: Kohlberg's theory of, 85–86; Rest's theory of, 86–88
Colle, R., 64
collective identity, 8, 40–42; individualism versus, 19, 52; Mannheim on, 35–36; Steele on, 31–32

colorblindness, 20
Conroy, M., 122
consumer ethics scale (CES), 103–105
contingency theory, 23–24
Cooper, T. L., 92, 129
corruption, 121, 127, 137, 148
Craft, J. L., 93–94
Craig, J. S., 106
Cross, T., 12
Crowson, H. M., 103
cultural competency, 12
"Cuspers," 32–33
customer-oriented service, 131
"cyclical speculum," 40

Dalton, K. M., 67
Dávid-Barrett, E., 121
Davies, F., 17–18
Dawis, R. V., 23
defining issues test (DIT), 88, 128; Bebeau on, 109; multidimensional ethics scale and, 103; Rest on, 100–103, 129; Trevino on, 102; Welton on, 105
dental ethical reasoning and judgment test (DERJT), 109
dental ethical sensitivity test (DEST), 102, 109
deontology. *See* teleology-deontology dichotomy
Dimock, M., 62
DIT. *See* defining issues test
diversity, 7–12, 19; cultural competency and, 12; definitions of, 7–8, 14; dimensions of, 8; European view of, 12; generational, 29–33; negative effects of, 16–19; positive effects of, 8–9, 18; types of, 8–11; visible/invisible, 11–12
diversity management, 13–16; approaches to, 19–26; dimensions of, 8; disabilities and, 9
Dornoff, R. J., 104
Doverspike, D., 30
Downe, J., 113
Downs, H., 75
Dubinsky, A. J., 91, 106
DuPont, A. M., 106
Dwyer, R. J., 49

EDM. *See* ethical decision-making
Ely, R. J., 21–22
Emerson, T. L., 101
Emler, N., 103
Employment Non-Discrimination Act (ENDA), 10
entrepreneurship, moral, 116–117
environmental antecedents, 120–122
equal employment opportunities: affirmative action and, 14, 15; legislation on, 13–14
Ericsson Corporation, 27
Ermasova, N., 123
Esau, M., 115–116
EST (ethical sensitivity test), 109
ethical beliefs, 99
ethical climate, 117–120
ethical codes, 112–113
ethical decision-making (EDM), 92–94, 112–116, 125; of Cooper, 92; of Dubinsky, 90; of Ferrell, 89; of Hunt, 89–90; of Jones, 90–91; of Kohlberg, 85–86; of O'Fallon, 107; of Rest, 86–88; of Schwartz, 91–92; of Witmer, 92
ethical evaluations, 99
ethical judgment, 96–107, 125; definitions of, 94–95; empirical studies of, 95–96; measurement of, 98–107; nomenclature of, 98–99
ethical sensitivity, 107–111, 125, 128–130, 136–137; definition of, 107; measures of, 108–110; public

service ethos and, 132–134, 136t, 140–146, 149–150
ethical sensitivity test (EST), 109
ethics position questionnaire, 93, 101–102

Farazmand, A., 123
Fazekas, M., 121
Ferrell, O. C., 89, 91
Fishbein, M., 128
Flory, S. M., 95
Forrester Research, 64–65
Forsyth, D. R., 93, 101–102
Forte, A., 98
Fraone, J., 74, 79–80
Frink, D. D., 18
functionalist management, 16

Gafni, R., 62
Gan, C., 114
Garcia-Sanchez, I. M., 112
Gazley, B., 12
gender diversity, 9, 18, 122
gender wage gap, 9
generation(s): archetypes of, 42–48; definitions of, 31–32; dominant/recessive, 42; foundation of, 33–39
Generation X (1961–1981), 2, 46, 54, 141t, 143t
Generation Y (1982–2005), 2, 43–44, 57–60; Baby Boomers and, 46, 123; cohorts of, 132–134, 138, 139t; Gen X and, 141t, 143t; Gen Z and, 69–71; G.I. Generation and, 52; public service interests of, 50–51, 126, 132, 138, 142–144, 149–150; technological use patterns of, 65–68
Generation Z (2005–present), 2, 44, 46, 55–56; Gen Y and, 69–71; Silent Generation and, 56–57
generational gaps, 41, 47–51, 76–78
generational theories: of Mannheim, 34–36; of McCourt, 37–39; of Pilcher, 36–37; of Strauss, 32, 39–43
Geri, N., 62
German Youth Movement, 35–36
G.I. Generation (1901–1924), 41, 44, 51–52
Gilbert, J. A., 14
Glass, A., 66
Gorsira, M., 118
Gould-Williams, J., 17–18
Great Depression, 36; G.I. Generation and, 51; Silent Generation and, 52
Gursoy, D., 50

Hannam, S. E., 80–81
Harasymiw, B., 120–121
Harber, J. G., 74–75
Hassan, S., 114–115, 148
Heidenheimer, A. J., 148
Herek, G. M., 10
Herndon, N. C., 99
Heskett, J., 79
Holocaust, 139t
Homan, A., 17
Honeycutt, E. D., 106
Howe, N., 32, 39–49; archetypes of, 42–49; on character values, 42; cyclical model of, 41–43; on dominant/recessive generations, 42; on Gen Y, 2, 59; generational theory of, 32, 39–43, 47; LifeCourse website of, 40n1; on Silent Generation, 53
Hungary, 121
Hunt, S. D., 91; on ethical judgment, 94, 95, 105–106; on marketing ethics, 89–90
Hyman, M. R., 104

individualism, 8, 19, 40–42, 52
Indonesia, 115

institutional approach to diversity, 24–25
intergenerational gaps, 60–61; social media usage and, 68–69; technology and, 61–65
intersectionality, 11
issue contingent model, 90–91
Ivancevich, J. M., 14

Jilke, S., 122
Johnson, L., 31
Johnson, M., 31
Jones, T. M., 90–91
Jordan, J., 108

Kane, S, 66
Kast, F., 23
Kidwell, J. M., 97
knowledge structure, 130
knowledge transfer, 79
Kochan, T. A., 26
Kohlberg, Lawrence, 85–86, 100, 128
Konrad, A. M., 12, 24
Kooij, D. T., 30
Kupperschmidt, B. R., 31

Lancaster, L. C., 51; on G.I. Generation, 52; on Silent Generation, 53
Leung, P., 108, 110
Lewis, C. W., 115
Lewis, G. B., 76
LGBT rights, 9–11, 56
LifeCourse website, 40n1
Lilly, J., 118
Lim, A. S., 30
Lim Choi, D., 129
Loden, M., 7
Loken, B., 91
Lost Generation (born before 1901), 51

Madden, C., 69
Mannheim, Karl, 34–39
marketing ethics, 89–90
Martins, L., 17
Mason, E. S., 98–101
Massey, D., 103
Mayer, D., 118
McCormick, K., 13
McCourt, W., 24, 37–38
McKay, P., 24–25
"media generations," 71
Mee, L. S, 128
Meister, J. C., 80
Mentré, François, 47
methodology, 25–26, 134–140; limitations of, 135, 148–149
Millennials. *See* Generation Y
Milliken, F., 17
Molyneux, G., 77
moral entrepreneurship, 116–117
moral intensity, 90
moral judgment test (MJT), 100. *See also* ethical judgment
Mudrack, P. E., 98–101
multiculturalism, 20–21
multidimensional ethics scale (MES), 93, 99, 101; consumer ethics scale versus, 103–105; defining issues test and, 103
multigenerational public sector reforms, 78–82
multigenerational workforce, 73–75
Muncy J., 105
Mustafa, D., 115

National Association of Colleges and Employers (NACE), 2–3, 49
Naudé, A., 107
Ndalamba, K., 115–116
new public management (NPM), 111, 131, 147
Newton, C., 69
Nguyen, N. T., 97, 104

Nigeria, 113–114

O'Fallon, M. J., 93, 106
#OKBoomer, 34
Oliver, S., 122
Orange telecommunications company, 27
organizational characteristics, 112–116
organizational cognition, 126
organizational integration and learning, 21–22

Pakistan, 122–123
Pan, Y., 89–90; on ethical judgment, 94–96, 98, 99; on multidimensional ethics scale, 105; on multiple-item measures, 106; on student samples, 107
Paolillo J. G., 97–98
Park, J., 50
Perry, J. L., 118–119, 129
person-situation interactionist model, 88–89
Pilcher, J., 36–37
Pitts, D. W., 14–15
Prensky, Marc, 63, 72, 82
public service ethos (PSE), 5–6, 111, 126–127, 130–132, 137; categories of, 148; ethical sensitivity and, 132–134, 136t, 140–146, 149–150
public service interest, 50–51, 126, 132, 138, 142–144, 149–150
public service motivation (PSM), 118–120, 131
public service practice, 131–132, 138, 144–146, 148
Pugh, D. S., 25

race, 8, 20
Ramsey, R. P., 133
Rao, T., 68
Rayner, J., 131–132, 137, 138
regulative institutions, 24
Reidenbach, R. E., 93, 103–104
resource-based approach, 25–26
Rest, James, 90–91; defining issues test of, 88, 100–103, 129; on ethical judgment, 94; on ethical sensitivity, 108, 128–129; four-component model of, 86–88, 95, 129; Kohlberg and, 86; Trevino on, 102; Welton and, 105
Rittenburg T. L., 94, 96–97
Robbin, D. P., 93, 103–104
Robbins, S., 7
Roberson, Q. M., 25
Rokeach value survey (RVS), 93, 101
Roman, R., 64
Rosener, J. B., 7
Rosenzweig, J., 23
"rule-bending" actions, 137. *See also* corruption
Russia, 123

sales ethics vignettes, 104, 106. *See also* consumer ethics scale
Schwartz, M. S., 91–92
Schwepker, C. H., 94
Scott, W. R., 24
Seitel, S., 73
sexual orientation, 9–11, 56
Shaub, M. K., 103, 108–109
Silent Generation (1925–1942), 44, 52–53, 56–57
SIS (standard issue scoring), 100
Skipper, R., 104
Smith, P. B., 48
social justice, 13
social media, 68–69
Society for Human Resource Management, 10
Sparks, J. R., 89–90, 94–99, 105–107
Sprinthall, N. A., 129
Sri Lanka, 121–122

standard issue scoring (SIS), 100
Steele, B., 31–32
Stefaniak, A., 51, 58
Sterns, H. L., 30
Stevens, C. K., 25
Stewart, D. W., 129
Stillman, D., 51–53
Stillman, Richard, 112
Strauss, W., 32, 39–49; archetypes of, 42–49; on character values, 42; cyclical model of, 41–43; on dominant/recessive generations, 42; on Gen Y, 2, 59; generational theory of, 32, 39–43, 47; LifeCourse website of, 40n1; on Silent Generation, 53
Sullivan, S. E., 29–30
Sumra, K., 122–123
Swaidan, Z., 97

Tankersley, C. B., 104
Tanzania, 113
Teixeira, R., 77
teleology-deontology dichotomy, 89, 91, 106
test for ethical sensitivity in science (TESS), 110
Thoma, S. J., 109
Thomas, D. T., 14, 21–22
Thompson, C. A., 32–33, 49
Title VII of Civil Rights Act, 13
Tolbize, A., 52
transformational leadership, 73
Trevino, L. K., 91; on defining issues test, 102; on Kohlberg, 86; person-situation interactionist model of, 88–89
Truman, Harry S., 13
Tschirhart M., 7–8, 118–119

Valentine, S. R., 94, 96–97; on ethical decision making, 87–88, 91
value survey, 93
Vandenabeele, W., 119
Vaterlaus, J. M., 61–62, 63–64
Veale, M., 117
Vetter, C., 51, 58
Villanueva, P. A. G., 121
Vitell, S. J., 97–98, 105

Walker, S. K., 64
Walsh, J. P., 126, 130
Weeks, W. A., 97
Weigand, R. A., 18–19
Welton, R. E., 105
Williams, A., 56–57
Williams, S., 58–59
Willmott, H., 16
Willyerd, K., 80
Wise, L. R., 7–8, 118–119
Wittmer, D., 92, 108–110, 129
Wood, W., 78
work teams, 8
Wyatt-Nichol, H., 12

Yang, Y., 24
Yang, Z. V., 48, 76, 77
Yordi, B., 80–81

Zemke, R., 53, 58

www.ingramcontent.com/pod-product-compliance
Lightning Source LLC
LaVergne TN
LVHW050152080826
844660LV00002B/183

* 9 7 8 1 4 3 8 4 9 0 7 7 9 *